America's Supreme Deity

Cooper, Radin, Schmidt, Speck, Voegelin

Jay Miller. PhD, ed

© 2020

footnotes #1-238

Godhead Supreme

Throughout Native America, the precedent for everything else was a potency, sometimes called power and vitality. Often it was deified as a high god, the crux of the cosmos. Mortals tapped into it via immortals, also called supernaturals and spirits. Each of these had reserves of power consistent with its position along a great chain of being dependent upon the ultimate power broker, whether a high god, first cause, or deified vitality conceived as neutral, epicene, male, or female.

For over half a millenium, this potency has been identified as the essential force in Native American religion(s), ramified into many spiritual and artifactual facets. For example, a few years after landfall by Columbus, Father Ramon Pane wrote that the Caribbean Arawak concept of *cemis* [*zemis*] simultaneously meant idol, building, and power.[1]

Since then, many others have further considered the concept of power, usually within smaller regional contexts. Often, however, the close overlap in beliefs across the continent has been attributed the zeal of Christian missionaries, building a new foundation upon the ravages of severe depopulation and societal collapse.

While new conditions call for novel adaptations, the loss of ancient beliefs among surviving native communities, however, is more apparent than real. Traditional religions have always been accepting of any and all sources of potency, so they were quite willing to graft Christianity into existing beliefs. Despite strong intolerance and repression by missionaries, natives have been able to blend European beliefs with their own, instead of abandoning one for the other.

According to the native view, the amazing diversity of American cultures, languages, and societies is a consequence of their different religions. Each culture has traditions which were divinely instituted for that tribe specifically. Other cultures had their own practices, which also were part of the universal scheme, and so all were respected as valid but alien alternatives.

Thus, long before anthropology, Native America acknowledged a religiously-based doctrine of cultural relativity, influenced by particular features of its terrain, kinship patterns, and ritual relations with the environment. Yet, throughout the continent, the cardinal principal uniting these many religions was the desire to "learn from the land," as one Lushootseed elder expressed it. This learning was more religious than ecological, although these are not native distinctions. The religious was primary because it expressed the importance of potency for vivifying the ecological and for indicating the nodes along the great chain of being occupied by the immortals (often called bosses) in charge of various species.

In most cases, the sources for this learning were beings who were localized at specific sites, giving worthy petitioners a glimpse of themselves - in essentially human form - and a message allowing continued access to potency proportional with their place within the existential chain.

While a holistic entity, potency is also divisible into different concentrations, providing particular qualities to various immortals. Continued partnership between human and source required proper conduct, respectful use of nature's bounty, and a personal song, given at the time of the encounter to evoke the universal rhythms, harmony, and pulsations so characteristic of all manifestations of potency.

Among those people who relied on the Soul Redeeming Ceremony, power in its fullest

---

[1] Edward Gaylord Bourne, Columbus, Ramon Pane, and the Beginnings of American Anthropology. *Proceedings of the American Antiquarian Society* 19: 310-348 1906.

form was called _xaxa_, the source and summary of existence. One elder said it was like the mind of the universe, but whenever you start to think or talk about spirit things, they wiggle away from you. Although deified and personified, it was vague, yet personal in the sense that it was named, rational, and aware of itself and others.

Among the Coast Salish, a larger grouping that includes Lushootseed, Straits, Tsamosan, and other divisions as far north as the Bella Coola and as far south as the Tillamook on the Oregon coast.

> Nooksak and closely related Salish languages have a term, _xae'xae_, which is untranslateable but includes within its purview both the positive and negative aspects of the sacred - that is, both "holy" and "dangerous."... [It] refers not only to the supernatural itself but also to the distinguishing characteristics of the relationship between the everyday world and the supernatural. The relationship is one of disjunction. Man and his works are one series, one kind of reality; the supernatural is another series, another kind of reality. The passage from one to the other is fraught with danger.[2]

While the above agrees with my own data, Amoss goes on to say that supernatural power is "impersonal and diffuse ... [and] does not emanate from any single source and it is never totally under the control of any personalized being." As mentioned above, my information indicates that it has personal qualities and intelligence in its own right, and is occasionally addressed as a divinity. It is my impression that the potency itself is greater than its deification. Both Amoss and I agree "This power has no moral quality until [some of] it is harnessed by some personalized being."

In practice, this power has at least two aspects, related to its control by immortals or by mortals. Among the Lushootseed, the immortals were known as _sqəlalitut_ (derived from the verb _qəlalitut_, 'to dream, envision'), who provided access to the facet of power called _syud_, a partnership with an immortal conferring _pig^wəd_, 'song and dance attuned to power'.[3]

The most significant type of _sqəlalitut_, some say a separate kind, is _x^wdab_, the gift of healing-curing given to shamans, whether men or women, enabling them to treat specific illnesses and accomplish particular tasks, such as going to the land of the dead to recover stolen souls.

The other facet of potency was _xəcadad_, knowledge of special prayers passed down through elite families. The term means 'to mesmerize or ensorcel', implying the ability to impel absolutely, derived from the term _xəc_, "mind, inner thoughts, understanding, sense, count'.[4]

Against this background of the Lushooteed beliefs, we can draw comparisons with other regions.

Durkheim[5] was the first major scholar to notice that many linguistic terms from North America (and elsewhere) referred to a similar idea of potency, which he unfortunately called "impersonal religious force". It is represented by words ranging as widely as _wakan_ of the Siouians, _orenda_ of the Iroquois, _pokunt_ of the Shoshonians (now called Numic), _manitou_ of the Algonkians, _nauala_ of the Kwakiutl (now called Kwagiulth, Kwakwaka'wakw), _yek_ of the

---

[2] Pamela Amoss, _Coast Salish Spirit Dancing_, The Survival of an Ancestral Religion, Seattle: University of Washington Press 1978: 42.

[3] Thom Hess, _Dictionary of Puget Salish_ 1976: 374.4.

[4] Thom Hess, _Dictionary of Puget Salish_, Seattle: University of Washington Press 1976: 590, 589.3.

[5] Emile Durkheim, _The Elementary Forms of the Religious Life_, New York: Free Press 1965: 220ff [1912].

Godhead

Tlingit, and _sgana_ of the Haida (also the word for orca killerwhale).

In these and other cases, the referent seems to be an ultimate, active force (kinesis) pervading the cosmos. Using the same or closely related tribes discussed in terms of death beliefs, we will now consider this concept of potency.

Northwest

The Lushootseed data, while also being representative of many of the other Coast Salish, is also comparable to the Quileute term _tibiita_ meaning "mind, soul, spirit, and power," with connotations of heartiness and strength.[6] For the matrilineal north, Durkheim noted the concept among the Tlingit and Haida, in addition to the ambilateral Kwagiulth of the central coast. Each of these analogous to that of the Tsimshian, considered shortly.

With greater authority gained from extensive fieldwork, Boas[7] reported that the Kwagiulth use the term _na'walak_{w}_ with a wide range of meanings expressive of many aspects of the supernatural, whether as person, attribute, quality, or abstraction; all of them more than anthropomorphic. Boas compared it to English terms like saint, saintly, sanctity, and sanctuary and to German ones like _der Heilige, Heiligkeit_, and _Heiligtum_.

His analogy was misplaced, however, because these words are nominals; they refer to a stasis that is contrary to the potent dynamism of Native America. By its very nature, terms for power are usually predicates, verbs indicating dynamic totalities.

Even when they are nominal, their intent is cohesive, not selective. The Tlingit term _yek_ is a distributive, like multiples in other Northwest languages. In lieu of plurals like English, neighboring Tsimshian uses the distributive for anatomical terms. Hence the word "arms" means something like 'each their own arm'. For the Tlingit concept of power, "this means that instead of thinking of so many different objects, they think of one diffused into many".[8] Potency is regarded as a vast immensity: dispersed, inscrutable, but manifesting itself as a personalized, anthropomorphic entity when appearing to humans.

Amplifying the work of Swanton, de Laguna[9] saw _yek_ as "vital force, the expression of animate energy wherever and however it is manifested...[and] there seems to be no underlying concept of power which was not ultimately associated with living things, persons, or spirits." While power does exist in close conjunction with all of life, the Tlingit portray the supernatural in their art with human heads, faces, and, sometimes, bodies,[10] probably to convey that it has sentience and emotions like humans and, in this sense, is anthropomorphic.

Tsimshian

According to Boas,[11] the Tsimshian use _naxnox_ as an all purpose term for anything

---

[6] JV Powell and Fred Woodruff, _Quileute Dictionary_, Northwest Anthropological Research Notes, Memoir 3 1976: 151, 213, 384.

[7] Franz Boas, _Kwakiutl Ethnography_, Helen Codere, ed, University of Chicago Press 1966: 167.

[8] Frederica de Laguna, _Under Mount Saint Elias_: The History and Culture of the Yakutat Tlingit, Washington: Smithsonian Institution Press. Three Volumes 1972: 810.

[9] Frederica de Laguna, _Under Mount Saint Elias_:1972: 811.

[10] Frederica de Laguna, _Under Mount Saint Elias_:1972: 812.

[11] Franz Boas, _Tsimshian Mythology_, Bureau of American Ethnology, Annual Report 31: 29-

mysterious, including, but not limited to, supernatural helper(s), secret society whistles, religious paraphernalia, and any display dramatizing such power, ultimately derived from a deity called Heaven. Adams[12] limited the term to spirits and displays of power, while Dunn,[13] in his careful dictionary, defines it as "supernatural; having supernatural power...a supernatural being."

As part of her astute analysis of the Tsimshian crest system, Halpin[14] identified the social context for this potency as the winter ceremonial system, the mirror image of the crest system so important during the potlatches of the summer economic season.

During winter, the summer economic and political role of chiefs became a priestly one, characterized by the assumption of _naxnox_ names, rather than inherited ones associated with a crest. In this guise, they managed or performed astounding displays attributed to the _haleyt_, secret shamanic cults. Each used masks, whistles, and more elaborate trappings to show off their access to power, sometimes to overawe "cowering" commoners.

They also used the occasion to correct other members of the elite, even belittling haughty chiefs. Some displays (called _sedulsa naxnox_) of powerful wonders both popularized important name-titles and reinforced the existing heirarchy, as each chief, by order of rank, tried to restore a lifeless patient, who, by prearrangement, was finally cured by the one of highest rank.

In all, the presence of _naxnox_ served to define the winter as the religious season and to grade the chiefs and _haleyt_ members into a hierarchy reflecting their differential access to potency. Contact with immortals and their reserves of power served as the basis of both the crest and the _naxnox_ systems, producing overlapping heirarchies. Yet potency itself was most immediate during the winter _naxnox_ displays. The crests had access to it only indirectly by means of heirlooms.

The crest system used heraldic animal designs to set up elaborate distinctions among pseudo-species of matrilineages, each of which was internally distinguished by class and rank. The _naxnox_ system gave access to an absolute quality that was the means for exalting leadership, monitoring social roles, and entertaining public gatherings, colorful diversions during gloomy winters.

While the crest system has survived an enthusiastic conversion to Christianity, the _naxnox_ system has not, leaving uncertain manner its names were transmitted. The term and concept are still in use by the Tsimshian, however.

Plateau

Sanpoil

Among the Interior Salish bands, the overall potent unity is called _shumix_, allowing for regional vowel shifts among the speakers of the dialect chains. It continues to occupy a vital role in the thought and public expressions of the Salish on the Colville Reservation. It has also

---

1037 1916: 543.

[12] John Adams, _The Gitksan Potlatch_: _Population Flux, Resource Ownership, and Reciprocity_, Toronto: Holt, Rinehart and Winston of Canada 1973: 42.

[13] John Dunn, _A Practical Dictionary of the Coast Tsimshian Language_, National Museum of Man, Mercury Series, Canadian Ethnology Service Paper 42: 1-145 1978: 78 #1518.

[14] Marjorie Myers Halpin, The Tsimshian Crest System: A Study Based on Museum Specimens and the Marius Barbeau and William Beynon Field Notes, PhD Dissertation, University of British Columbia 1973: 127ff.

benefitted from the leniency of the Jesuits who have ministered to this population for two centuries.

Shumix exists in perpetuity both as an abstract whole and as aspects conferred to humans by particularized immortals. As with other Salish, it is linked to a larger mystery called *xaxa*. In accord with their modern life, Colvile elders say that power is a special ability given to natives by God, who is now a blend of the Christian God and the earlier high god called Sweatlodge.

According to mythology, the Timeless Age was a steady state inhabited by beings simultaneously spiritual, humanoid, and biological. Thus, the same being was simultaneously a spirit, a man, and a bush, or a deity, woman, and bird, or any combination of these. When this world changed to usher in the present one, Sweatlodge was a leader who decided to give up his arms, legs, body, and head to assume the hemispherical form of a sudatory to be of benefit to future humans.

The world change was preordained to coincide with the first arrival of humans. Many events mentioned in the sagas were deliberately intended to prepare the world because, in an oft repeated phrase, "human people are coming soon." When all was ready, Sweatlodge called a grand council of all the immortals, where each one assumed a name reflective of the role it would play in ignoring, hindering, or helping humans during the coming age.

In addition, objects were cached throughout the landscape to potency. Generally, the locations of these were passed down in kindreds as private knowledge, encouraging the same career in a family over many generations.

When the last detail was fixed and the last name assumed, generally by rabbit, the world instantly changed into its present form. Yet, some things were still left unsettled because the change was so sudden. Beings caught off-guard became solidified in precarious positions, fearsome monsters escaped to devastate the world, and not all the necessary knowledge, skills, and abilities had been provided for humans.

For these reasons, Sweatlodge appointed Coyote to remedy the new world. Coyote had distinguished himself during the Naming by trying to get the name of a more important animal, instead of Imitator, the one intended for him. Thus, he was the first being to think for himself, although not always in the most benevolent manner. This independence got him through the most difficult tasks, further complicated by his own penchant to be reckless, foolish, and driven by lust, greed, and hunger.

At the start of each adventure, he often messed things up, died, or was killed. As a hedge against this impetuous lack of judgement, Fox was given the ability to revive Coyote by stepping over him five times. Refreshed but ungrateful, Coyote then went on to finish the task, progessively moving eastward until he went to live in a glass house floating on the ocean. People say that he will return again when he is needed. Some hope he will eventually smash up the many dams blocking the Columbia River, allowing the salmon and ancient landscape to return.

Most of Coyote's adventures left some permanent mark on the landscape as a memento of his efforts. These variously include a cliff, rock, lake, mountain, plant, or commandment stating how a locale was to be respected. Collectively, these are called the "proofs" of his acts, each with lasting consequences for humans.

At the Change and during subsequent modifications, beings were confined to distinctive public forms, although all remained basically humanoid at home. While outside, each wore the cover characteristic of its species. Similarly, objects cached around the landscape were transformed into loci of concentrated potency, each marked by short white lines along the rock edges of outcrops or talus slopes.[15]

---

[15] Jay Miller, Rock Art on the Amero-Canadian Plateau, Paper Read at New Directions in

Knowledge of the benefits of each location was inherited by the members of a kindred, linking generations with the same place, spirit, and power, as noted for general Native America by Radin.[16]

Hence, careers in fishing, hunting, warfare, gambling, doctoring, and so forth inherited along bilateral family lines, not because children learn from parents, but, in native belief, because they went to the same locales to acquire related facets of a power.

All of this indicates, therefore, that _shumix_ is a generic concept originating from the beginning of the world and differentially apportioned among knowledgeable families. Its potency rests on its being primordial, a true precedent for all that is universal, diffuse, and fluctuating. While Sweatlodge has the controlling interest, other intermediaries shared proportional access to it.

At the most esoteric level, among shamans, power has facets that occur in multiples of five, with 5x5 being the ideal, comparable to the 4x4 arrangement used by Lakota shamans. Since five is a Salish pattern number, as is four among the Lakota, these schematics accord with expectable cultural parameters (see below).

Among the Sanpoil and other Interior Salish, potency uses immortal conduits to reach humans. It refers to a time when the world was in flux and behavior was not rigidly governed by the plethora of commandments specifying how and when women sit, the type and size of spear used in a particular stream, where to hunt deer, when and what to fish, the treatment of berries, various rights to locales, and much more.

Yet, someone with a sure sense of his or her proportional access to power could ignore or modify commandments with impunity as long as this was consistent with the dictates of an immortal. This seems to be the reason why the Plateau was the source for several widely diffused prophet cults.[17]

California

The large population and rugged terrain of Native California made it one of the most diverse regions of the continent. In addition, settlements were usually small and widely scattered, fostering further differentiation. Therefore, it is all the more significant that a generalized belief in power has been summarized for the entire area by Bean.[18]

The origin of power is usually explained in either of two ways.

(1) power is created from a void in which two forces, usually male and female, come together in a cataclysmic event that forms a creative force; or (2) power and creators appear simultaneously in the universe without explanation, and a creative force begins thereupon to form or alter the world.[19]

Native American Art History, October 24-26, Albuquerque, New Mexico 1979.

[16] Paul Radin, Religion of the North American Indians, _Journal of American Folklore_ 27 (106): 335-373 1914: 372.

[17] Leslie Spier, _The Prophet Dance of the Northwest and its Derivatives_: The Source of the Ghost Dance, Mensha: General Series in Anthropology 1 1935.

[18] Lowell Bean and Thomas Blackburn, _Native Californians_: A Theoretical Perspective, Ramona, California: Ballena Press 1976: 407-20.

[19] Bean and Blackburn, _Native Californians_: 407.

Moreover, the concept of power depends on four basic philosophical assumptions.

(1) power is sentient and the principal causative agent in the universe; (2) power is distributed differentially throughout the three realms of the universe and possessed by anything having "life" or the will "to act": (3) the universe is in a state of dynamic equilibrium in relation to power; and (4) man is the central figure in an interacting system of power holders[20] ... Since power is sentient and personalized, man can interact with power or conduits of power much as he would with humans. Power can be dealt with rationally through a system of reciprocal rules (expectations), which were established or handed down to man in early cosmic times. Without individual and community action by man through such rituals as world renewal ceremonies, the balance of power in the universe would be upset, and one side of the system might be disproportionally favored over another. Individually acquired power (knowledge) and traditionally acquired power (held by priests or shamans) must continually be employed by man to maintain the dynamic equilibrium or harmony of the universe.[21]

This discussion applies equally well to the rest of Native America, as will be seen. In all, power can be acquired by quest, dreaming, praying, calling upon areas of concentrations such as shrines and leaving offerings, or the purchase of knowledge, bundles, or consecrated equipment.[22] A person can become more receptive to power by altering mental and bodily sensibilities through the single and multiple means of

Hallucinogenic plants, the handling of power-containing objects, and various forms of sensory deprivation or acts designed to concentrate attention, such as meditation, fasting, imposed periods of sleeplessness, isolation, induced sweating, listening to music, singing drumming, chanting, and hyperventilation.[23]

While almost all of this summary applies equally well to beliefs in the rest of Native America, an exception is a statement that power is entropic, gradually diminishing

since the beginning of time in quality, quantity, and availability ... because man at various times treated it or its conduits improperly, failing in his reciprocal responsibilities within an interdependent system.[24]

In contrast, my own analysis indicates that power is usually believed to flow in a closed system, but as people lose interest in obtaining it or the knowledge needed to control it is not passed on, potency shuns humanity. Visionary encounters, revived rituals, invented cults, and Christianity have all contributed to providing renewed access to power, but many of these are not as effective as were ancient ones. In other words, the modern attitude is that potency remains

---

[20] Bean and Blackburn, *Native Californians*: 409-10.

[21] Bean and Blackburn, *Native Californians*: 410.

[22] Bean and Blackburn, *Native Californians*: 414.

[23] Bean and Blackburn, *Native Californians*: 414.

[24] Bean and Blackburn, *Native Californians*: 411.

undiminished, but it has become less accessible as the details of tradition have been ignored, lost, forgotten, or modified beyond recall.

Basin

Numic

The term used by Durkheim to refer to potency among the Shoshonean Numic is incorrect. _Pokunt_ is his corruption of the word for shaman _puhaganti_, which combines lexicals for power (_puha_) and "one who has". In my full study of the concept in the Basin,[25] potency is described in terms of a pulsating web with each intersection linked to a mountain peak and the central nexus located upon the highest one in the area. This figurative web ordering the flow of power in terms of mountains duplicates the natural pattern in which the diffuse scatter of moisture is also concentrated into rivulets, streams, and springs. Throughout this arid region where water is of vital importance, _puha_, or a close linguistic variant, designates potency in all of the American branches of the Uto-Aztecan language stock, including Hopi.

Southwest

Hopi

The Hopi continue the use of _puha_ as a Basin legacy, which they have blended with the elaborate farming ritualism of the Pueblos. Its derivations include terms _powaqa_ "spirit" and _pavan_ "force, strength, might".[26]

Navaho

The term _jish_ is used by Navaho for an entire medicine bundle along with all of its contents, for just the wrapping, and for each one of the items included inside it. Citing Gladys Reichard as the source of this insight, Witherspoon[27] described it as a linguistic synecdoche, the same term used for a whole and its parts or selected aspects.

Durkheim[28] made the more general observation that

When a sacred thing is subdivided, each of its parts remains equal to the thing

---

[25] Jay Miller, Numic Religion: An Overview of Power in the Great Basin of Native North America, _Anthropos_ 78: 337-354 1983; Great Basin Religion and Theology: A Comparative Study of Power (Puha), _Journal of California and Great Basin Anthropology_ 1984.

[26] Charles and Florence Voegelin, _Hopi Domains_ ~ A Lexical Approach to the Problem of Selection. _International Journal of American Linguistics_, Memoir 14: 1-82 1957: 44 C 4.3, 45 C 4.4.

[27] Gary Witherspoon, _Language and Art in the Navajo Universe_, Ann Arbor: University of Michigan Press 1977.

[28] Emile Durkheim, _The Elementary Forms of the Religious Life_, New York: Free Press 1965: 261.

itself ... he part is equal to the whole; it has the same powers, the same efficacy.

Similarly, a recent analysis of the concept of the Holy Wind indicates that it is a whole serving as the universal mediator of the Navaho cosmos, the medium making possible the motion/pause axiom echoing throughout this culture. Each Navaho is animated by a facet of this Wind swirling through the finger tips and taking the forms of several in-dwelling winds. As McNeley[29] sagely noted

> Navajo naming of a particular aspect of Wind does not differentiate it as a kind of Wind having no relation to the whole of which it is a part, just as our naming of a sea does not imply that the waters referred to are distinct from the great body of water encompassing the whole earth.

Apachean

The Mescalero and Chiricahua, along with the other Apacheans (Southern Athapaskans), believed the universe was flooded with a diffuse, animating force that had no single name and was instead labeled in terms of its use for good or harm. Morris Opler[30] identified this root ($-\gamma\underset{\cdot}{\imath}^{h}$) which is distinct from that used to refer to the witchcraft complex ($-t'\underset{\cdot}{\imath}^{\uparrow}$). He concluded "In other words, by utilizing the radical element, which expresses the basic idea, all sorts of actions and attitudes involving the basic idea can be expressed. Many of these radicals or stems are quite standard throughout Apachean and have a wide distribution in Athapaskan as well." The source for power was Giver-of-Life and

> One might say that this deity has been invoked to lend conceptual wholeness to the supernatural world of the Apache... Power is thought of as a mighty force that pervades the universe. Some of it filters through to the hands of man. But to become manifest to man, power must approach him through the medium of certain agencies and channels, must 'work through' something.[31]

> When an Apache received a visit from one of these conductors and accepted the bestowal of power, he or she was given instructions for a personal ceremony of benefit to others, mostly family members. Each rite specified songs, prayers, four ceremonial gifts offered whenever it is held, and, perhaps, taboos placed on themselves and/or patients.[32]

There are many kinds of ceremonies, but the real ceremonies are those which deal with

---

[29] James Kale McNeley, *Holy Wind In Navajo Philosophy*, Tucson: University of Arizona Press 1981.

[30] Letter of 25 May 1984 giving Lipan and Mescalero forms, with [h] marking aspiration and [↑] high tone.

[31] Morris Opler, The Concept of Supernatural Power among the Chiricahua and Mescalero Apache, *American Anthropologist* 37: 65-70 1935: 66.

[32] Morris Opler, The Concept of Supernatural Power among the Chiricahua and Mescalero Apache 1935: 67.

the heavenly bodies and forces ... A ceremony is usually transferred to a ... close relative. But the power has to be consulted before the transfer of a ceremony. If power is satisfied, it is all right. If the person isn't fit for it the power refuses. This is shown by the fact that the man cannot learn the songs and keep in mind what to do. If the power is willing to have the transfer made, the man will learn the ceremony in less than four days.[33]

Plains

Lakota

The Siouian concept of _wakan_ has been the subject of considerable scholarly attention. Assessing this work, Powers[34] regards the term as connoting something ancient, old, enduring, and difficult to understand, particularly in the 4x4 or 16 cell typology used by shamans to grasp its range. It is most closely related to the idea of knowledge, as opposed to ignorance,[35] particularly in terms of memory since a shaman (_wakan_ + person) retired when he or she could no longer effectively remember important information.[36]

Among the Omaha, speakers of another Siouian language, potency is indefinite, ineffable, non-existent without a locus, and double faceted as _wakonda_: the animating life-force of the universe, manifested by _xube_: the emotional impact produced within a person by contact with it.[37]

In all, _wakonda_ is the abstract power latent in the cosmos, causing a jolt (_xube_) when directly experienced by a human. In this combination, it is an affecting presence instilling the most profound of religious feelings, consubstantial yet variable, because the strength of the jolt corrolates with the amount of power involved in the event.

In his important but vituperative review of Americanist treatments of religion, Radin[38] vehemently insisted that Winnebago _wakan_ and Ojibwa _manitu_, respectively Siouian and Algonkian, did not refer to a concept of potency. Rather, they represented a pervasive belief in localized spirits, each accepted by the laity and systematized by shamans into a higher order immortal such as a deity, boss of a species, mythic hero, or ultimate high god. Where other scholars viewed these as facets of power, Radin argued they misrepresented data and over-extended the range of meaning.

While work before and after Radin indicates that his position is untenable, he does make some valid points. He correctly noted the association of local spirits with families rather than single individuals, and the virtually automatic ability of a particular offering to engender a specific benefits. Further, he described immortals mourning for their dead human partners as

---

[33] Morris Opler, Myth and Practice in Jicarilla Apache Eschatology, _Journal of American Folklore_ 60:133-153 1947: 5.

[34] William Powers, _Oglala Religion_, Lincoln: University of Nebraska Press 1977: 47, 63, 184.

[35] William Powers, _Oglala Religion_ 1977: 184.

[36] William Powers, _Oglala Religion_ 1977: 63.

[37] Raymond DeMalle and Robert Lavanda, _Wakan_: Plains Siouan Concepts of Power, _Anthropology of Power: Ethnographic Studeis from Asia, Oceania, and the New World._ Raymond Fogelson and Richard Adams, eds, NY: Academic Press 1977: 161, 164.

[38] Paul Radin, Religion of the North American Indians, _Journal of American Folklore_ 27 (106): 335-373 1914.

acting like forlorn pets, actively seeking out another tie within the same family or household. Many tribes use this analogy, but it has been overlooked.

With considerable insight, he treated religion as a dynamic institution, supporting cultural values while also molding to new conditions. Innovations had to be congruent with changes in the environment, redirecting ancient emotional outlets and behaviors into new forms. Strong feelings, rooted in earlier tradition, became attributed to new stimuli. On occasion, they were adapted into ritual to provide reassuring comfort during stressful change.

As illustrated by several anecdotes, Radin noted that the intensity of mental concentration were proportional to efficacy of prayer, ritual, or quest, but the most vital feature of all was memory (a watchful, reflective awareness rather than a general consciousness of the past). Throughout the Americas and elsewhere, memory had this crucial role because it supplies relevant teachings and procedures of proven effectiveness.

Therefore, memory is the key to potency, if not its source. It is the primordial Mind within all sentient beings: universally aware, sensitive, and personalized. Hence, Durkheim[39] was incorrect in saying "_wakan_ is in no way a personal being"; although in a footnote, he contradicts himself by citing Alice Fletcher that among the Dakota "a certain anthropomorphism has attached to this conception. But this anthropomorphism concerns the various manifestations of the Wakonda", all of which attest to the "essential consubstantiality of all sacred things".

East

Lenape Delaware

Like other Algonkians, the Delaware believe in spirit-deities or immortals called _manitu_ (plural: _manituwak_), with the attributes of immortality, thought, language, and supernatural potency.[40] They mediate between mortals, biota who must reproduce themselves, and the Creator, whose name translates as "The One Who Created Us By His Thoughts." He is the apex of the chain of being, a complex referral system based on differential powers.

Potency, an abstract unity called _manituwakan_, is possessed in fullest form by the Creator in His guise as _gitmanitu_ - Great Spirit - and variously apportioned among the _manituwak_, who in turn confer some of it upon human partners, who gained the attention of an immortal through prayer, fasting, suffering, and petitioning them in the Lenape language.

This was the proper language for spoken communication with the immortals. Now that few people speak it, contacts with the old sources have become very infrequent and new religions, ranging from Christianity to Peyotism (The Native American Church), are finding favor among modern Delaware. As long as the language was viable, however, it appears that some immortals were willing to maintain contact with the Delaware during their perambulations from the east coast to Oklahoma and Ontario, where most now live.

Among the traditional Delaware, the universe is threefold. Everything is an aspect of either Man or Woman, mediated by Mind as thought, intelligence, sapience, and memory.

Anything in the category Man involves form, container, and externals, while anything Woman is content, contained, and internal. Mind is inclosive, sharing qualities of both genders,

---

[39] Emile Durkheim, _The Elementary Forms of the Religious Life_ 1965: 221, 221 #11, 228.

[40] Jay Miller, Delaware Alternative Classifications, _Anthropological Linguistics_ 17: 434-444 1975.

in addition to the special ability to permeate and enfold. Mind and power are synonymous: both deriving from the Creator, pervading the universe, and individualized by localized immortals.

For the Central Algonkians of the Great Lakes, William Jones[41], who was both a Harvard-trained anthropologist and a member of the Fox tribe, wrote of *manitu* as a miraculous potentiality that

> takes on the character of conscious personality with some attributes of immanence and design ... [and] can be transferred from one object to another.

It is most commonly experienced as

> being overwhelmed by an all-encompassing presence ... Often one will cut one's self over the arms and legs, slitting one's self only through the skin. It is done to open up many passages for the manitou to pass into the body ... The term manitou beings is but an intelligible form of expressing the exciting cause; it is more natural to identify the communication with animate beings, in spite of the consciousness that the beings themselves are vague and inarticulate ... Where one differs from another is in the nature of its function, and in the degree of the possession of the cosmic substance. But the investment of a common, mythic virtue gives them all a common name, and that name is Manitou.

Power is never static or isolated. Among the Iroquoian-speaking Cherokee of the Southeast, *ulanigvgv* means everything characterized by a flow or current within a distinct unity, including lightning, spirits of running water, electricity, notions of ethnic power, and the influence of the Bible on believing Christians.[42]

Indeed, power is often equated with energy, especially electricity, but, while this is sometimes apt, its limitations will be considered below.

Discussion

Native America was a place of permeable contacts among the scattered population, interlinked by trade routes and regional congregations for transmitting news, innovations, and goods. Whether the concept of power arrived with the first people or developed later and spread via these networks, the continent acknowledged, directly or indirectly, an underlying belief in a deified Mind, emanating potency throughout a web of localized immortals and shrines which could tranfer it to mortal use.

While none are fully satisfactory, attempts to come to terms with this concept of potency have treated it as distributive, consubstantial, and synechdochal. Each has its own advantages and disadvantages. The distributive recognizes that power is divisible, but treats each part as equivalent rather than proportional. Consubstantiality attests to a common quality shared among

---

[41] William Jones, The Algonkin Manitou, *Journal of American Folklore* 18 (70): 183-190 1905: 184, 187, 189.

[42] Raymond Fogelson, Cherokee Notions of Power, *The Anthropology of Power*: Ethnographic Studies from Asia, Oceania, and the New World, Raymond Fogelson and Richard Adams, eds, New York: Academic Press 1977: 185-194.

the whole and parts, while highlighting it as an emotional charge or mystical stirring. The synechdoche or metonymic, whole and part sequencing, acknowledges that some parts are more crucial than others for grasping the whole.

The limitations of these different models can be illustrated by considering the equation of potency with electricity. Like power, electricity is everywhere, but it is most effective when concentrated with varying intensities in different locations. It has a current that can be directed along set courses by means of conductors or conduits, and, in this sense, it is distributive. However, the distribution is not equal because the intensities can fluctuate within a wide range.

On the Plains, the renewal of potency coincided with natural displays of electricity. Thus, at the first sound of thunder in the spring, individuals and tribes opened their medicine bundles (power packs) to refresh them as the world was reviving. Thunder and lightning are integral manifestations of power on the Plains, so they are specially propitiated.

Power is both consubstantial and synechdochal in that the slightest pulse of electricity still carries a tingle, which can increase to fatal intensity. In consequence, the strength of any emanation is considered to be proportional with the amount of access it has to the whole.

Like potency, lightning as electricity is considered to have an ultimate source and summary in divinity, but, unlike power, it lacks inherent rationality. Sometimes, lightning, as in Norse mythology, is only the tool of an immortal. In Native America, however, it is often a manifestation of the Thundebird. Like electricity, potency in the hands of mortals can be used to help or abused for selfish ends. Among immortals, by contrast, such applications become minor in terms of the overall patterns of flow, rational balance, and complementarity pervading the cosmos.

Control of power rests on special bonds among the generating nexus, immortals, and mortals. In most cases, it must be localized, as though to give it a base (conductor-conduit) for regulating its output. A wise Menomini once described a medicine bundle (portable shrine) as a power pack most like a radio, able to function effectively only when particular items were correctly assembled and activated.

Throughout the Americas, the means for regulating the outpourings around the intersections in the potency web were immortals and sacra, particularly shrines and bundles. All of life is believed to be basically humanoid, sharing sentiments in common with humans. Each species, however, wore a particular covering outside its domicile, complementary to other existences.

These existences are, by and large, undifferentiated. As Laird[43] explained for the Chemahuevi, these immortals have a "rainbow-shimmer" because they hover between definite forms. This iridescence is the mark of their sacred immortality. It is also expressed by iridescent feathers, shells, fish scales, and quartz crystals.

Of the three sources of potency, immortals were the most volitionally mobile, shrines the most inert, and bundles could be moved with care. It was immortals, therefore, who managed the endless redistribution of power and directed its various flowings.

Among humans, bundles were important for amassing a section of flow, usually proportional to its personal or tribal use. Each personal pack was assembled by a human after an initial encounter with an immortal, who promised success at a particular career. The degree of potency attributed to each bundle matched the successes of that individual, and provided him or her with a relative standing within the community.

---

[43] Carobeth Laird, *The Chemehuevis*, Banning, California: Malki Museum Press 1976: 110; Chemehuevi Shamanism, Sorcery, and Charms, *Journal of California and Great Basin Anthropology* 2 (1): 80-87 1980: 82.

Tribal bundles, which sometimes developed out of personal ones that became famous and powerful, are managed by a priest or priesthood. Among the Skidi Pawnee, Caddoan speakers of the Plains, each village bundle in the confederacy was subsumed by four bundles associated with the semi-cardinal directions and, ultimately, by those of the Wonderful Person Skull and of the Evening Star Woman. The entire hierarchy depended on a high god called _Tirawa_, Expanse of the Heavens, reminiscent of the Tsimshian deity called Heaven. Each bundle was attended by three officials: an owner, a warrior, and a priest, representing a fundamental Pawnee triad necessary for the deployment of power.[44]

The contrast between immortal and bundle reflects a difference observed by Flannery[45] between power given provisionally and absolutely. The former relies on an on-going contract, but the latter was an outright gift for beneficial or malevolent use.

Both bundles and shrines are focusing mechanisms orienting person, community, or tribe throughout the Americas. In ancient Mexico, "all villages and towns had a main bundle called _altepetlyyollo_ − the heart of the town," while the Mayan Popul Vuh refers to four important bundles known as 'power-tied-up' ".[46]

As these examples indicate, the Americas had several important centering metaphors. In ever widening rings, these were the heart as the nexus of a person, the hearth of the home or family, the rotunda of the community, and the bundle, palladium, or sacred fire of the tribe. Each provided increasingly stronger amounts of power. Some of them, particularly the heart, were applied at many levels of integration, each metaphorically equated with a total person.

In the same way that each form of existence wears an external covering to differentiate it from others, so all of creation has to maintain important distinctions to keep potency accessible to the greatest number. Otherwise, the more poweful flowings would absorb lesser ones and all would fuse together. The function of the ritual taboos and injunctions, therefore, is to maintain proper alignments of power.

Among the modern Dunne-za (Beaver), Northern Athapaskans of northeastern British Columbia, successful visionaries have to be careful to avoid certain experiences forbidden by their immortal partner. Usually, they have to respect sensory inputs and intervening boundaries scrupulously.[47]

For example, someone with power from Frog could not eat any food that might contain fly eggs because these are frog food. Someone gifted by Spider could not overhear the sound of a plucked string, since it was too much like webbing. Anyone linked with Eagle avoids camera flashes and bright lights because Eagle causes lightning.

If these injunctions were broken, even inadventently, the visionary became "too strong, too powerful" because they had taken on too many attributes of their special immortal and were in danger of becoming a Wechuge, a giant cannibal who eats his or her own lips before

---

[44] Susan Golla, Skidi Pawnee Religion: A Structural Analysis, Master of Arts Thesis, George Washington University 1975.

[45] Regina Flannery, Two Concepts of Power, _Acts of the International Congress of Americanists_ 19: 185-189 1952.

[46] Werner Stenzel, The Sacred Bundles in Mesoamerican Religion, _Verhandlungen International Congress of Americanists_ 38, band 2: 347-352 1968.

[47] Robin Ridington, _Swan People_: _A Study of the Dunne-za Prophet Dance._ National Museums of Canada, Mercury Series 38: 1-132 1978; ms(a) Wechuge and Windigo: A Comparison of Cannibal Belief among Boreal Forest Athapaskans and Algonkians; ms(b) Trails of Meaning.

devouring friends and relatives.

The most universal expression of such avoidance is the taboo against menstruating women coming into contact with men's gear or sacred objects. Usually, it is said that women are too polluting at this time. In terms of potency, however, menstruating women are in a position to fuse other powerful flows and short circuit them, particularly since they are then congruent with the rhythmic cyclicity of the moon, the earth, and the tides.

Among the HoChunk ~ Winnebago[48] and others, families carry the burden of maintaining these distinctions. Each bundle had its own set of restrictions watched over by an enveloping mystical poison, which automatically killed anyone violating its taboos. The owner of a bundle could use this poison to cause harm, even though the bundle within was beneficial. As with the Dunne-za, any neutralizing of opposites intensifies potency into a stronger and more dangerous swirling.

For example, if a menstruating girl came into contact with a war bundle, an intensely female entity encountering a stronger male one, her menstrual flow continuously increased until she bled to death. Since a bundle is more powerful than an individual, anyone caught up within its currents could be drowned, sometimes in their own blood.

Throughout the Americas, as illustrated by the Interior Salish, access to power could release someone from moralistic conventions. Like the doctrine of revelation among Mormons, however, this does not negate the rigidity of society; rather it reinforces the rules by showing that only special people can flaunt breaches motivated by religious conviction. On the whole, therefore, the important configuration of potency, immortal, and visionary stays integrated. Categories are not confounded, and the reciprocity among everything in the great chain of being maintains all.

Surveying the guardian spirit complex, Swanson[49] found it distinctive to Native America and attributed it to the characteristically diffuse polity. Authority coincides with maturity, so adulthood emerges as an office serving both personal and communal interests, empowered by charisma. Following Max Weber, he derived charismatic power from a special relationship with whatever a culture considered to be of "ultimate value," whether God, truth, tradition, potency, or something else. Like Radin, Swanson was preoccupied with spirits.

He defined them by seven important attributes. They are selective in their choices, had separate existences, bestowed power, enabled a human to be more independent, remained autonomous, were perceived as real, and made a positive contribution to the person and society.

Ignoring the overall hierarchy or chain of being associated with power, his often redundant attributes make no mention of the different proportional amounts of power usually attributed to such spirits. This issue is complex and deserves careful attention. Some accounts indicate that sometimes a higher order immortal will test a human by impersonating a lower order one. Thus, a Thunderer might appear as an antmouse to test the sincerity of a quester, but an Ant could never effectively take the form of a Thunderer. At least, that is the way it appears. Yet, during the Timeless Age, to which immortals still belong, no one was limited to any particular shape.

Visionaries become charismatic because they mediate among an immortal, their own kin, and the community. The ultimate value-source of their ability, of course, is potency attributable to the high god, creator, or first cause. As source and summary, it is essentially deified thought or anthropomorphized Mind, with the qualities of a permeating nexus - an ordered series of radiating and ringing conduits filling the cosmos, like the pattern of a spider web, sweathouse

---

[48] Paul Radin, *The Winnebago Tribe*, Lincoln: University of Nebraska Press; BAE-AR 1923.

[49] Guy Swanson, The Search for a Guardian Spirit: A Process of Empowerment in Simpler Societies, *Ethnology* 12 (3): 359-378 1973.

frame, and circulatory system, as recognized by the Numic and Delaware.[50]

A succinct example comes from the Gros Ventre or Atsina, Algonkians of the northern Plains.[51] According to The Boy, a remarkable native thinker, the divinity is called "The One Who Has Control Over Everything By His Thought-Wish-Will," and the spider serves as his avatar, nicely linking Mind and web.

This wish-thought is also available to humans, having its clearest expression in public opinion. When "it is from the heart," the Atsina believe that its focused application can fulfill any wish, bolster any leader, or kill any deserving victim.

In the final analysis, potency is typified by memory, the aspect of Mind with the greatest significance in societies based on tradition, transmitted by oral, personal instruction. As a body of remembered knowledge, tradition leads to reverence of the elderly because they are the sources of and for ancient wisdom.

Memory is emphasized in at least three ways. First, the dead seem to take with them to the afterworld a distillation of their memories from life. Second, power has its source in the Mind of the universe, the precedent for all else. Third, the deity or divinity can be understood as functioning like a primordial synapse transforming remembrances into power surges among immortals, bundles, and shrines for use by humans. The outcome of all this networking is the past-oriented, concentrically-organized, and obliquely-responsible societies of the Americas, where the Golden Rule was both preached and practiced. Across the continent, the actions and thoughts of anyone had consequences for everyone.

These were communal, humanely sensitive societies where everyone was more responsible for others than for themselves. Hence, reciprocity and complementarity discouraged directly personal goals in favor of those in which each contributed to the needs of the whole. Therefore, personal aims were considered selfish, and were equated with sorcery and other harmful intentions. Leaders were honored and respected for giving to others, instead of keeping for themselves.

Memory is a recognition of the past imagined as a pulsating web. Its nexus is creation and its tendrils are accumulated remembrances. In tribal rituals recreating the origin of the world, the process is evoked by the text and rhythm of a sacred song. Of all acts, song best represents this universal kinesis of ebb and flow, rhythm and harmony, diffusion and concentration, rings and radials.

The Huron and Iroquoian term for power (*orenda*) derives from a root meaning 'song'. Having a tune, melody, rhythm, and flow, it was only appropriate that the bond between an immortal and a human be represented by the song passed between them. Thereafter, it marshalls power when needed to help self or others. The Dunne-za say that the melodic line of the song represents a trail that must be grabbed hold of with the mind.[52] Thus, most tribes greatly admire anyone with an excellent memory for songs.

Lastly, the analogy between potency and song can be extended to the land. Indeed, a native idiom for acquiring a song from an immortal is "learning from the land," not as a static place, but as an interflowing of contours, lives, winds, and waters.

---

[50] Jay Miller, A Strucon Model of Delaware Culture and the Positioning of Mediators, *American Ethnologist* 6 (4): 791-802 1979.

[51] John Cooper, *The Gros Ventre of Montana*: Religion and Ritual, Volume II, Regina Flannery, ed, Washington, DC: The Catholic University of America Press 1956.

[52] Robin Ridington, *Swan People: A Study of the Dunne-za Prophet Dance*, National Museums of Canada, Mercury Series 38 1978: 24.

As Jenness[53] expressed it so well,

For power, though universal perhaps, was graded, and whatever had little power could safely be neglected. [The world was peopled] with numerous 'powers', some great, mysterious, and awe-inspiring, some small of little or no account. Furthermore, following man's [*sic*] tendency everywhere, he gave them such anthropomorphic traits as speech and knowledge, even ascribed to them human or partly human forms ... [a] name heightened its individuality, giving it the status of a definite supernatural being.

The power of a species was believed immanent in each member, and especially personified as its boss, warder, or master. Ultimately, however, these were no more than nodes among the mysterious forces of nature, each and all of them having human attributes.

In English, the word 'earth', like the concept of potency, refers to the tiniest speck of dirt and to the entire planet. It is nothing and it is everything. This is its mystery. In native terms, "Earth is alive with potency and, therefore, especially sacred."

---

[53] Diamond Jenness, *Indians of Canada*, National Museum of Canada, Bulletin 65: 169-70.

Proteans[54]

In a shadowy world, being existed in iridescence. They had neither firm form nor fixed habits nor se abodes. Instead these people shimmered. But there were no humans among them until the Creator decided that humans would arrive on earth and, using telepathy, let everyone know they must have names and characteristics. For this Name Day, a place and time was set for the very first instance, putting these in motion throughout the world. Everyone was to be ready at dawn on that day, and those there first could choose their own name until all available names were assigned, and each given roles and duties in the coming age.

Of these First People one was different, he was Coyote, known mockingly as Imitator. During the shadowy world, beings had inherent personal powers which they could draw upon to help, hinder, or harm themselves and others. Everyone else was able to tap into the universal flow of forceful energy power called *shumesh*, Coyote pointed to his gut as the source of his powers, and indeed he was able to summon five 'poops' for advice on what to do in any situation. But then he would pretend that "He knew it all along" and acted on it as though it were his own idea. Still, in this way, unlike other beings, Coyote could think for himself.

Coyote's wife was Mole and they had children, but he was inept as a provider and was a philanderer if there was an opportunity. And he was very boastful, to cover his faults. When he learned about Name Day, he immediately began proclaiming that he would be first in line and known by the name of a mighty being, such as Eagle, Grizzly Bear, Salmon. These names would lead birds of the air, the four-footed of the land, and the fish of the water. He mocked Mole that he would then need a better wife. She was long suffering and did not respond to his taunts knowing from her lifetime with him that this was not to be. Fox, a relative, remarked that Coyote's name would always be available to him as no one else wanted it.

Coyote was still boasting loudly as everyone retired to their lodges to get a good night's sleep before the dawn of Name Day. Coyote decided he stay awake all night to be there first at dawn. When he did go home, his sons greeted in hopes that he had brought food, but their hope were again dashed. Mole gathered some old bone and stone boiled them in a basket to provide broth to feed their children. The she and they went to sleep.

Coyote sat by the fire, awaiting dawn. Late in the night he got sleepy so he propped his eyes open with tiny sticks, but still he fell asleep. Long after the sun was up, he awoke, as punishment for his abuse, his family did not wake him at dawn. Mole loved her husband, in spite of himself, and did not want him to get another name.

Now half-awake, Coyote rushed from the lodge to find empty space as though he was indeed the first in line. When he got to the Creator, he demanded the Grizzly, but Creator said it and all other names had already been taken by what were now known as Animal People. Coyote was crest fallen and now stuck with his name of Imitator forever.

Creator took pity though, and assigned Coyote the job of preparing the world for the humans who were coming soon. For this role, he also retained his unique ability to think, for good, bad, or ill, for himself. He was to change bad things to good, lay down the laws for those soon to come, and teach culturally useful skills. He transformed cannibals and monsters into

---

[54] Proteus was a Greek god who could tell the future, but when he was asked a question he didn't want to answer, he would change shapes. With someone or something protean, you get all the power of shape-shifting, plus some of the menace of a god you cannot control.

useful beings, calmed places that had been turbulent, and instructed how and when humans were to harvest the bounty of various places.

The powers in his gut were strengthened so he could continue to call upon them, and continue to pretend he already knew what they had suggested to him. In addition, because blundering was his way, Fox was given the ability to revive a dead Coyote by stepping over him four times, as long as one of his hairs remained.

Thus, after all, Coyote became a leader of sorts. Became of the prop sticks that held his eyes open, Coyote thereafter had slanted eyes, as did the humans who came later.

Finally, Creator decided that humans could receive lasting benefit by turning into Sweathouse. Inside, humans would purify, pray for strength and good luck, summon up their medicine powers, and overcome sickness, turmoil, and troubles.

Creator's ribs became the frame of Sweatlodge, skin its cover, and its ever mindfulness benefited the minds, hearts, and health of those in a sweat, both immediately and long term. From this central position, Creator served as source and summary for the flow of *shumesh* among and throughout the cosmos, available for other spirits, beings, and humans in need, in pity, and in force.

Iridescent Immortals

In his excellent treatment of the "irony of the masculine condition" expressed through the parrot among the Bororo, Crocker[55] made some observations on iridescence that I would like to pursue here. Among the Bororo, both whiteness and all colors are believed to be expressions of spirit. For them, all colors include hues which are variegated, stippled, and mottled. Crocker compared this belief with the spiritual beauty of stippled trout and finches' wings evoked in "Pied Beauty" ("Glory be to God for dappled things") by English Jesuit Gerard Manley Hopkins. Crocker concludes "One might even suppose that such iridescence is often found characteristic of liminal conditions or entities, a possibility which find confirmation in at least one other culture (Kaguru) beside the Bororo and our own Catholic one."

To explore this possibility, I will consider three examples from western Native North America where the Tsimshian, Salish, and Chemehuevi provide data regarding the iridescence of shells, feathers, scales, and crystals. Instead of liminality, these cases suggest that this shimmering, rainbow-like quality is an indication of the sacred, elevated, and immortal.

Among the Tsimshian, the group in the Canadian North Pacific associated with the saga of Asdiwal, iridescence is a prerogative of the royal families. As Halpin[56] has noted, their system of Crests (*pteex*) consists of twin axes; one for the generic emblems and another for ranking them. Crests derive from names which are inherited matrilinally within the households belonging to the semi-moieties of Blackfish-Wolf and of Raven-Eagle. The highest Crests are often called "Prince of X", and the artifacts depicting them are decorated with abalone shell inlay. For example, the Crest named Prince of Grizzlies, attributed to the Blackfish, has abalone panels on its frontlet and ceremonial hat.

Tsimshian social organization changes with the contrasting seasons. The Crests are

---

[55] Christopher Crocker, "My Brother The Parrot", *Social Use of Metaphor ~ Essays on the Anthropology of Rhetoric*, University of Pennsylvania Press 1977: 164-192.

[56] Marjorie Halpin, The Structure of Tsimshian Totemism: 16-35, *The Tsimshian and Their Neighbors of the North Pacific Coast*, Jay Miller and Carol Eastman, eds, Seattle: University of Washington Press 1984: 30, 29 Table 4.

emphasized during the summer when the people used to live in camps and engaged in economic pursuits under the direction of the chief as a political leader. During the winter, the Tsimshian gathered into their towns composed of plank houses and devoted themselves to religious matters sponsored by a chief in his priestly guise. During the winter, the Tsimshian articulated themselves in terms of wonders (_naxnox_), each derived from a name inherited through a household. With the spring runs of candlefish and salmon, Crests again replaced wonders.

As the Crests had hats as their primary vehicles, so the wonders had masks. The most dramatic wonders also included stupendous feats of engineering designed by special artists. When a member of the royalty sponsored a public display of wonders, such artists were employed to produce wonderfully elaborate displays. They worked in secret; outsiders who saw any of their preparations were killed on the spot.

The more important of the elite masks and other Wonders often evoked light and the iridescent of abalone and flames. Set into the finely polished sheen of carved cedar, the entire surface reflected the light of the open hearth fire.

The culminating image of thirty centuries of stone sculpture, if not also of the Naxnox masking tradition, is a pair of stone masks. The outer one is solid ("blind") but the inner has bored eye holes. The impression is that a dancer first appeared wearing the heavy, blank mask and then in an instant of high drama suddenly became sighted, what was blind became visionary, what was closed became open to the light.[57]

Among the Tsimshian, light is symbolized by the rainbow shimmering iridescence. It is an expression of pure light, of mystical power, and of the essence of knowledge, wisdom, and cosmic force. It is most analogous to the Levi-Straussian concept of "Mind."

Light is also emphasized in mythology. From time to time, earth has been visited by Shinning Youths who came down from Heaven, announced by four claps of thunder and four bolts of lightning. Foremost among them was the big man who eventually became Raven, the transformer linked to a cloak of black iridescent feathers reflecting the sunlight.

Iridescence is inherent to many types of feathers and shells, yet it is not always culturally emphasized or elaborated. For example, further south along the shores of Puget Sound, the Lushootseed (Puget Salish) recognize the beauty of abalone only in myth but not in practice. In the story "Crow Looks For A Husband", she eventually decides on the son of Shell because his constantly flickering colors and "pearliness" were very nice.[58] The word (_s'učəlgʷəcits_) used for pearliness also translates as iridescence. When asked about the import of this pearliness, the most articulate of Salish elders said that iridescence is an expression of immortal power; another, influenced by modern science fiction on TV and in the movies, said that iridescence was caused when different dimensions came into contact. The colorful flickering showed that the immortals were always moving, never staying still. The advantage of this account is that it shows how modern conditions can occasionally enable someone to better express ancient ideas. By referring to the media, it was easier for both of us to understand what the other had in mind.

Shell and feathers are not the only mediums which figure in this belief. Like the trout

---

[57] Wilson Duff, _Images, Stone, BC ~ Thirty Centuries of Northwest Coast Indian Sculptures_. Vancouver: Hancock House 1975; Marjorie Halpin, 'Seeing' in Stone ~ Tsimshian Masking and the Twin Stone Masks: 269-287. _The World Is As Sharp As a Knife ~ An Anthology In Honor of Wilson Duff_, Donald Abbot, ed, Victoria: British Columbia Provincial Museum 1981.

[58] Vi Hilbert, _A Lushootseed Reader_, Seattle: Lushootseed Press 1983.

evoked by Hopkins, the combined effects of light and water further highlighted the beauty of the staple food. Salmon, their bodies sleek from fighting upstream to spawn, caught the glint of the sun on their scales.

This is hardly unique to Tsimshian or Lushootseed. In his summary of a Californian Modoc story, Levi-Strauss[59] describes a salmon as beautiful: "all blue, gold and green." Later, he refers to "its gleaming iridescent scales," and also notes the analogy to shell: "the prose of Modoc myths is as brilliantly colorful as the pearly luster of the haliotis or ear-shell. It is shot through with vivid glints of red, violet, blue, green and gold".

South of the Modoc are the Chemahuevi, a Basin group on the California-Arizona border. Their traditions, as expressed by George Laird, a resident Cherokee, have been admirably preserved through the efforts of his wife, Carobeth. She has wisely urged the adoption of the term "immortal" to replace the incorrect, but frequently used, term "supernatural" to refer to the class of personages of the Mythic Age. Furthermore, she goes one better and characterizes them as shimmering between forms, able simultaneously to appear as humans, animals, plants, and spirits.[60]

It is these immortals who appear to recent humans and agree to share some of their power, guaranteeing the basis of any successful career. One of the most prominent of these belonged to the shaman. In this instance, the shared power always came from one of the immortal shamans mentioned in mythology, such as the Duck. According to George Laird, one Duck, probably the mallard, was noted for the iridescence of its feathers. In Chemehuevi, a Numic language, this is literally called the 'water-purple' of the feathers: more poetically, it is their "'rainbow-shimmer".[61]

The dynamism evoked by this shimmering duality is a hallmark of the concept of power espoused throughout Native North (and South) America. A review of other representative examples would be monotonous, taxing of space and salience. It would merely confirm the aptness of the above cases. Against the charge that they are only from western America, I need only broaden them with the example of the rock crystal, an emblem of shamans and of power throughout the Americas, if not also the world. Underhill[62] assigned the rock crystal to the basic strata of Americanist beliefs, together with girl's puberty and first foods rites.

Can these examples be related to liminality? In his classic statement, Turner[63] calls it a state or process that is betwixt and between. Its characteristics are ambiguous and indeterminate; it is "frequently likened to death, to being in the womb, to invisibility, to darkness, to bisexuality, to the wilderness, and to the eclipse of the sun or moon."

As the previous cases illustrate, however, the role of iridescence among these tribes has to do with the class of beings called the immortals, who are anything but temporary or transitional. The association, therefore, is with the sacred and the mystical, though they can

---

[59] Claude Levi-Strauss, *The Naked Man ~ Introduction to the Science of Mythology ~* Volume 4. New York: Harper and Row 1981: 66, 77, 85.

[60] Carobeth Laird, *The Chemehuevis*, Banning, California: Malki Museum Press 1976: 110.

[61] Carobeth Laird, Chemehuevi Shamanism, Sorcery, and Charms. *Journal of California and Great Basin Anthropology* 2 (1): 80-87 1980: 82.

[62] Ruth Underhill, *Red Man's Religions ~ Beliefs and Practices of the Indians North of Mexico*, University of Chicago Press 1965: 63.

[63] Victor Turner, *The Ritual Process*, Chicago: Aldine Publishing Co 1969: 95.

appear to shimmer. Needham[64] has observed that "The most prominent images of the mystical ... are darkness, femininity, passivity, and the left."

Granted that universals do not always apply in specific cases, the association between iridescence and darkness is particularly suspect. Light, movement, and color are to be expected, often expressed through the medium of fire and water.

The associations of iridescence, thus, are not directly with liminality, but rather with the movement out of or away from it and into revelation. It is the sign of a new, holy, and wise state. It marks the getting of wisdom and the coming into the light. What comes before may be liminal, sometimes leaving a dark afterimage or residue; but, this is influence not identity; after darkness comes the light, the shimmer of the rainbow that marked the end of the Flood for Noah.

Concentration takes place during the dark and quiet, but it is made manifest by sharing it publicly around the fire. It is this message that the demiurge of the Coos of Oregon passed on to Melville Jacobs and then Levi-Strauss[65] "I will send ten sounds around the world, and you must shut your eyes then, otherwise you will have no knowledge."

[64] Rodney Needham, *Reconnaissances*, University of Toronto Press 1980: 89.
[65] Claude Levi-Strauss, *The Naked Man ~ Introduction to the Science of Mythology ~* Volume 4, New York: Harper and Row 1981: 581 #4.

High-Minded High Gods in North America

In his Manchester College lectures at Oxford in 1932, Fr Wilhelm Schmidt, SDV,[66] considered the ethnographic evidence for the belief and cults concerned with the notion of a (monotheistic) High God in Native North America. While his interpretations of the relative antiquity of the three ethno-linguistic groups with which he was concerned are no longer tenable, the ethnographic reality of a High God for each of these groupings remains confirmed. According to Schmidt's argument, the Yuki of California with their singularity as an unaffiliated language group were the oldest stratum; the Algonkians represented an intermediate stage that was individualistic since they "no longer practice collective tribal initiation of boys, still less of girls";[67] and the Interior Salish (whom he called "Inland Selish") were the most recent with the belief but no cult.

Through the succeeding years, other High Gods have been reported for Amerind tribes either without further comment or with the parenthetical remark that they may have originated under the stimulation of Christian missionization. The fact of the matter is that no one, except theologians, has presented a plausible explanation for the existence of the North American High Gods. Because I have recently been involved in fieldwork among many of the tribes discussed by Schmidt and I have surveyed the Americanist literature to locate other High Gods, I feel that this background enables me to present a structuralist explanation for High Gods as an ultimate projection and personification of the symbolism of Mind (Intellect) so basic to many Amerind cultures. I see in the High God phenomenon an empirical vindication of the theoretical importance which Claude Levi-Strauss has placed on the Mind as the apical mediator for all human societies. The occurrence of the High God in North America, thereby, represents a particular example of the more general phenomenon. The personification aspect derives from the prevalence of anthropocentrism, the Precopernican perspective,[68] in Amerind cultures. The usual explanation offered throughout Native North America as to the nature of the world is that everything (animal, plant, spirit, celestial bodies) is at base a Man or a Woman who assumes the "cloak" of their species or identity when trafficking with the Human World.

With this précis of the argument, we can now consider the ethnographic data before summarizing this new understanding of the role of the High God as mediating Intellect, as mindful master. We will first review evidence from the Yuki, Delaware, and Sanpoil before assessing data from the Naskapi, Creek, Pawnee, Keres Pueblos, and Lakota Sioux.

---

[66] Wilhelm Schmidt, *High Gods in North America*, Oxford: U Press 1933. From 1912 to his death in 1954, he published 12 volumes of *Der Ursprung der Gottesidee* (*The Origin of the Idea of God*), asserting Urmonotheism for almost all tribal peoples believing in a high god – usually a sky god – as benevolent creator who was First Cause of all things and Ruler of Heaven and Earth before men and women began to worship many gods. Schmidt was an ordained Roman Catholic priest in the Society of the Divine Word (SDV), founder and editor of the journal *Anthropos*, and linguist famous for his comparative work on Mon-Khemer and wider Austronesian family.

[67] Wilhelm Schmidt, *High Gods in North America*, Oxford: U Press 1933: 63.

[68] Mary Douglas, *Purity and Danger*: An Analysis of Concepts of Pollution and Taboo, London: Pelican Books 1970.

According to Yuki mythology, the Creator *Taikomal* ~ The One Who Walks Alone first appears as down, floating on the primal water, which changed into himself to the accompaniment of an all-pervading song.[69] After he had created the world and travelled around to inspect and improve it, he rose into the sky where his continued existence is known because thunder is his voice, wind his breath, lightning his punishment, and wild tobacco smoke his preferred offering. Because of his ubiquity, *Taikomal* can be equated with all-pervading thought or consciousness. Since he remains in the sky, his appearance to the candidates of the highest ranking degree of Yuki shamanism, the sky shamans, must take place through the medium of thought. The young boys being initiated into the Creator Cult must remain silent, fasting, motionless for four days; again presumably to facilitate mental contact with the Creator. Now that *Taikomal* has physically left the earth, therefore, his essential intellectual quality has emerged with particular clarity.

The Delaware Creator is *Kishalamukong* ~ The One Who Created Us By His Thoughts so his cerebral asset is blatantly emphasized.[70] He entrusted the care of the world to the Atlantean Cosmic Turtle, who is also believed to be sapient by the Delaware.[71] The Creator is visualized as eternally sitting in the twelfth or highest heavenly tier above the earth. If and when he communicates with these earth, it is by means of his thoughts, or what some modern Delaware prefer to call the "astroprojection" of his mind. His worship in the Big House rite, summarized by Schmidt,[72] was specifically explained to me as involved with the Delaware sending their good thoughts and prays up to him.

During research with the Sanpoil division of Interior Salish, I had occasion to note the emphasis which they place on the mind or consciousness. When probing the memories of various elders, each of them could recollect events back to the time when they "came to." In American English, "to come to" usually refers to regaining consciousness after some traumatic experience. For the Sanpoil, however, "coming to" means to gain mental awareness as a distinct individual sometime about the age of two years old.[73] In Sanpoil belief, their version of the Interior Salish High God is called Sweat Lodge. He was once a Man during the Myth Age, but near its terminus he decided to become eyeless, armless, and legless by transforming into the first semi-hemispherical sweat lodge.[74] Since that time, people who seek continued health or solution to a quandary have entered the sweat lodge to clarify 'their minds and commune with the Creator. In the Sanpoil case then, too, the creator has become a quintessential embodiment of the mind. Moreover, as part of the origin myth. Coyote receives the charge from the Creator to modify and transform the world because Coyote was the first character to think for himself. In addition to these examples initially discussed by Schmidt in some detail, there are additional

---

[69] George M Foster, A Summary of Yuki Culture, *Anthropological Records* 5 (3): 154-244 1944.

[70] This and other data derive from my fieldnotes taken during over six years of research with Delaware-Lenape now living in the state of Oklahoma.

[71] Jay Miller, Why the World is on the Back of a Turtle, *Man* 9 (2): 306-308 1974.

[72] Wilhelm Schmidt, *High Gods in North America*, Oxford: U Press 1933: 94-102.

[73] These data are drawn from my 1977-78 fieldnotes concerned with Sanpoil and other tribes now together on the Colville Reservation, north central Washington State.

[74] Verne F Ray, The Sanpoil and Nespelem: Salishan Tribes of Northeastern Washington. *University of Washington Publications in Anthropology* #5: 1-237 1931. The legend of sweat lodge continues to be told by Sanpoils and other Colvilles.

High Gods whose consideration provides further support for my argument.

At nearly the same time that Schmidt was examining the data discussed above, Father John Cooper was probing the belief in a High God in the eastern subarctic of Canada along the west coast of James Bay. There he found an unquestionable belief in a High God in addition to a trinity composed of the Master of Food, the Master of Life, and the Master of Death. The High God is equated with Manitu, the source of supernatural power. This is an important equation because Cooper[75] cites the word *sokadis'u* as meaning either someone "has supernatural power or mind power" as distinct from mere physical strength.

Among the Creek (Mvskoki, Muskogee), the Creator is called Ohfvngv (Above) or Breath-Holder and breath is equated with life.[76] Creek shaman-priests use techniques of blowing and breathing in their cures and rituals. As life was equated with breath so the essence of life was equated with "clear thought and vision." In one account of the origin of the world, seven people were able to expand the parameters of dry land "by extending their thoughts".[77] Similarly, although all Creek are endowed with life-breath, the most important men, those who are the foundation of the most complex religious ceremony, the Green Corn or Busk rite, are respectfully called the brains or mind of the Busk.[78]

The Pawnee High God is called *Tirawahat* ~ Expanse of the Heavens ~ *Tirawa* ('The One Supreme Power In The Heavens Who Created The World').[79] Here the data are not entirely clear and the example may be spurious in terms of monotheism since he was a wife called Vault of the Heavens; however, Weltfish[80] does note that for the Pawnee "the primary level of reality is thought ... the Pawnee deity ... began the process of creation with thoughts and so created the universe and the stars, and they in turn were to create man in their own image ... In the Pawnee context, the thinking man was the essential human being."

The Keres example is especially instructive because here the Creator is a Woman rather than a Man and she created and articulated the world by the sheer power of her thoughts. For this reason, her name *Tsityostinako* is often translated as Thought-Woman,[81] but careful probing of the meaning of *Tsityosti* (*-nako* indicates a woman's name) leads me to suggest that this term indicates full consciousness or complete mental awareness.[82]

Out of deference to the Sioux, whom Schmidt[83] unjustly characterized as blood-thirsty, warlike, sun-worshippers, I feel compelled to also add the Great Mystery (*Wakan Tanka*) of the

---

[75] John M Cooper, The Northern Algonquian Supreme Being, The Catholic U of America, Anthropological Series 2: 1-78 1934: 38. {included herein}

[76] John Swanton, Religious Beliefs and Medical Practices of the Creek Indians, Washington, DC: *Bureau of American Ethnology – Annual Report* 1924-1925 #42: 473-672 1928: 481.

[77] John Swanton, Religious Beliefs and Medical Practices of the Creek Indians 1928: 487.

[78] John Swanton, Religious Beliefs and Medical Practices of the Creek Indians 1928: 302.

[79] Susan S Golla, Skidi Pawnee Religion: A Structural Analysis, DC: MA, George Washington U 1975.

[80] Gene Weltfish, *The Lost Universe*, New York: Ballantine Books 1971: 16; *Lost Universe ~ Pawnee Life and Culture*, University of Nebraska Press 1977.

[81] Franz Boas, Keresan Texts, Publications of the American Ethnological Society #8, 1 & 2: 1-300 1928.

[82] My research on the Keres Pueblos occupied 1968-69 and 1972.

[83] Wilhelm Schmidt, *High Gods in North America*, Oxford: U Press 1933: 60.

Lakota division to the listing of High Gods.[84] According to the holy men, the great mystery is simultaneously formless yet tetradic (quartered along various axes), not identifiable yet everywhere, and incomprehensible yet worthy of serious reflection by analogy to a universal intelligent sentience.[85]

Based on these eight examples, I find support for my assertion that the role of the High God is a projection and personification of human thoughtful intelligence, of Mind. Other examples might also be cited if the data were more complete and conclusive. For the present, however, these eight will do nicely. A corollary of my assertion is that [919] the personification is necessary because these and other tribal cultures live with an anthropomorphic world view. This corollary is also supported most strongly by the Keres example of a Woman Creator. In other words, while almost all High God Creators are personified as men, the underlying rule of anthropomorphization rather than straight masculinization permits the occasional Woman Creator to appear. Since both are projections of human thought, the Precopernican world view exists without challenge from some other strategy such as zoomorphization or deification.

This projection and anthropomorphization also provides support, at least in terms of Native North America, for the assertion by Levi-Strauss that the Mind serves as the ultimate mediator between Nature/Culture. As all-pervasive, monotheistic personifications, these High Gods indeed do mediate the culturally-constructed natural world of their adherents. Until now, Levi-Strauss has provided us with such examples of the importance of the mind as the incest taboo, cooking, classification systems, and language. As suggested by the eight Amerind cases summarized above, we may now add an even more potent if intangible metaphor for the mind: The pre-existent High God ~ Creator who has both baffled and intrigued Americanists for so long because no one was properly mindful of the role he/she/one plays in human thought and expression.

Jay Miller, High-Minded High Gods in North America, *Anthropos* 75: 916-919 1980.

---

[84] Ross Hassick, The Sioux Life and Customs of a Warrior Society, Norman: U of Oklahoma Press 1964.

[85] Additional support for the equation of *Wakan Tanka* with Mind as knowledge is found in William Powers, *Oglala Religion*, Lincoln: U of Nebraska Press 1977: 172, 182.

The Matter of the (Thoughtful) Heart:
Centrality, Focality, or Overlap

Throughout Native North America, and elsewhere in the world, the heart is often considered to be the locus of thought. After examining interpretations for this phenomenon as centrality or focality, we concentrate on an explanation of overlap as redundancy in order to discuss the main quality of mediators and the emic objectivization of the Levi-Strausian concept of Mind as mediator between Nature and Culture. Focus on the heart as a singularity provides further support for the importance of a high god/deity also associated with mindfulness.

THE ULTIMATE TEST of any scientific explanation is its ability to integrate, or account for, more data than any alternative attempts. The most salient characteristic of this integration is its redundancy throughout the data, its organization of diversity. For this reason the most powerful anthropological explanation generally available at present is the structuralism of Claude Levi-Strauss. The notion of structure enables the recognition of the redundancy of the opposition of Nature and Culture as mediated by Mind throughout all human enterprise.

This redundancy is not limited to straight parallels, however, but can take other forms of relationship. Levi-Strauss has shown that data is never only what it seems; it is more, intricately more. Behind the intricacy is the process of transformation, code switching, that can occur as equation, reversal, segregation, and neutralization. Equation is the straightforward relationship of direct parallels between the terms involved in the relation, e.g, $A : B :: C : D$. Reversal inverts this relationship, generally reversing the most frequent association, eg, $A : B :: D : C$. By segregation, the relationship between the terms is extended or overdrawn, eg, $A : B :: Y : Z$. Alternatively, neutralization narrows the relationship between the terms, eg, $A : B :: A_1 : B_1$. This explication is necessary because structuralism is often accused of being a mentalistic exercise, without any empirical basis. This is patently false, because as part of anthropology, structuralism must be empirical: "That anthropology is first of all an empirical science is obvious: each culture that we approach confronts us with an entirely new situation which can only be described and understood at the cost of the most concrete and painstaking scrutiny".[86]

Nonetheless, structuralism parts company with the rest of empirical anthropology because its goals are "understanding" rather than "proof." It recognizes the primacy of form over content, so that concepts and ideas are given precedence over behavior and events. While the focus of analysis is upon relationships, the understanding emerges from inductive rethinking of the ideas represented by the data. As Levi-Strauss[87] has said explicitly, quoting Durkheim, "if sociological phenomena are just objectivated systems of ideas, to explain them is to re-think them in their logical order and this explanation finds in itself its own proof; at most, a few examples could be added as confirmation."

The constraints on this rethinking are those imposed by universal features of human thought processes and by localized factors of the techno-environment of a given human

---

[86] Claude Levi-Strauss, Structuralism and Ecology, *Barnard Alumnae Magazine* 1972.

[87] French Sociology, *Twentieth Century Sociology*, G Gurvitch and WE Moore, eds, New York: Philosophical Library 1945: 528.

community. Every culture selects from the range of meaningful relationships and expresses them in terms of available signs and symbols derived from common human experiences and from the local ecology. [339]

Rather than apply this theoretical background to particular cultural data, I will use it to explore one of the most fundamental aspects of structuralism – Mind. If ideas are to have anthropological relevence they need objectivization in social pheonomena; their currency and redundancy rests on their empirical representation. In an earlier paper I explored the objectivization of Mind in terms of the so-called high gods widely reported from Native North America. There I argued that these high gods, bereft of all attributes save intelligence, serve as personifications of the ubiquitous, cosmic mediation of Mind for these cultures. In the present paper I would like to focus more intensely on the widely reported emic interpretation from all over Native America that the heart is the locus of thought, and sometimes also of emotions. First I will present a brief survey of such ethnographic reports from throughout the continent, and then I will individually examine three alternative explanations for the thoughtful heart as based on the recognition of centrality, focality, or overlap. This examination will lead us into the works of Aristotle, who also glimpsed the importance of this problem.

Ethnographic Reports

The broad spread of this phenomenon, regardless of linguistic, cultural, or geographical differences, can be seen from the following representative sample, organized for convenience from the Atlantic to the Pacific coasts of North America. This phenomena is actually much more widespread, probably once quite explicit even in Indo-European,[88] so the Native American examples are also indicative of global ones.

My initial experience with the thoughtful heart occurred during fieldwork with Delaware people, whose ancestors once dwelt along the Atlantic slope of the eastern United States. The Delaware believe that the heart is the source of thought and of emotions.[89] Farther west, in the Plains culture area, the gestural lingua franca usually called the sign language represented the words "to think" or "thought" by pointing to the heart before bringing the hand forward "to gesture thought coming forth from the heart".[90] For the American Southwest, we have the report of Carl Jung[91] that members of the pueblo of Taos in New Mexico believe they think with the heart. In Arizona, Spier[92] found that "the Maricopa believed that one thinks with his heart," and that one's emotions were registered by the heart beat.

In the Northwest, the widely used trade pidgin called Chinook jargon expressed the word for thinking as literally "to use the heart".[93] More specifically within this area, the word for

---

[88]   Jay Miller, Delaware Anatomy: With Linguistic, Social, and Medical Aspects, *Anthropological Linguistics* 19 (4): 144-66 1977.

[89]   Jay Miller, Delaware Anatomy 1977: 147.

[90]   D Umiker-Sebeok and T Sebeok, *Aboriginal Sign Languages of the Americans and Australia*, The Americas and Australia, vol. #2, New York: Plenum Press 1978: 120.

[91]   Tony Hillerman, *The Spell of New Mexico*, Albuquerque: University of New Mexico Press 1976: 38.

[92]   Leslie Spier, Yuman Tribes of the Gila River, Chicago: University of Chicago Press 1933: 33.

[93]   J Gill, *Gill's Dictionary* of the Chinook Jargon, Portland: JK Gill 1933.

'heart' in the Salishan language of the Snkyius ~ Moses-Columbia is based on the root for 'think'.[94] Also in the Pacific drainage, the Kalapuya had many expressions relating the heart to thought and emotions. For example, the phrase, "Heart is not good" meant "I am angry" and "How is your heart" meant "What do you think?"[95] Similar idiomatic usage equating the heart, thought, and emotions is reported for other areas, such as the Great Lakes.[96] These few examples should indicate the ubiquity of the thoughtful heart; especially telling are the illustrations from such international means of communication as the Plains sign language and Chinook jargon.

To initiate our discussion of the more general explanation of these occurrences, [341] we must revert to the classical roots of European intellectualism and follow the lead of Aristotle.

Alternative Explanations

The thoughtful heart is not only widespread, it is also ancient, attracting the attention of no less a figure than Aristotle.[97] In discussing animal life, some of which is bloodless, he nonetheless observes: "For in all animals there must be some central and commanding part of the body, to lodge the sensory portion of the soul and the source of life."

In the higher animals there was blood, and a heart in the commanding center of the body. Of all animals only humans stand erect, with the upper part of the body directed toward the upper realms of the universe. After arguing that the brain was a cold organ thickly covered with flesh and not the sensory center that some had claimed, Aristotle argued that the central location of the heart and its greater abundance of heat-generating blood explained the human upright stance:

"Heat ... tends to make the body erect;
and thus it is that man is the most erect of animals."

Aristotle was led to disparage the brain because it was cold, bloodless, and enclosed. But the heart was the same as or analogous to organs in all animals; warm, full of blood, "in anatomical connection, through the blood vessels, with all the sense-organs," and "in a central position befitting the supreme organ". Included within these attributes are glimpses of the three alternative explanations to which we will now turn.

Great reliance was placed on the central position of the heart, explicitly because such centrality provided a commanding position within the body. In more general terms, I view this argument as based on a synecdoche, having the part stand for the whole; in this case, the center of the body represents the entire organism. The difficulty with this explanation is that while the

---

[94] MD Kinkade, The Lexical Domain of Anatomy in Columbian Salish, Peter de Ridder Press Publications on Salish Languages # 1 1975.

[95] Melville Jacobs, Kalapuya Texts, *University of Washington Publications in Anthropology* # 11: 1-394, Seattle 1945: 95, 137.

[96] Vernon Kinietz, *The Indians of the Western Great Lakes* 1615-1760, University of Michigan, Museum of Anthropology, Occasional Contributions #10 1940: 200.

[97] Aristotle, *De Portibus Animalism*, vol. #5 of The Works of Aristotle, WD Ross, ed, Oxford: Clarendon Press 1931: 655b, 669b, 656a #3.

synecdoche accounts for the emphasis on the heart as a metaphor for the body, it does not explain why the heart should also serve as the locus of thought.

Therefore we might consider the heart as an example of focality, the condensation of a complex relationship around a fixed, central position in the body. Focality appears to be a better explanation, because it includes not only the location of the heart, but also its direct links with the rest of the body by means of the circulation of the blood. Similarly the circulation of the blood might be equated with the circulation of ideas and hence with thought. However, we are still unable to suggest a clear association of Mind and thoughts with the heart rather than with the more analogous blood. To complete the explanations and trace the relationships involved, we must carefully consider the process of objectifying ideas.

While the notions of centrality or focality have explanatory power for dealing with various signs as metaphors, they are inadequate for dealing with the relationships between Mind and heart. This relationship characterizes these objectivized ideas not as metaphors but rather as mediators. Mediators have special properties, which enable them both to synthesize the members of an oppositional pair and to bear an identity with other mediators recognized by a culture.[98] Generally all mediators form an identifiable grouping, because each shares the property of being a "permeating nexus." A mediator functions as a permeating nexus when it has a central point from which some tendril-like appendages emanate to permeate, engulf, and encompass everything else in the cultural realm. On this basis the frequent references to mediators such as spiders, crosses, and other nexi become understandable as variant or diverse permutations on this quality of mediators. More importantly Mind itself as a mediator is also associated with this shared property. Some ethnographic reports explicitly state that thought proceeds from a fixed point, such as a creator, to permeate the world.

This quality of nexal permeation is at the heart of the objectivization of Mind. It is neither centrality nor locality, because its characteristic is that of overlap into all cultural domains, and of redundancy throughout the culture. It is the organization of diversity, rather than some form of diminution through substitution of part for whole or condensation; the range of variation is organized, rather than simplified.

On the basis of this argument the identity of heart and Mind should be obvious. As Mind is the ultimate mediator, the permeating nexus, so the heart becomes its locus because the heart and circulatory system of blood vessels are a graphic objectivization of this mediator. The heart is the nexus and the vessels its permeations. Together they redundantly overlap through the entire body. In the extremely rational world that was Native America, logical consistency was an important adjunct to the entire world view. In this as in any other pre-Copernican universe – to use Mary Douglas's phrase[99] – body symbolism played the crucial role in organizing a culture. Now that science has usurped the explanatory power of logical constructs for the modem world, we are less likely to grasp the satisfaction that derived from the equation of heart and Mind.

---

[98]   Jay Miller, American Humanity and Other Monsters ~ A Structuralist Analysis Of Frankenstein, The Mummy, Dracula, and The Wolfman; Anthropology of the Unknown, International Conference On Humanoid Monsters, U of British Columbia, May 10-13 1978.

[99]   Mary Douglas, *Purity and Danger: An Analysis of Concepts of Pollution and Taboo*, London: Pelican Books 1966.

They were isomorphic not only for understanding the cosmos, but also for rationally articulating an individual. As body is usually equated with house for the communal group, and with the cosmos for the entire realm of living things, the human form is usually the most powerful metaphor for a small-scale society.

The total integration of the world is accomplished by the isomorphism of heart and Mind. As the body articulated a metaphor that pervaded the cultural world, so did the heart and mind of an individual serve to mediate this world on three levels. First, at the level of sensory experience, heart and thought mediated the conceptualization of the individual. In some cultures centrality is given limited recognition at this level in that the concentric triad of center, inside, outside is usually expressed as heart, right side, and left side. Second, at the level of community interaction, the heart and mind together serve to integrate the individual members in terms of shared thoughts. Third, at the level of the cosmos. Mind as the ultimate mediator is directly linked with the heart of an individual, overlapping and crosscutting all other divisions.

The consistent reports situating the locus of thought at the heart are indicative more of certain universal characteristics of mediators than they are of any particular process or perspective revealed by these data. The heart as a nexus with the vessel system as its permeations serves as an objectivized idea for organizing diverse data in terms of a center and an infinitely expanding set of emanations. The thoughtful mind overlaps other phenomena, giving it a redundant, rational, and coherent unity.

In the last analysis, however, the only "improvement" science has made to our thought has been to replace the heart with its vessel tendrils by the brain with its neural lattice work.

Jay Miller, The Matter of the (Thoughtful) Heart:
Centrality, Focality, or Overlap,
Journal of Anthropological Research 36 (3): 338-342 1980.

Deified Mind among the Keresan Pueblos

Stanley Newman did not introduce me to the literature on the Keresan Pueblos, but he certainly made me more aware of its complexities. As my undergraduate advisor, he had the difficult task of guiding me through shifting loyalties to archaeology, linguistics, and symbolic anthropology. My rudder through it all was a fascination with the Keres that was continually reinforced by my exposure to their prehistory as a member of the Anasazi Origins Project, their ethnography through reading, their public rituals as an observer, and their language via examples used by Newman from his fieldwork with Laguna.

My increasing concern became Keresan belief in a supreme deity, who has been called Thought Woman in the literature, revolves around many dimensions with symbolic oppositions involving Man / Woman, Sacred / Secular, and Nature / Culture. As an androgynous being, with the potential to assume any form but particularly that of a spider, this creator truly presides over a rational universe.

Eventually, the Keres took me to graduate school and provided a dissertation. They continue to fascinate me, but now in comparison with other Native American tribes where I have done more sustained field work.[100]

Yet one aspect of Keres culture stands out above all others. This is their belief in a high god or supreme deity who has been often called Thought Woman in the literature. Recently, several authors, themselves belonging to Laguna Pueblo,[101] have also provided commentary on this being. Among the things that impressed me in Newman's classes was his interest in the more subjective side of linguistics, particularly his interest in the sound symbolism and psychiatric dimensions of speech.

Assessing both the older literature on this deity and modern commentary, our understanding of this "female" deity should improve. It is not that such a being is unique to the Keres, after all the Shawnee pray to Grandmother and the southern Numic to Ocean Woman.

The earliest account in this century occurs in the curious volume by Gunn:[102]

> Their theory is that reason (personified) is the supreme power, a master mind that has always existed, which they call *Sitch-tche-na-ko*. This is the feminine form for thought or reason. She had one sister, Shro-tu-me-na-ko, memory or instinct. Their belief is that *Sitch-tche-na-ko* is the Creator of all, and to her they offer their most devout prayers, but never to *Shro-tu-me-na-ko*. They say it is bad to do so. This shows that they know of the two divisions of the mind, reason and instinct, and also that they are aware of the apparent uselessness, and possible evil consequences, of cultivating the subjective mind.

---

[100] High-Minded High Gods in North America, *Anthropos* 75: 916-19 1980; Shamanism in western Native America: Numic, Salish, and Keres Pueblo; *Woman, Poet, Scientist:* Essays in New World Anthropology, honoring Dr Emma Louise Davis; Great Basin Foundation, Los Altos, California: Ballena Press 1985.

[101] Elsie Clews Parsons, *Laguna Genealogies*, American Museum of Natural History, Anthropological Papers 19 (5): 131-282 1923.

[102] John Gunn, *Schat-Chen: history, traditions and narratives of the Queres Indians of Laguna and Acoma*, Albuquerque: Albright and Anderson 1917: 89.

While there is much in his book which is questionable, as in some of this paragraph, his basic statement does hold. The creator at Laguna is something like personified thought or reason. This was confirmed a few years later in the work of Parsons,[103] where she names the four sisters who figure in the Origin Saga: *iyetiku, tsichinnako, naustiti, ushstiti.* In a footnote she adds, for the second, "The etymology given is *tsichu,* think, *chinnaku,* femaleness."

Again from Laguna, Boas,[104] building on the fieldwork of Parsons, makes reference to *ts'its'i.'na.k'o* and to "Thought Woman (the Spider?)." He includes the only available text in Keresan (Keresic) making reference to her role as creator of the universe.

At the end of their discussion of the ceremonial calendar at Laguna, Dutton and Marmon[105] call attention to "Reason, a great power − the Great Spirit, we might call it − had created earth, the sun, the stars, and all living creatures." This is again the deity in the guise of an English equivalent.

The most careful statement, however, has come from a member of the pueblo, attempting to compare Keres and Christian notions of the deity. For Purley,[106] the hallmarks of Thought Woman are the concepts of a supreme being, a female, a fused godhead, and a denial of human dominion over the world.

In the course of this, he reports

> *Tse che nako* is all-comprehensive and in no need to be worshipped, therefore she does not demand worship for herself to satisfy "Her Own." "Her Own" includes all life possibilities within herself.

> The Keres people believe that *Tse che nako* has more female than male attributes: therefore she is referred to and approached as if she is female.

> *Tse che nako* is not limited to a female role in the total theology ... she is both Mother and Father to all people and to all creatures. She can function in whichever role she chooses and very often does ...

> She did not restrict the process of creation only to herself. Tse che nako included the power to create individual thought in all human beings and all creatures. In other words, all living things can create, although it is a matter of degree.

> Keres holy men hesitate to mention *Tse che nako*'s name, especially for purely secular discussions. Thought Woman's name is reserved for use only in

---

[103] Elsie Clews Parsons, *Notes on Ceremonialism at Laguna,* Anthropological Papers of the American Museum of Natural History 19 (Part 4): 85-131 1920: 114 #3.

[104] Franz Boas, Keresan Texts, Publications of the American Ethnological Society # 8, 1 & 2: 1-300 1928: 7, 276.

[105] Bertha Dutton and Miriam Marmon, *The Laguna Calendar,* University of New Mexico Bulletin 283. Anthropological Series 1 (2): 1-21 1936: 20.

[106] Anthony Purley, Keres Pueblo Concepts of Deity, *American Indian Culture and Research Journal* 1 (1): 29-32 1974: 30, 31, 32.

sacred ceremonies. In secular discussions and teachings, *Tse che nako* is often symbolically referred to as Old Spider Woman or Spider Woman.

> ... evil, while it is a separate, recognized force, is not so strong that it must be blamed for mankind's wrongdoing. Mankind is responsible for its own behavior.

Curiously, Purley does not mention that aspect of the Christian tradition which is closest to Keresan notions of divinity, namely Sophia as Wisdom and feminized Mind.

Lastly, we have the poem that begins the famous novel by Silko,[107] herself of Laguna ancestry, paying homage to "*Ts'its'tsi'nako*, Thought-Woman" (line 1), Thought-Woman, the spider (line 10), who is "sitting in a room" (line 14) thinking the story we are about to be told.

Laguna is one of seven contemporary Keres pueblos in central New Mexico, and, to some extent, the most divergent. About 1870, after the railroad came through their lands, the pueblo split into different groups. While all of the other Keres are nominally Roman Catholic, Laguna had a sizeable Protestant segment, the outcome of intermarriage with American men of authority. The more traditionally conservative and Catholic party left Old Laguna and settled at Isleta, a Tiwa Pueblo just south of Albuquerque. After a few years, many of them came back to Laguna land and built the town of Mesita, although their religious paraphernalia, or much of it, stayed at Isleta.[108]

As I have reconstructed it, Keres social organization is binary at many levels, all of them pervaded by an axiomatic concern with gender. Thus, of the seven modern towns, three (Cochiti, Santo Domingo, and San Felipe) are manly, characterized by leaders drawn from the priesthoods and by the initiation of only boys into the cult of the masked Katsina.

The other four (Santa Ana, Sia, Acoma, and Laguna) are womanly, with leaders selected for both matri-clan and priesthood and the Katsina initiation of both boys and girls. Further, there is also something like an intensity scale in which Cochiti and Santa Ana are the most strongly consistent with this ideology and Santo Domingo and Laguna, both of which have many external links with other cultures, are the most diffuse.

Hence, we need to consider the belief in this deity among other Keres before we can properly appreciate all of these references from Laguna.

To date, the best published statement on this deity appears in the last volume of Leslie White's comparative study of the Keresan towns.[109]

> The most important deity in Sia cosmology is *Tsityosti.nako*, "Prophesying Woman" ... This deity is found at Santa Ana ... and at Laguna ... also. But everywhere the conception appears to be unclear and even inconsistent. Stevenson treats this deity as a male, but in her emergence myth *Sussistinnako* is addressed as "our mother" (in Keresan pueblos the cacique, a man, is ceremonially addressed as "mother"). The ending *-nako* means 'woman.' But at Laguna she "looked like a man" (Boas 1925: 221, 228). Stevenson says that

---

[107] Leslie Marmon Silko, *Ceremony*, New York: New American Library 1977.

[108] Byron Harvey, Masks at a Maskless Pueblo: the Laguna Colony Katsina Organization at Isleta, *Ethnology* 2 (4): 278-289 1963.

[109] Leslie White, *The Pueblo of Sia, New Mexico*, Bureau of American Ethnology, Bulletin # 184 1962: 113.

Sussistinnako was a spider; my ~~informants~~, that *Tsityostinako* "had the shape of a certain kind of spider."

Tsityostinako is called Prophesying Woman because "she knows [rather than deciding or determining] what is going to happen;" one ~~informant~~ added: "when a person is thinking about something that is *Tsityostinako* expressing herself in him."

Tsityostinako lives at *Shipop* in the Yellow world, "but she is everywhere, like God," one ~~informant~~ said. She is the creator in Sia cosmology as she is at Laguna (Gunn 1917: 89). She bore two daughters, *Utctsiti,* the mother of the Indians, and *Naotsiti,* the mother of other races and peoples.

As this quote confirms, this deity is associated with thought in several modes, with spider, and with creation as an ongoing process. The 'thought' etymology is supported by recent grammars. For Santa Ana, Davis[110] lists *c'id^{y}ustA* as 'to think, to worry.' From Acoma, Wick Miller[111] has *'ic'itistaan'i* 'mind, willpower' and *–'uc'itistaaN* 'to think'. In a text, Spider Woman gives aid to the War Twins.[112]

For the manner in which the original creation took place we must refer to two volumes dealing with the Acoma account. By a curious twist, the account of the saga was published by Stirling,[113] but the most important aspect of the process, the songs which enabled creation to occur, was published by Densmore.[114]

Together, these versions make clear that thought has a pulsating vitality most like song. It is this parallel that has been overlooked in previous accounts of the saga, such as the summary by White.[115]

The spider attribute relates both to the form of the arachnid body and its web: a center with extensions. The web is a particularly apt metaphor for thought because the rhythmic pulse of thought waves mirrored in the songs of creation and curing flows out as ripples and rays from the source and summary which is this deity. The presence of two terms for this deity is a reflection of the important distinction between the ordinary Keresan language used by everyone and the ceremonial vocabulary used by men in the kivas, first reported for Laguna by Hrdlicka[116]

---

[110] Irvine Davis, The Language of Santa Ana, *Bureau of American Ethnology, Bulletin 191, Anthropological Paper* 69: 53-190 1964: 170 #455.

[111] Wick Miller, *Acoma Grammar and Texts*, Berkeley: University of California Publications in Linguistics 40 1965: #84, 109.

[112] Wick Miller, *Acoma Grammar and* Texts 1965: 2, 53.

[113] Mathew Stirling, *Origin Myth of Acoma and other records*, Bureau of American Ethnology, Bulletin 135 1942; Edward Proctor Hunt, *Origin Myth of Acoma* Pueblo, Peter Nabokov, ed, Penguin 2015.

[114] Frances Densmore, Music of Acoma, Isleta, Cochiti, and Zuni, *Bureau of American Ethnology, Bulletin #165 1957.

[115] Leslie White, The World of the Keresan Pueblo Indians: 53-64, *Culture in History ~ Essays in Honor of Paul Radin*, New York: Columbia University Press for Brandeis University 1960.

[116] Aleš Hrdlička, A Laguna ceremonial language, *American Anthropologist* 5: 730-2 1903.

(1903) and since confirmed for all Keres.[117]

All of the evidence assembled indicates that Thought Woman, as Mind, is not so much an entity as a nexus of many important dimensions, the crux of a series of symbolic oppositions, involving Man / Woman, Sacred / Secular, and Nature / Culture. As a manlike being with female attributes, with the potential to assume any form but particularly that of a spider, this creator truly presides over a rational universe.

Jay Miller, Deified Mind Among the Keresan Pueblos,
General and Amerindian Ethnolinguistics ~
In Remembrance of Stanley Newman,
Mary Ritchie Key and Henry M. Koeningswald, eds,
Contributions To the Sociology of Languages 55,
Berlin: Mouton De Gruyter Press 1989: 151-156.

---

[117] Leslie White, A Ceremonial Vocabulary among the Pueblos, *International Journal of American Linguistics* 10: 161-67 1944; Robin Fox, A Note on Cochiti Linguistics, in Charles Lange, *Cochiti ~ A New Mexico Pueblo, past and present*; Carbondale: Southern Illinois University Press 1968: 557-72.

The Catholic University of America Anthropological Series # 2

The Northern Algonquian Supreme Being

by

Rev John M Cooper

The Catholic University of America Washington, DC.

1934

The Northern Algonquian Supreme Being[118]

JOHN M COOPER

Introduction

Most of the field data which constitute the basic evidence in the present paper were gathered by the writer in the summer of 1933 among the Cree-speaking peoples of the west coast of James Bay, the southern extension of Hudson Bay. The appended unpublished field data from the Montagnais-speaking peoples of the east coast and of northern Labrador have been generously put at my disposal by Miss {!?} Regina Flannery of the anthropological staff of The Catholic University of America and by Dr William D Strong of the Bureau of American Ethnology. The field study of 1933 was made possible by a grant-in-aid from the Social Science Research Council. To the Council as well as to Miss Flannery and to Dr Strong I desire to express my cordial appreciation.

From our older sources we can sketch a crude picture of the general culture of the eastern Cree of the York Factory district on the west coast of Hudson Bay proper, and in these sources there are several significant references, to be cited later, to a Supreme Being belief and cult. But our extremely scant sources on James Bay, from the time of Hudson's ill-starred voyage of 1610-11 to the dawn of the present century, give us almost no information on any phase of native culture in the Bay. It is not surprising therefore [2] that we find very little information therein on native religious culture around the Bay. In fact, only five of our sources, early or recent, contain, to my knowledge, data on native religion, and, of these five, two of the three more Important, Oldmixon and Skinner, are in flat contradiction to each other so far as belief in or cult of a Supreme Being is concerned.

Oldmixon, drawing seemingly upon Thomas Gorst's manuscript journal of 1670-75, ascribes to the natives of the southeastern end of James Bay a belief in "two *Monetoes* or Spirits, the one sends all the good things they have, and the other all the bad ". Skinner who make two trips to James Bay, in 1908 and 1909, denies the existence of such a belief among the Indians whom he calls the "Eastern Cree", and among whom he includes the Cree-speaking bands of the west coast of James Bay and the Montagnais-speaking bands of the east coast. "Certain it is," he writes, "that they were, as is so universal in North America, polytheistic, and that the idea of a single great spirit (*Kitche-manitou*) is entirely a European importation; and none are more positive of this than the Cree themselves".[119] Our field problem was, first of all, that of

---

[118] As we plan to publish, so soon as funds become available, the other and general results of our 1933 and earlier James Bay field studies in the Anthropological Series of The Catholic University of America and as *Primitive Man* and the Anthropological Series do not reach the same circle of readers, the present paper is being simultaneously issued as number 2 of this series and as numbers 3-4 of volume vi of *Primitive Man*.

[119] Oldmixon, *The British empire in America*, 2 v., 2d ed., London, 1741, i, 548; *manetoes* in 1st ed. of 1708, repr. in J.B Tyrrell, *Documents relating to the early history of Hudson Bay*, Toronto, 1931, 382; A. Skinner, *Notes on the eastern Cree and northern Saulteaux*, AMNH-AP, v.IX, pt.i, 1911, 59.

determining who was right, Oldmixon or Skinner.

The solution of the problem was complicated by the fact that white adventurers and traders have been active in the Bay continuously since 1668, that missionary work has been carried on on both the east and the west coast of the Bay since 1840, and particularly since 1847 and 1851, and that for the past several decades practically all Indians living on or near the Bay have been Christian.

The younger Indians today can give little or no information on whether any belief in and cult of a Supreme Being existed prior to the coming of Christianity, although much of the general pre-Columbian culture of the region is still intact, or else is well-known to them. Even the Indians of [3] middle age, with rare exceptions, have little information to give regarding pre-Christian theism. Consequently our task was one of gathering and reconstructing, so far as was possible, what could be salvaged from the older ~~informants~~. During a very short visit to the Bay in the summer of 1927, the present writer had gotten some hint as to a pre-Christian belief in a Supreme Being at Albany, but the account then gotten was so fragmentary and confused that reliance could not safely be placed upon it. During a somewhat longer reconnaissance in the summer of 1932, some further scattered hints were obtained, but again these were not definite enough to justify publication. Following up some lucky clues obtained during the first days of our stay at Moosonee in August and September 1933, much fuller, and we believe reasonably conclusive, information was obtained.

In the present paper we shall give this information, somewhat summarized, and an interpretation thereof. It has been deemed advisable to present the more important evidence verbatim as obtained from the respective ~~informant~~s, so as to put before the reader as fully as space limits permit, all the evidence on which our conclusions are based and to give him opportunity to form his own judgment as to whether these conclusions are valid or not.

In presenting the evidence we shall begin with that from Albany and the adjacent area on the west coast of James Bay, then present that from the Moose and Kesagami district on the southwest and southern end of the Bay, and finally append the data from the Eastmain area and northern Labrador. The Albany, Moose and Kesagami Indians are all Cree-speaking; the Eastmain and northern Labrador Indians, Montagnais-speaking.

Direct information on west coast theism was gotten from fourteen of the older people, with some additional confirmation from the missionaries on the Bay. In only one case, that of the ~~informant~~ from whom we obtained the first clear clue, was it feasible to get a more complete native text. Prayer formulas, however, and a number of other important details could be and were obtained in Cree. [4]

Conditions were such that it seemed more advisable, all things considered, to work through an interpreter. The present writer has some little speaking knowledge of Cree, but not a sufficient understanding of or fluency in it to use it as the ordinary means of direct communication. He has been fortunate in having an extremely capable, dependable and experienced interpreter, Mr Willie McLeod, a pensioner of the Hudson Bay Company, who was born and reared in the southern James Bay area, who is thoroughly at home in both Cree and English, and who has been trained by me during two summers both as to the importance of exact and literal translation and as to the hazards of direct questioning. Through these two summers' intimate association with him, the writer has been able on literally scores of points to check up and verify his general reliability and intelligence in interpretation, and, through later analysis of texts gotten with his help, his accuracy in translation.

These necessary preliminary statements on the problem and its background having been outlined, we shall now proceed to give the field information gathered from the respective ~~informants~~.

FIELD EVIDENCE. A ~ Albany and Atawapiskat Bands

Frank Rickard. The ages of natives are seldom known accurately by them. Frank is probably around fifty-five years old. He has lived twenty-seven years of his life up on the northern half of the West coast, – two years on Cape Henrietta and twenty-five years in the Atawapiskat and Agamiski Island region. He was a very intelligent, dependable, and satisfactory ~~informant~~ with whom I spent many hours going over various phases of native culture. His information on the pre-Christian religious beliefs regarding the Supreme Being had been given to him by his grandmother, a Cree Indian, – as Frank himself is, – who was born at Albany, and who lived there all her life. She died twelve years ago at a very advanced age. Frank thinks that she may have been close to a hundred years old. We may put her age at somewhere between eighty and ninety and possibly above that. We shall first give the text obtained [5] from Frank. It was written by him in Cree syllabic, phonetically transcribed from dictation by him, translated by Willie McLeod, and analyzed later on the writer's return to Washington.[120]

1. āwạ kicē'skwe'o ka tipatcimut mask^{w}ūdj mītā'tu mitā'nạ pipūnạ kī pimātis^i'u. Nī'cūcap pipū'nạ mā'kạ kā punipimā'tisīt.

2. Pâ'maci ạyā'mihā'win itāk^{w}ok itā'u manitū it^{w}ewạ'k ili'liwạk. Mu'lạ mū'gạ kiskelimē'wạk kē'kō manitūwạ. I'cpimik ma'kạ tatelimē'wạk. Mū'cạk ma'kạ alimūmēwạk.

3. Nē'stạ ma'kā kē'kwạn kā nipạta'niwạk, mu'lạ ki mucena'mạk kā ācamitutci'k; ka'tạ wā'pạtạm manitū. Mū'cạk ak^{w}onạha'muk ku'tạk mī'kiwam ē itōtạtā'tcik.

4. Mi'siwē kē'gwạn manatcitā'wạk tatō kā nipạtā'tcik. Mu'lạ [ki] kā mīlekōnā'o kica'cpin pakwạnitā'o tōtạma'kwe itelitạmdk.

5. Matci'kạ āwā'cic nī'ctam ē nēpạhat pēlēli'cạ mu'lạ wāyēc [or wī'yec] ikin tankē ispī'tci apicī'cicit kīsis^{w}ākanēwạn. Mi'siwē ma'kạ muwē'wạk ētacī'tcik. Ēkwŏne ēspitci manatcitā'djik. Mu'lạ ka'tạ mī'likō manitūwạ it^{w}ē'wạk.

6. Mu'lạ nē'ctạ ūtci wī'ạkwēwạk.

7. Ē'ko ma'kạ ka peta'newạk masmạhī'gạn kīwētinạk. Kī otō'tewạk ili'liwạk nī'cuwạk Pensiwēdjūwe'nŏk. Ki wītạmāwākāncwiwạk kutŏs kīcikā'wā ki'tci nanā'tāwihōtci'k, pē'yạk ma'kạ ēkī'cikak ēạyā'mihēkī'cikak kitci

---

[120] The following phonetic symbols are used in this and other Cree texts in the present paper: *ā*, as in *father; a*, as in *hat; ạ*, as *u* in *but; â*, as *aw* in *awl; ē*, as *a* in *fate; e*, as in *met; ī*, as in *pique; i*, as in *pin; ō*, as in *note; ŏ*, as in *hot; o*, as in German *voll; ū*, as in *rule; u*, as in *put;* weak vowels and voiceless semivowels, as superiors {superscript}; consonants, as in *Phonetic transcription of Indian languages,* Smithsonian Misc. coll., v. 66, no.6, 1916: 4-7. I cannot vouch in all cases for correctness of vowel length. Aspirates are common in James Bay Cree, but very often so weak as to he barely or doubtfully distinguishable. They are not recorded in the text from Frank Rickard. The ending *-a'o* is diphthongal, but the two vowel sounds are not as fully blended as *-ow* in English *how.*

manadjitā'tcik.　Ma'tinawē'kī'cikak ma'kạ mēsiwē kē'kwŏn ōlastā'wạk [6] kē āpātcitā'tcik.　Me'tạ napạtē'iskwâtē'mik peskostāwạk, mī'nạ kwēskitēisk^wātē'mik kōna pekitinē'wạk, pī'tukamik ma'kạ otci oti'namuk.

8.　Kēyapạtc manatcihē'wạk ā'nihi manitō'wạ kā alimumā'tcik.　Ispi ma'kạ kā wītạmā'tcik ki'tci manitūwa, mō'cạk kicē'manitū' ki itewạk.　Mū'lạ kī ŏtci alimōmē'wạk k^wōtạkī'yạ manitū'wạ.

1.　This old woman who tells the story perhaps lived one hundred winters. It is now twelve winters that she died.

2.　Before prayer [Christianity] is, the *Manitū* is, the Indians say.　But they do not know what sort of *Manitū*.　But they always think of him as being above. And always speak of him.

3.　And what is killed they did not carry uncovered when they gave [it] to one another to eat; the *Manitū* will see it.　They always cover it when they take it to another lodge.

4.　They respect everything that they kill.　The *Manitū* will not give to us [incl.] if we do wrong, they think.

5.　You see, when a boy for the first time kills a little bird, it does not matter at all how small it is, they [French *on*] cook it.　Then all who are present eat it all.　It is to this degree that they respect [the meat].　Else it will not be given to them by the *Manitū*, they say.

6.　On this account also they do not curse [blaspheme].

7.　And it is then that the book is brought from the north.　Two men arrived from York Factory.　They [the people] were told that they should work six days, but on one day the praying day [Sunday] that they should respect it.　When then it is Saturday they put in its place everything that they will use.　They pile up firewood on one side of the door, and on the other side of the door they lay down snow, and thus from within doors they take it.

8.　And they respect that *Manitū* about whom they speak.　And when they are [were] told about *Kitci Manitū*, they always [thereafter] called him 'Old *Manitū*'.　They did not after that speak of the other *Manitū*. [7]

So much for the text itself.　Further and explanatory data from Frank here follow.　Before the Indians had heard about God from the missionaries, " they knew there was a *Manitū* but did not know who or what the *Manitū* was.　He was just called *Manitū*, not *Ki'tci Manitū*".　"When Christianity was first introduced," so Frank's grandmother had told him, "the Indians thought it very strange that it was so much like what they had previously had, and that the Christian God was so much like the old *Manitū* they had known in pre-Christian days."　Frank's old grandmother used to say to him: "When I hear about the real [Christian] God, I wonder how we knew all this before.　It must have been given to us by the real God.　Dreams must have had much to do with it, for the people often dreamed about the *Manitū* they used to serve".

"The only difference was that instead of calling him *Manitū* they called him thereafter *Kicē'manitū* ('Old *Manitū*') or else *Kistcī'manitū* ('Great *Manitū*).　These two latter names came into use only after the missionaries [or the York Factory men] came."　"They did not know much about the *Manitū* but they knew that he was *icpemik* ('above') and that there was only one *Manitū*", and Frank was very positive on both these points. "They knew about no *ma'tci manitū* [the devil in the Christian sense, or supreme evil spirit] but only about the *Manitū* first spoken of." "The *Manitū* provided food for the Indians". "He also sent them dreams to let them know where they could find beaver, caribou, and other animals".

"When the Indians had meat, and there were two tents close together, they did not know how the *Manitū* would take it if they gave the meat away. So when they took part of the meat to the next tent, they used to cover the meat so the *Manitū* would not see it". "The Indians were very careful how they used the meat and they knew they must not waste it, for, if they did so, this would displease the *Manitū* ". " If a man wasted meat the *Manitū* would punish him just as we punish a child. The Indians were afraid that if they wasted meat they would be hard up and would lack food". [8]

"When a small boy killed his first bird, even though it was a small bird, everybody in the tent had to be given a piece of the bird [to eat], in order to please the *Manitū*".

"If a man lied or stole, this did not concern the *Manitū* ", so far as Frank had heard.

Frank had heard nothing from his grandmother regarding old beliefs as to the future life.

Jeannette Sagạbạ'kiskạm. Jeannette is Cree. She was born in the region near the mouth of the Atawapiskat River, but she was reared around Albany, before there was a resident minister there, that is before at least 1860. She was still tied in a mossbag as an infant when the Catholic priest first visited Albany, which, as we know, was in 1848. She should consequently be about eighty-five years old, and certainly looks it. Her information regarding the aboriginal Supreme-Being belief was obtained from her father and her paternal grandfather, both Albany Indians. Jeannette was very positive and emphatic that it was from these sources she had obtained her information. While she is very advanced in years, her mind is quite clear. Here and there, however, in her testimony could be detected some post-Christian influence, but this represented an inconsiderable element in her data and on nearly all points she was perfectly clear as to what was pre-Christian and what was post-Christian.

"No one knew where *Manitū* was, just as we do not know now, but they knew there was some being". "He was called *Manitū*". "There was only one *Manitū*". " He was always above. He could see what the people were doing, and was looking down on them, but they never saw him and could not see him". There was a *Matci Manitū* who was wicked. "The *Matci Manitū* was the same as Wihtiko." "The Indians used to pray to the good *Manitū* to keep the bad *Manitū* away."

The people believed in *Atihk^wạtcak,* a human being who had turned into a caribou and who had become a sort of master of the caribou. He was, however, quite distinct from *Manitū*. *Manitū* was also quite distinct from the [9] *pōwā'gạn* ("guardian spirit"), and from *Mikenak*, the spokesman or chief being {Turtle} who comes into the conjuring tent. "The Indians knew nothing about the appearance of *Manitū*." "They made no statues of him". "The Wihtiko could be killed but it was impossible to hurt or kill the good *Manitū*". "The *Manitū* had no son. His son was never known until the first missionaries came. The old people ", Jeannette added, "looked upon *Manitū* just as you whites look upon God today". "*Manitū* was looked upon as the boss of the whole world. The earth and everything were made by *Manitū*". "It was *Manitū* who made the caribou. *Manitū* is head of everything."

Jeannette gave a considerable number of details on the making of the first man and woman by *Manitū*. She distinguished two beginnings of the race, that of the second or Christian Adam and Eve after the flood and that of the first couple which occurred before the flood. In her account of human origins.' however, there was a certain confusion, which I could not entirely straighten out, between Christian and pre-Christian elements.

"The people looked to *Manitū* for their living just as people look to God today. He would drive the animals into the traps for them." "While the people were on earth *Manitū* looked after them". "*Manitū* put into the Indians' minds the idea of how to make fire with the bow-drill". Jeannette had never heard of *Manitū* sending dreams.

"*Manitū* was never sung to", as is done in conjuring. "This," Jeannette, a devout Christian, commented, "would be 'awful'". "Cursing or speaking badly of *Manitū* never occurred", Jeannette being very emphatic on this point. " *Manitū* made it very hard for anyone who stole or murdered. Such a man had a hard time getting along". " If the Indians wasted the meat this would make *Manitū* angry and he would not let them have any more ". " When meat was carried from one tent to another, it was always covered over so that *Manitū* would not see them taking it away ".

"*Manitū* was prayed to to thank him for the food and health he was giving the Indians". "The people would [10] ask him for what they needed to live on and they would get it. They did not exactly say prayers, but they would just let him know they were hard up for food in the bush and would thank him when they got it". "Before eating they would take a bit of grease or other food and would throw this into the fire, and the smoke would go up. When doing this they never said anything aloud, but only in their minds. The putting of the grease or meat in the fire was done very reverently. Everybody remained silent, and when the smoke had gone up, all was over. They looked at the smoke going up in hopes that *Manitū* would receive the offering, because the smoke was going up above where *Manitū* was. They would just say in their own minds, not aloud, and nearly all had the same thought:

Kī pākuselimī'tinan kitci mī'liak mī'tcim
('We [excl.] expect [depend on, have confidence in]
thee that thou givest us [excl.] food').

While doing this, all remained silent and very serious. No one would speak until all this had been done". Jeannette had seen the above done. "After food was shared out, they were very careful not to let any bit of food fall on the brush in the lodge. In those days there was no white man's grub, and the Indians were very much afraid of *Manitū* because he was the only one they were getting anything from." The above prayer is the only one Jeannette remembered.

"There was no idea as to where people went after death. The Indians did not know what happened to the dead". Although the dead were supposed to survive bodily death, neither Jeannette nor her daughter Dinah Williams, about fifty-five or sixty years old. – a very intelligent woman and quite well informed herself on the old customs and beliefs, who was present throughout the interviews with her mother, – had ever heard of souls going to live with *Manitū* or of crossing a river to arrive at their future destination. " The people looked to *Manitū* only while living."

Patrick Steven. Patrick is probably about sixty-five years old. He was born at Albany. His father's father [11] was an Otchipwe, who had been born up the Albany River a little below its junction with English River, but who had always lived at Albany. Patrick's father was born and reared at Albany and lived his life there, Patrick's father's name was *Kicē'nābēcīc* ("Old Little Man"). His father practised conjuring but not with the use of the conjuring tent. Patrick himself was destined to be a conjurer, but instead followed the ways of the Book. Patrick is extremely well informed regarding the old customs, not only in religious but in general culture. He is also an unusually intelligent man, and was very anxious to give exact answers to all questions. He was one of the most intelligent and best equipped ~~informants~~ the present writer has ever met anywhere in the North. The data given by him in the non-religious field have been checked up from independent ~~informants~~ and from published Algonquian sources in scores of cases and invariably found accurate.

"The *Manitū* was thought to be a real *Manitū*. He was the one to whom the Indians always looked for help. But the ministers told the Indians that the *Manitū* was not the real Kitci *Manitū*. Before the ministers came the Indians knew only *Manitū* and there was no Kitci *Manitū*. There were only one *Manitū* ", and Patrick was very emphatic on this point.

In a later interview with Patrick and without any thought on my part or even indirect questioning, – we were speaking about conjuring at the time, – he volunteered the information that the conjurers addressed three beings or used three different names for the one *Manitū* or appealed to him under three different aspects. "This three-being concept came from the conjurers who made the people believe there were three [beings], but in reality there was only one *Manitū*. The three had no special names except the following:

> *Ka tibelitā'mạn mī'tcim,* ('Thou who hast mastery over food'), who is the one in charge of all the animals and was looked to by the Indians for their meat; *Kā tibelitā'mạn pīmā'tisiwin,* ('Thou who hast mastery over life'), who is the one who had charge of the Indians' life during their life-time and who was appealed to if anyone was sick; [12] *Kā tibelitā'mạn nipiwin* ('Thou who hast mastery over death'), who was the one who caused death".

Patrick had heard about these three from a great many old men at Albany of the same age as his father, not merely from his father alone from whom he had obtained most of his information on the other phases of pre-Christian religious culture, and Patrick was very positive regarding his sources on this point. "If through the machinations of a conjurer an Indian lost his luck in hunting, he would get a second conjurer to conjure for him and this second conjurer would conjure to the 'Master of Food' so the man would get his food as before, and thus things would come right again for him". "The conjurers used to conjure to the 'Master of Life' when anybody was sick so that the sick person would recover. They did not conjure to the 'Master of Death' for they had no use for him as he caused only grief to them. Of course they believed it was always to *Manitū* that they were conjuring. The three masters were really only one".

Patrick was very positive that these three were after all only one, the one great *Manitū*, but I could not determine clearly, in spite of considerable time spent with him on the matter, whether these three represented in his mind merely three different forms of address to the *Manitū* or whether they were, as he put it, "as if different parts of the one *Manitū* had charge of the three different things", namely, food, life and death, Patrick expressed the matter as follows:

> *Nictiwạk isạ e nanạkatcitā'tcik kēkwāniu, pēyạko mā'gạ ma'mō manitū'*
> ('They are three then who look after everything,
> but all together the *Manitū* is one',
> or as Willie McLeod translated a little more freely,
> 'all are one *Manitū*').

All through my conversations and interviews with Patrick on the *Manitū*, the unity of the *Manitū* was emphasized both explicitly and implicitly. And in one later interview he expressed the relationship as follows: "All the three are [13] one and are the one *Manitū*. They are not the same as three different people but are just three different parts of the same one. My Father," he added, "told me that the old people before him had always said this same thing".

The Indians did not know exactly where *Manitū* lived. He was never seen. He was not the same at all as *Mikenak*, the being who came into the conjuring tent. *Manitū* was the master and boss of *Mikena'k*. *Mikenak*, so everyone said, was under *Manitū*. He was a servant of *Manitū*. It was *Manitū* who would send *Mikenak* to the conjuring tent. "*Mikenak*, after he had performed the duty on which he had been sent by *Manitū*, would go back to *Manitū*. *Mikenak* was master of the *pōwā'gaṇak,* ('the guardian spirits or dream beings'):

Kā tibelitạk pōwā'gaṇak
('He who has mastery over the powagans')."

Manitū was also quite distinct from the powagans and from the young man [*Atihk*^w*atcahk*] who was metamorphosed into a caribou.

"The Indians never knew about the *Matci Manitū* [the 'Devil' or great evil spirit] till they got the Bible. My father told me this same. They had only one *Manitū*. But they believed in Wihtiko long ago".

Patrick's father had never told him anything about who made the world or anything about the first man or woman. His father had told him that the discoverer of the art of fire-making was a human being.

"It was *Manitū* who used to give the Indians everything. But this was done through the conjurer who would tell the people where to find caribou and everything else they needed." It was *Mikenak* who brought dreams to the people.

Patrick had never heard of any statue or representation made of the *Manitū*, The Albany Cree were very careful regarding the disposal of the bones of animals killed. After considerable indirect questioning which elicited no definite information, I had to put a rather direct question to Patrick as to whether, if the bones were not properly disposed of, *Manitū* or the respective animals or both would be angry. He replied, – but the reply must be taken with reservations [14] in view of the direct question put, – that " really it was the respective animals who would be angry although it was *Manitū* who caused the animals to be angry."

"When meat was carried abroad outside of the tent it was never carried without being covered. The Indians had so much respect for the meat that they did not want to show it at all. To carry it abroad uncovered would make *Manitū* angry", "*Manitū* would sometimes get angry with the Indians and the Indian with whom he was angry would soon know it for he would have a hard time and would starve ". Patrick could not recall just what precisely would make *Manitū* angry. "The Indians would say: 'There must be something we are doing wrong or not doing, for which *Manitū* is punishing us thus'. But they did not know exactly what it was." Whether or not *Manitū* was offended when a man lied or stole, Patrick could not say.

"In times of starvation the Indians would try to stand it as long as possible and at last would appeal to a conjurer for aid. If there were no conjurer available the starving Indian himself would appeal to the Master of Food. He would lift up his eyes and say:

Ni manitū'm kī pakwạse'limitin kitci mīlīydạn kē ō'tci pīmadisī'yan
('My *Manitū* I depend on thee that thou givest (me) that I may live').

45

After this he would not receive the meat immediately but the meat would come before he and his family actually starved". "If one of the children were sick in the tent and there were no conjurer at hand the child's father would say to the *Manitū*:

Ki pakwōsē'limi'tin kitci milōayat āwạ kā a'kwōsit kīca'cpm i'sạ nāhelitạmạ'ne kītci wītcihạt
('I depend on thee that this one who is sick may be well if now thou wiliest to help him')".

Then, too, "in olden times the *Manitū*'s name was used when the Indians were having a quarrel. They would say: 'I depend on the *Manitū*' or 'The *Manitū* helps me'." [15] Patrick had never heard of the *Manitū*'s name used in cursing or swearing proper. One particular obscene word *akai* ("female genitals") was and still is very commonly used.

"At feasts only men were present; women were not allowed to sit with them. All would sit around. One man was head man. He would take a piece off the choice part of the meat, a bit about the size of the end of a finger, and throw it in the fire saying: '*Pape'we, papewe, pape'we't* This was done to bring good luck, so as to get plenty more meat. It was done before starting to eat." "It was done for the dead," so Patrick said, but possibly in view of the purpose expressed of getting more meat and in view of other evidence gathered by me from other ~~informants~~, there may have been some reference also to the *Manitū*.

At any rate a somewhat similar offering, and clearly to the *Manitū*, was made. "An Indian would hold up a piece of meat to the *Manitū* saying:

Ē milotūtāwī'yen wēt'ci ni mītcicinamatan mī'tcim
('Thou doing good to me is the reason why I hold up food to thee in my hand').

The holder of the food would then put it in his mouth and eat it. The above words were addressed to the *Manitū*".

Patrick had no knowledge of the pre-Christian concept of the soul. In fact he stated that "there was no belief in a soul", that "when a person was buried he was buried like an animal", that "when he was dead he was dead forever and this was the last of him." He had never heard from his father where the dead go after death. "My father told me that the Indians used to respect the dead to the extent of giving them decent burial but that there was no thought of the person having a soul." Probably Patrick referred here to the more abstruse Christian idea of the soul, as he knows well the old saying that the Northern Lights were believed, − "by some people, though not by all," − to be the spirits of the dead who are dancing. "There was no belief that at death the soul went to live with *Manitū*". [16]

David Wynn. David is an Albany Cree Indian now living at Moose Factory. Information obtained from him had been told to him by his grandfather, Peter Wynn, an Albany Cree Indian. David is probably about sixty-five years old. He was emphatic in stating that the data on religion referred to conditions before the missionaries came and before the two men from York Factory came. He was a very satisfactory ~~informant~~ but had not as detailed knowledge as Jeannette and Patrick.

"There were three *manitū*s, a lowest, a middle, and a highest one. The lowest one, *Kā tibelitā'mạn misiwē mī'tcim* ('Thou who hast mastery over all food'), was master and ruler of everything on land and sea. When the Indians were in want, the conjuring tent was put up and this was the *Manitū* that was asked for help in the meat line. The middle one, *Kā tibelitā'mạn pīmā'tisiwin* ('Thou who hast mastery over life'), had all to do with man's lifetime. When anyone was sick this one was called upon for help. The third and highest one, *Kā tibelitā'mạn nipiwin* ('Thou who hast mastery over death'), was the head of all and master of everything and the master of death. The conjuring-tent rite had nothing to do with this Master of Death. The powagans used to tell the conjurers that there was even a greater spirit yet [than these three] and my grandfather used to say that this greatest spirit must have been the Christian God. Often the conjurers tried to get this real *Manitū* to come to them so he could be better known, but they could not succeed. The conjurers told the people there was a great *Manitū*. The three above *Manitū*s used to say they were not the greatest, but that there was one greater one above them. The people called this greatest one just *Manitū*".

Whether these three were ruled by this greater spirit was not known by David. He volunteered however the following story in illustration: "Some people were starving to death. They killed a whiskey jack. They came to a lake. They pulled the gizzard out of the whiskey jack, chiseled a hole in the ice covering the lake, put the gizzard on a hook, let down the hook and line in the water and said: 'Let us [17] see if there really is a greater one than the three'. If they caught a fish, this would mean that there was a greater one; if no fish were caught, this would mean there was no greater one than the three. They put the hook down and soon began pulling up fish as fast as they could take them in. So they said: 'Really there is a greater good being than these three'. That is all they knew about the great being. They supposed he had given the fish. This saved their lives".

"My grandfather always told me about *these three,* but the three said there was one greater than they. After the Christian ministers came and told the Indians about *Kitci Manitū* the Indians said at once: 'This is the greatest one who was talked about'." "There was only one after all, but when the people asked for anything they asked that one of the three who was master of what they were asking for. They never asked the Master of Death for anything. They had nothing to do with him. They asked only the other two for what they wanted".

David had never heard where the three or the one over them lived, except that it was always above, but "exactly where in the above I never heard". "The three were never seen. They only just spoke and spoke for themselves."

"In olden times the Indians never knew of the *Matci Manitū*. There was just one *Manitū*." "They were much afraid of *Wihtiko*."

David had never heard from his grandfather who was the maker of everything. He had only heard of the great *Manitū* and the three great masters.

"The Indians were always very particular not to waste meat". David then told the following story to illustrate this: "A certain Indian did not have good sense. He killed a caribou and threw it all away saying: 'We will just leave this caribou. If we run out of meat, we can ask the One who is Master of Food to give us some more'. The Indian took with him only a very little bit of the caribou and left the rest there because he was depending on the Master of Food to give them more. He and his family soon ate up what they took with them. They then tried their very best [18] to get more meat, but they couldn't. They said to themselves: 'We shall really starve to death'. Then they put up a conjuring lodge. They said: 'You who are Master of Food, I want you to come to the conjuring house'. The conjurer went into the tent with his rattle in his hand and the tent started to shake. The Master of Food came to the top of the tent and said: 'I have come. What do you want?' The conjurer replied: 'We are starving to death. Give us more meat to eat'. The Master of Food replied: "Huh! We are not master of everything. There is another one above us who is master of everything'. The conjurer asked: 'Who is that?' The Master of Food replied: " *We* cannot name him.' The conjurer said: 'Well, then we shall have to starve'. So they starved to death, for they got nothing more. The above conjurer was the same man who had thrown away the meat. This story which was told to me by my grandfather was another thing that taught the people to be careful not to waste meat."

"The Indians used to ask the One who was Master of Food to help them when they were hard up for food. The conjurer himself when he wanted meat, used to ask the same Master of Food for help." "At a feast, but not at ordinary meals, the head of the feast would put a small piece of meat in the fire before eating and used to say:

Ē'oko ūmạ kī'lạ ēcạmita'n
('This here I give to thee to eat').

"This was given," so David said, "to the one who was giving them the meat". The prayer formula suggests, however, more an offering to the dead. And in fact David's grandfather told him that meat used to be so offered to the dead. "At the first feast held after the burial, this was done, with the words:

Ē'oko ūmạ kī'lạ ēcạmita'n kā ki pōnipimādis'īạn
('This here I give to thee to eat thou who hast died')."

"Everything belonging to the dead was put around the-grave or hung up nearby. This had been done since the [19] time of Mistakalac [a well-known folklore character on the west coast of James Bay] because the Indians thought that the rest of the people would rise from the grave as Mistakalac had done and would need these things. This is what my grandfather told me." "There was no thought of any one having a soul or spirit. But the people would say when they would see the northern lights:

Tcīpāyạk nīmiwạk
('The dead are dancing')."

Jimmie Acickīc ("Mud"). Jimmie is a Cree Indian, about sixty-five or seventy years old, from Atawapiskat, about one hundred miles north of Albany. The fragmentary information obtained from him had been told him by his father. There are indications of some Otchipwe and possibly Christian influence in his data. There is and has been at Atawapiskat a good deal of visiting by and intermarriage with Otchipwe from up inland.

The Supreme Being was addressed as *Nōtāwinan* (Cree: "Our Father") or as *Nūs* (Otchipwe: "My Father"). "My father did not tell me who 'Nus' was, but he knew there was something beyond".

"The Indians never wasted meat in the old days. There was lots of starvation then, my father told me". "When meat is carried abroad, it is always covered. Only frozen rabbits can be carried abroad uncovered. Meat need not be covered when being passed around within the tent. I do not know the reason for covering it".

"The first thing before eating, a bit of meat or grease or hard liquor used to be put in the fire. I do not know why." "They also used to hold up a piece of meat in the right hand and say *Nōtāwinan*". "When lots of people were in the tent, the meat would be cut up in mouthfuls and be all in a big pan. Before eating, they would hold up a piece of meat and say *Nus*. I heard this from my father. After holding up the meat, they would put the same piece in their mouth".

Willy Allen.   A very intelligent man of middle age, who is an excellent ~~informant~~ on contemporary culture but who has only slight knowledge of the pre-Christian religious [20] beliefs proper. He represents the Albany and Atawapiskat culture.

"The Indians still believe that if they waste meat or do not use it right they will not have luck in hunting. If a man does that, *ka pastahūn* ('he will bring evil or vengeance upon himself). When carrying meat abroad, they always wrap or cover it with cloth, a bag, or something. I do not know the reason for doing this ".

William Loutitt.   One of my most valuable and intelligent ~~informants~~ on the general and magico-religious culture of the Albany area, but not so well informed on the pre-Christian *Manitū* belief. He is an Albany Cree, is about sixty or sixty-five years old, and had been, up to last year, forty years in the service of the Hudson's Bay Company at Albany, as interpreter and in other capacities.

"In the old days", he told me in 1927 when I first met him, "a bit of meat or grease, or a bone with a bit of meat on it would be thrown into the fire, the thrower saying:

Kinwic kītci pīmadisīan
('May I live long!')."

Sam Sutherland.   He now lives at Moose Factory, but he comes from the barren grounds up near Cape Henrietta where he lived as a boy. He must be about sixty years old. The following data were obtained from him in 1927, and refer to the Cape Henrietta region.

"After a big killing of caribou, the best of the meat was kept until there were lots of visitors. Then a big lodge was erected and a feast held. The oldest man present, among hosts or visitors, was in charge of the feast. The feast was held at dusk or just after dark. At the feast, this old man took a spoonful of grease from the top of where the meat was boiling and threw it on the fire, saying. 'Here is to the one who gives us all the meat to kill'. The grease in the fire lit up the whole place ". Speeches also were made, and there was singing in unintelligible words. Pieces of meat were also, so Sam said, thrown into the fire, apparently at the same feast. While Sam did not think "the one who gives us all the meat" was "God", it seems probable, in view of the evidence gathered in 1933 from other ~~informants~~ that this " one " was the supreme *Manitū*. [21]

Father Emile Saindon.   Father Saindon, of the Oblate Fathers, who has been among the Indians of the west coast of James Bay as a resident missionary for eleven years and who speaks Cree fluently, told me that the Indians of the northern part of the west coast had some idea of a Supreme Being before their conversion to Christianity. Father Saindon also writes in his

> "En missionnant: Essai sur les missions des Pères Oblats de Marie Immaculée a la Baie James", Ottawa 1928: 38; "Païen, il [the west coast Cree] ne connaissait pas l'ête mystérieux dont il soupçon-nait l'existence et la puissance. ... Ilcroyait à l'existence de deux êtres, l'un bon, l'autre mauvais, à la vie heureuse que donne l'esprit bon, à la vie malheureuse que donne l'esprit méchant. Il redoutait, jusqu'au tremblement, l'Esprit méchant. Cependant, il entrait en communication avec lui pour être favorisé a la chasse, savoir des choses secrètes, jeter des sorts, etc. C'est par toutes sortes de sorcelleries que ces relations s'entretenaient".

It may here be added parenthetically that the Reverend RA Joselyn, the Church of England missionary, resident at Albany, has also, so I was told, been informed by the old natives there about a pre-Christian belief in a supreme Deity, but I had not the opportunity to obtain details from him, as I was told this only at his departure from Moose last summer for Albany. His information, I understand, came to him especially from old man Goodwin at Albany.

FIELD EVIDENCE. B ~ Moose Factory and Kesagami Bands

Charlotte Sutherland. Charlotte must be nearly eighty years old, possibly a little older. Her parents were Cree Indians from Moose, as were also her grandparents, or at least her grandfathers. Her parents went up the coast to live on Cape Henrietta after her sister's birth but before her own. When she first remembered, the missionaries had come to James Bay or Albany. The information she gave on pre-Christian beliefs had been told her by her parents. Whether this information refers to Cape Henrietta and [22] Albany culture, or to Moose culture, is hard to say. It is here being given as more probably Moose culture. She is very old and feeble, and does not enunciate very clearly; so it was necessary to use tandem interpreters, Willy McLeod, and her son-in-law Frank Rickard (cited above) who is used to her way of talking. Charlotte, in spite of her poor enunciation, turned out to be an intelligent, clear-headed, and valuable ~~informant~~.

"The name *Kitci Manitū* was first used after the two men from York Factory came. Before that time only the name *Manitū* [without *Kitci*] was used." Charlotte was very positive in emphasizing that the *belief itself* existed among the Indians before the two men from York Factory came, which visit occurred at Cape Henrietta [about 1843, as we know from a contemporary source to be cited later] when her parents were there and while her older sister was still in the cradleboard.

Charlotte also knew the three terms, *Kā tibelitā'mạn mī'tcim, Kā tibelitā'mạn pīmātisiwin,* and *Kā tibelitā'mdn nipiwin.* The first was appealed to when meat was needed, the second when any one was sick. She was very emphatic however that there was "one *Manitū* only". She explained the above three very much as Patrick Steven had done, in the following words: "These were not three but all one. What the Indians said or asked was said to or asked of the one, but they would mention the three different cases. If a person was sick, they would say, *Kā tibelitā'mạn pīmātisiwin,* and would ask him to help the sick person. After all there was only one *Manitū.* The one who was master of the food and the one who was master of the sick are both one. The Indians used different ways of speaking according to what they wanted".

"There was only one *Manitū* to look to but the Indians did not know who *Manitū* was". "*Manitū* was always above", and Charlotte was very positive about this. "The Indians could not help but think that He was good, for He always gave them what they asked for". "*Manitū* was never seen". "They thought that He had a body just the same as human beings have, and always thought this until [23] they were taught [by missionaries or the two York Factory men] that He was a spirit". "People never saw *Manitū*, but *Manitū* saw them. They were afraid to do wrong lest He should see them".

"*Manitū* was not at all the same as powagan. *Manitū* was looked upon as good, but powagan was looked upon as the [or a] Matci *manitū* and no good [this latter evidently a post-Christian attitude on the part of Charlotte]". Charlotte had never heard of a "boss of the caribou". "Not until the two men came from York Factory did we hear about *Manitū* having a son".

"We never heard who had made the world, until the missionaries came. No one had any idea about this before, nor even wondered or thought or bothered about it". "We never heard who were the first man and woman until the missionaries came". "*Manitū* was looked upon as boss of everything, and of the Indians too". *Manitū* gave meat to the people, Charlotte emphatically held, and "when any hunt was made successfully, *Manitū* was thanked for giving the game". To the question put at another time, Who gave the meat to the Indians?, she replied: "You know whom we [Christians] thank now for the meat. That is the one who was thanked for it then".

Charlotte was very positive too in asserting that the *Manitū* sent dreams. "The Indians thought dreams told them where and how to find food. The dreams came from *Manitū*, – such as, how to make a successful hunt for caribou, – and the people thanked the *Manitū* for giving them the dreams".

"I have never heard of anything like a statue made of *Manitū*. " "No such thing as using *Manitū*'s name disrespectfully ever occurred in the old days. Cursing", she added, "started about the same time that praying [Christianity] started". "No one could hurt or kill *Manitū* [as they could *Wihtiko*]. No such thought ever came into people's minds. *Manitū* was invisible. I cannot see how people could think that at all".

"Meat was always covered when being taken from tent to tent", but Charlotte could not give the reason. "It was [24] considered bad to waste meat. The Indians were very particular about this, for they feared the one who gave it". To the question, Did the *Manitū* ever get angry at men?, Charlotte replied: "We had no chance to know that, for there was no one to tell us. He may have gotten angry, but we did not know it." Later she said: "I do not know of anything in particular the people were afraid to do on account of *Manitū*, but there were things they were afraid to do in the presence of *Manitū*. They had an idea of what was right and wrong, but I do not know exactly what it was". She had never heard that the *Manitū* would be cross if, for example, some one was guilty of theft. Apparently the obligations to *Manitū* were so far as Charlotte knew, of the ritual or non-social taboo order, such as, not wasting meat, and perhaps covering the meat. Charlotte had never heard of throwing meat or grease in the fire to *Manitū*, nor of holding it up to *Manitū* before eating.

"There was no fear of ghosts in the old days. The Indians did not even think there was such a thing as a ghost". "At death people did not go to the *Manitū* in the future life. There were no such hopes of going to or of seeing *Manitū*." "When a person died it was believed he was gone forever. It was thought he would rise again [this sounds Christian, but more probably it was a reference to the *Mistakalac* story cited above], but there was no notion that he would go to any place, heaven or hell".

Harvey Smallboy. Harvey is a man of about sixty years of age, the son of old Simon and Ellen Smallboy whose testimony will be given infra. He is a man of very superior intelligence, one of the best minds I have ever come in contact with in the North, – or, I believe, elsewhere. He is exceptionally well informed on contemporary and older Moose and Kesagami culture, as are his father and mother. In the matter of the Supreme Being, however, Harvey's parents were very reticent to me, whereas Harvey himself was quite willing to communicate whatever he knew. Most of his information on the Supreme Being belief and cult had been gotten from his grandfather, some from his great [25] grandfather. "My grandfather was not like my father. My grandfather believed in letting me know all about the old things, but my father [Simon, still living] does not believe in talking of such things". I got many evidences of Harvey's extraordinarily accurate and retentive memory during my many long chats with him over the old religious and non-religious culture; it was possible to check up his data at scores of points from independent ~~informants~~ as well as from older written sources on northern Algonquian culture.

Harvey had never heard from his grandfather the name *Manitū* applied to the Supreme Being. The only name he had ever heard was the odd one: *Kā umictikwa'skismiyan* ("Thou who hast the wooden shoes"), that is, shoes such as the whites wear, as distinct from moccasins.[121] None of my other ~~informants~~, – at least neither Jeannette, nor her daughter Dinah, nor Frank Rickard, nor Charlotte Sutherland, nor John Dick, – had ever heard of this name, though Harvey's father and mother were quite familiar with it. Jeanette and Frank Rickard were very much surprised when asked about it, while old Charlotte laughed outright at what she considered the absurdity of it as applied to the invisible *Manitū*. Harvey himself thinks it first came in when the two men from York Factory came to Moose, and probably in consequence of these two Indians wearing white men's shoes, as the ministers do. Harvey's theory is probably as plausible as any. At any rate, apart from the name, the concept clearly antedates the coming of the York Factory men and of the missionaries. For short we shall use the term ' Wooden-shoe Wearer' in the following pages. Harvey had never heard of the names, Master of Food, Life and Death, nor of the name *Pēmigābō[wi]yạn to* be mentioned under John Dick.

"There was no other being than Wooden-shoe Wearer. There was just this one. All the Indians looked to this same one". "I have never heard of any *Matci Manitū* [supreme evil being] believed in in the old days before the [26] missionaries. The Indians looked only to the good being. There was no other, no bad one. They always knew they were under the good one, and under no other". Harvey repeatedly stated on various occasions during our many interviews, both explicitly and implicitly, that this good being lived somewhere above. He was never seen, although Harvey knew and gave me a short story from Abitibi of a glimpse once gotten at a distance of a being supposed to be perhaps this One by some Abitibi Indians.

"All the Indians knew, before ever any missionaries or whites came among them, that there was something above them [Wooden-shoe Wearer], and knew that this One gave them their living and looked out for them". "They looked upon Him as Christians look upon God". "They looked to Wooden-Shoe Wearer for everything. In those days they had no other one except Wooden-shoe Wearer. Even the conjurers thought they got all their help from Him". "No matter what it was, He was always looked to, and He was the only one they looked to".

He was quite distinct from the powagang and from the human being [*Atihkwatcahk*] who turned into a caribou. Of this latter Harvey gave me a full account which need not be detailed here. Harvey had not heard of this caribou-man being master of the caribou.

Wooden-shoe Wearer was above everyone. He was boss of the conjurers and of the powagans. "Everything was done under Wooden-shoe Wearer. Even the conjurers looked to Him and thought there was no harm in conjuring, because they thought all this was serving the One above". "He was the master of all, but I never heard from my grandfather anything about the creation of the world, men, or animals". Although Wooden-shoe Wearer was master of the conjurers, Harvey had never heard of Him coining into the conjuring tent.

"Wooden-shoe Wearer would help the Indians to hunt. If the Indians went out to hunt caribou and saw a large herd, and the caribou would not take flight when the first one was killed, and thus the Indians would be able to kill all of them, the Indians would then thank Wooden-shoe Wearer [27] for keeping the caribou from running off at the first kill". "When hard up for food, the Indians would look to Him to give them food".

---

[121] I should expect the ending *-ạn* here instead of *-an,* but *-an* was the ending as given by Harvey.

"Wooden-Shoe Wearer used to put into the Indians' heads how to do things when they were puzzled what to do. Sometimes they would learn in a dream what to do. My grandfather used to say that they got lots of things in dreams. The Indians took it that Wooden-shoe Wearer sent the dreams".

Wooden-Shoe Wearer was apparently not concerned with the socio-moral code, so far as Harvey was aware. "The Indians in the old days did not seem to know good from evil. although they looked to the One above. I never heard that He would be angry if one Indian trespassed on another Indian's family hunting territory. The trespasser would be killed right off and the furs taken. Wooden-shoe Wearer was not angry if an Indian murdered or stole. If one of your friends got murdered, you, if you were a conjurer, would try to conjure the murderer to death and in so doing you would be serving the One above with the wooden shoes". "If an Indian was seen doing something wrong, the other Indians would say to him: 'Take care or you will make Wooden-shoe Wearer angry'. One thing wrong was to neglect holding up a piece of meat before eating [see infra]." This was the only thing Harvey could think of offhand as being considered wrong. He mentioned however the custom of always covering meat when it was carried abroad "on account of the One above". He also said: "If any one teased a conjurer while the latter was in the conjuring tent, the teaser was stopped and was told that if he did this he would make Wooden-shoe Wearer angry". "The Indians always tried to use meat in the right way and not to waste it."

"The Indians never thought much of Wooden-Shoe Wearer in connection with the taboo on throwing the bones of animals to the dogs. They just used their own minds about this. They never thought of Him in matters of this kind. They just thought it would make the *animals themselves angry.*" He added however the following story: [28]

"One old woman knew there was a Being looking down on the earth. She starved her dog to death. She then took the dead dog and covered it with brush and said to the dog: 'You must not get me in trouble with Wooden-shoe Wearer for starving you to death'. This occurred here at Moose".

"When eating, the Indians would first cut off a piece of meat from any part of the animal. The piece was held up toward the sky with the right hand. The holder would then say something like a prayer, as follows:

Kī'la kā umictikwa'skisiniydn nī ką wi mī'cimī'ckākun ū'mā mī'cim,
('Thou who wearest the wooden shoes,
may it give me the feeling of a good feed this food').

Then he would put the bit of meat into his mouth and eat it. Then the rest of the caribou would be eaten. This same was done with any other kind of meat. They never put the meat in their mouth before doing this".

Harvey also knew well the custom of putting a bit of meat in the fire. "All used to do this. My grandfather and great grandfather had both seen this done. It was done to bring good luck. It was given to Wooden-shoe Wearer. The smoke went up to Him".

Harvey distinguished between the two types of sacrifice in the following way: "If the meal was only a family meal, or if the man was just eating alone, the bit of meat was held up and then put in the mouth. If however there was a big feast and there was a large crowd present, grease was put in the fire. I never heard that anything was said when grease was so spilled in the fire. All just sat quiet until it was spilled in the fire". "The meat was put in the fire for the One above," and Harvey was quite emphatic on this point. "When it was put in the fire for the dead, something was always said, but when put in the fire for the One above they never said anything". Harvey had heard of the sacrifice of a dog at Albany, but never at Moose.

Harvey had been told, quite explicitly it seems, by his grandfather that the custom of holding up the meat came in immediately after the coming of the two men from York [29] Factory [about 1843]. "The older custom was to throw the meat or grease or both into the fire".

"I have never heard that throwing meat in the fire for the dead was done in the olden times. But more recently this has been done here at Moose and is still done at Rupert House. Putting meat in the fire for the dead came in much later at Moose". In view however of the widespread diffusion of this manistic offering throughout the northern Algonquian area, I suspect strongly that Harvey may be mistaken on this point. In view too of the occurrence of the custom of holding up food or the calumet as an offering in other parts of northern North America.[122] I am not at all sure that Harvey is correctly informed as to the supposed recent introduction by the two York Factory men of the custom of holding up the bit of meat. At any rate, the existence at Moose in old times of the custom of throwing meat or grease into the fire seems clear from the testimony of Harvey and from other independent Moose informants.

"I do not know where the dead were believed to go in the future life. The Indians did not seem to bother at all about the future life. They just left the world. They thought of this life only, and did not worry about the next one". Harvey had heard of the "path of the spirits", but had never heard of the dead crossing a river to reach the abode of the departed, or of crossing such on an oscillating log.

Simon Smallboy, and his wife, *Ellen Smallboy.* From a copy of Simon's baptismal record which he showed me, he [30] is eighty years old; Ellen is very near the same age, probably not more than a year younger. They are extremely well informed on the older culture and highly intelligent, and gave me a great amount of invaluable data on general culture in 1927, 1932 and 1933, but in all three years, friendly and communicative as they were on all other matters, Ellen in particular, they proved very reticent on the question of pre-Christian theism. They are both very devoted members of the Church of England, and I have reason to believe that their reticence was due to religious considerations. But at any rate, they confirmed their son Harvey's account in general.

Simon told me in 1927 that long ago meat used to be thrown on the fire, but gave no further details. In 1932 the couple told me that meat or grease used to be thrown on the fire at Kesagami [occupied by Cree-speaking people closely allied by language, culture and marriage with the Moose Cree; the area adjoins Moose territory, on the south and southeast], and the

---

[122] During a short stay among the Blackfeet and Gros Ventres of Montana in 1931, I was informed by them that one type of sacrifice among them included first holding up a bit of meat and afterwards putting it in the fire (Blackfeet) or on the ground (Gros Ventres). Raising up bear meat as an offering to *Gitce Manitu* and, immediately after this, casting bits of the meat on the fire is mentioned as a Plains Cree custom by Alanson Skinner, *Political organization, cults and ceremonies of the Plains-Cree,* AMNH-AP, vxi, pt. vi, 1914: 542. The lifting of the pipe toward the sky as part of the "smoke sacrifice" is of course well known as widespread in North America. We may also add that Mrs. Morrison made mention of holding up the meat at Eastmain on the east coast, to which locality the influence of the two York Factory men did not, so far as I can discover, extend.

thrower would murmur something when doing it, but the purpose was not known to the Smallboys, they said.

The following data obtained in 1933 are brief but apparently decisive. Ellen had heard about Wooden-shoe Wearer and was emphatic in saying so. "It is very strange", she added, "that we had a Being called this. All of a sudden people stopped believing in Wooden-shoe Wearer. Then the two men came from York Factory, and I believe they were sent by this great Being", "The first time the people knew about Kitci *Manitū* [that is, this name] was when the two came from York Factory". Simon and Ellen both knew well Harvey's account of Wooden-shoe Wearer. "I heard it", Simon said to me, "from my father and my grandfather, and was present sometimes when Harvey was told about it. The same story about Wooden-shoe Wearer told to Harvey was also told to me, and where I saw Harvey was wrong I corrected him, and that is why he told it very well to you". It was quite evident from the whole interview on the point with Simon and Ellen that they knew very much more than they would talk about. [31] They very probably knew as much as Harvey did, or at least the main points in Harvey's account. This instance, by the way, is one of the rather exceptional cases of marked reticence I have met in the north. Nearly always, once friendly relations have been established, the older people show relatively few inhibitions, even on matters concerned with most phases of magico-religious culture.

John Dick. John is a Moose Cree Indian, probably between sixty and sixty-five years old. The data on the old religion were told him by his father, also a Moose Indian.

John had never heard of the form of address, Wooden-shoe Wearer. "The One above" was spoken of as *Pēmigābōyạn* and as *Kotā'wināo.* The latter word means "Our Father," and John was very positive that this form of name was pre-Christian. The former should in all probability be, not *Pēmigābōyạn,* but *Pēmigābowī'yạn.* The word was translated by my interpreter, Willie McLeod, as meaning "Thou who standest forever". Watkins (Dict. of Cree language) has *pimigapowew* for "he stands by". McLeod's translation may be somewhat free. Probably the meaning is just "Thou who standest."

John had heard something at least of the Master of Food, Life, and Death. "They sound to me like three beings, but really they were three in one. The Indians used to say to the sick: 'Will it please you to ask the One above to help you'. In curing the sick the drum was used. Nothing was ever said to the one who was Master of Death", and John was emphatic about this last point.

"The 'One who stands' lived up above." "He is the same whom we now call God Almighty". "There was only One so far as I know". "The people knew nothing about His having a Son. He was the only One, and they did not even know who He was. And this rather puzzled them. There was no way of finding out in the old days about His Son, but they had a notion there was someone over them". John had never heard of any belief in a supreme evil Being or *Matci manitū* [the Devil] in the old days. [32]

"The Indians knew it was the 'One who stands' who supplied all the meat", but John was vague in reply to questioning as to who made everything. "The people knew they were getting their food from the 'One who stands'". "The 'One who stands' used to come into the conjuring tent; other beings used also to come into the conjuring tent, but He too was there". John had heard of *Mikenak,* but did not seem to know of any relation of *Mikenak* to the ' One who stands'.

"It was through dreams that most of the Indians got their knowledge of the 'One who stands' and of what to do when hunting. It was the 'One who stands' who sent the dreams. Often people got up from sleep after a dream and followed out what their dream indicated, and were

successful in getting game. Such a dream was sent by the ' One who stands'".
" No image was ever made of the 'One who stands'," and John was quite emphatic on this point.
"If the Indians had bad luck in hunting, they would say:

'We must have done something wrong that has made the 'One who stands' angry". "If somebody stole something, the 'One who stands' would be angry", and John was positive about this, stating also that this was the case even before the missionaries came. "Soon after doing something wrong, a man would lose one of his children. Then it would be said: 'We have made the 'One who stands' angry. Look at what He has done to us'". Previously John had replied to the question, Did the 'One who stands' ever get angry?, as follows; "I do not know, but all the people were very particular not to make Him angry".

"I have seen meat put into the fire before eating at a feast. This is the first thing done before eating. A small bit of meat is cut off and thrown in the fire. If, for example, a brother-in-law has died recently, this is done for him, and while doing it the thrower says:

Nīctā'o ki mātcustehama'tin
('Brother-in-law, I am throwing this into the fire for thee')".

John then added: "A spoonful of grease would be thrown into the fire and the one who did so would say: *N^ehiliwē'se, Pemigābō[wi]yạn* ('Be in good [33] humor, Thou who standest [always]'). This was said to the One who had sent the meat. This One is above." ("They supposed" so Willie McLeod explained, "that this One was always standing in the same place"). John had never seen anyone hold up a piece of meat to the ' One who stands' before eating. "The old way of asking the 'One who stands' for anything was:

Nī kạ nātōtạmāwā'o kotā'windā kitci wītchī'tạk ō'mạ kē tātōskēyạk
('I shall ask our Father that He help us
as to that when [which] we shall work [do, hunt] ').

One of the Indians would take a drum and beat it and sing this".

Elijah Alisā'be (or *Alạsā'be*). Elijah is a Moose Cree Indian, probably about sixty or sixty-five years old. Some, − perhaps all, − of the information obtained from him on the ancient *Manitū* belief had been gotten by him from his old grandmother. I had the opportunity of only one short interview with him just before my departure. He apparently did not know much about the old religion.
"After the meat was all laid out and the people were ready to start eating, meat or grease was thrown into the fire. This was done after someone had died. While throwing the meat into the fire the thrower would say, giving the name [kinship term] of the deceased, *Kā wī nạhī'lạwēsin* ('That thou inayest be happy')."
"My grandmother told me", Elijah added, "that meat was put into the fire to thank the one who had given the people the meat. They did not know who he was, nor did she". "When putting in the meat, they would say:

Mī'gwetc kī kā wī Iǫkītǫmāwi'nan mī'tcim
('Thanks, thou wilt we hope increase for us meat)".

To a question as to whether there were more than one or only one who gave the meat, Elijah replied: "I have never heard there was more than one".

As to what happened to people after their death neither Elijah nor John Dick had ever heard. [34]

FIELD EVIDENCE. C ~ Eastmain Band

Our opportunities for gathering information on the possible earlier existence of a supreme *Manitū* belief and cult among the Montagnais-speaking Indians on the east coast of James Bay were meager, as ~~informants~~ were not available at Moosenee during our stay there in 1933. Some scattered data were however obtained by Miss {!} Regina Flannery from one ~~informant~~ and are here appended with Miss Flannery's kind permission. The date were obtained by her from Mrs. Jane Morrison, now living at Moose Factory, who is about seventy or seventy-five years old, and who lived nineteen years at Eastmain and forty-two years at Rupert House. Her information represents the earlier beliefs at Eastmain and perhaps at Rupert House. In any case the culture of these two contiguous areas is practically identical in all other respects at least, and almost certainly as regards earlier theism. Mrs Morrison is very intelligent and is particularly well informed as to the older culture. Reared all her life in Indian environment she is as much at home in Montagnais as in English.

Mrs. Morrison is familiar with the appellations, *Kā tibelitā'mǫn mī'tcim, pīmātisiwin, nipiwin.* "The Indians addressed the Master of Life when they needed help. They were always thankful to this one". "When they have nothing to eat and are hard up and hungry, they turn their faces up and ask for help".

"You may never take a dish of meat or fish or any kind of food from one tent to another without covering it". Mrs. Morrison thinks the Indians have a notion that otherwise they will lose their luck.

"The Indians believe in dreams. When they kill any animal they are very careful with the bones, lest the dogs eat them. They fancy that someone tells them in their dream that they are going to kill something and that they should be careful to treat it well." One old Indian told Mrs. Morrison he dreamed someone told him that he was going to kill a caribou and that he should be very careful to treat all his friends with it and should not let the dogs get any of the bones. So he dried all the meat and got the [35] grease or marrow out of the bones and made a feast. The one who spoke to him in his dream was the "one who gives us everything to live on".

"The Indians hold up a piece of meat before eating and tell the one who gives it to give them the same luck they had when they got that meat".

When asked what a man would say if he were starving, Mrs Morrison replied: "They always have this same call for help; 'Our father who art in heaven have pity on us when [for] we are poorly off'. A man wrote this on a stick when he was weak and could not rise to get help, and they found it in his hand". This last 'prayer' suggests modern Christian influence, particularly the appellation it starts with. Some further minor Christian influence is perhaps discernible in Mrs Morrison's data on the Eastmain Supreme Being belief, but on the whole they appear quite aboriginal.

FIELD EVIDENCE. D ~ Davis Inlet and
Barren Ground Bands (Labrador Peninsula)

The following information was secured by Dr William D Strong, of the Bureau of American Ethnology, among the Davis Inlet and Barren Ground bands of the northeastern section of the Labrador Peninsula. Dr Strong's stay in northern Labrador lasted from July, 1927, to August, 1928, as a member of the Rawson-MacMillan Sub-Arctic Expedition of the Field Museum. During the winter he spent three months traveling alone with the Davis Inlet band in the interior. (For further details and orthography, see *Amer. Anthrop,* 1929, n.s, xxxi: 277-79.) This information he has kindly put at my disposal for use in the present paper. It represents a brief outline of his material on this point which he will publish later.

According to Davis Inlet and Barren Ground ~~informants~~ the supreme deity, i.e, the caribou god, lives in the far north. His house, – not the Caribou house mentioned below, – has never been seen. He is vaguely described as manlike. [36]

According to Davis Inlet band ~~informants~~ the caribou god has five names, as follows: *tepēnamwēsū,* "Big Boss of Indians" (Chief Indian God); *kanapenekastcī'wh^u,* (no meaning remembered); *ū'tnimatcī'sū,* "Giver of Food:" *pu'kwicēmni'makin,* "Giver of food to hunters"; *tcạ'micūmi'nū,* "Grandfather of all."

He is said to be the supreme God of the people among both bands, and is definitely superior to *Nztan,* the chief of the caribou, who lives in *d'tiwitcudp* [the caribou house], a mythical mountain in northeastern Labrador which is believed to be the home and source of all the caribou. A Barren Ground conjurer *(mete'o),* it is said, once went to this house where he obtained a glimpse of the caribou god, being stricken unconscious as a result. Another subordinate of the caribou god is *Mistapw* ("Great Man") who is regarded as the "head man" of all conjurers. A design, consisting of an inverted isosceles triangle, with a short upright line resting on the middle of the inverted base and with the upper end of the line surmounted by a circle, represents the caribou god. A conjurer should have this design on his coat at the back (where the vent is in white men's garments). This picture, or design is called *mistapm,* also, and the plural guardian spirits of a conjurer are called *mistapzuits.* While there is thus a direct connection between the caribou god and the "head man" of all conjurers, they are distinct entities, and the caribou god is regarded as supreme with *Mistapm* and *Niton* as his main subordinates.

The will of the caribou god is brought to individuals in dreams. Likewise, individuals acquire songs from the caribou god by dreaming, and these songs, accompanied by the drum, are sung to bring success in hunting. According to a Davis Inlet band ~~informant~~, the caribou god sees all that a man does and knows what he thinks; consequently if a man does wrong, especially if he violates caribou tabus, he will have bad luck and will probably die soon. The nature of these dreams, and the relationship of the caribou god to the other religious and magical beliefs among these bands, must await the full presentation of the data. [37]

Synthesis of Field Evidence

Before taking up the discussion of the foregoing field data, it may help to clarify the situation if we present first a brief synthesis thereof.

The more common name by which the Supreme Deity was known was simply *Manitū.* particularly in the Albany area. The name *Kitci Manitū* seems to have come in after the arrival of the missionaries or of the two men from York Factory. The same may probably be said of the peculiar appellation "Thou who hast the wooden shoes", reported by the Smallboy family from Moose. The form of address, "My Father" or "Our Father" may possibly be post-Christian, but the greater probability seems to be in favor of pre-Christian origin, to judge from our own field evidence as well as from the evidence in the published sources. The name "Thou who standest" reported by only one ~~informant~~, from Moose, is pretty surely aboriginal. The three names "Thou who hast mastery over food", "Thou who hast mastery over life", and "Thou who hast mastery over death" seem quite clearly, in view of our own field evidence as well as of the many older sources in which the appellation "Master of life" occurs, to be likewise aboriginal.[123]

That there was but one Supreme Being is reasonably clear from the evidence. All ~~informants~~ were positive or even emphatic that there was only one. There is some question however as to whether the three, the Master of Food, of Life and of Death respectively, were conceived of as separate' from and subordinate to the supreme one. or as phases or parts of the supreme one, or merely as different forms by which he was addressed. The greater weight of evidence [38] leans rather towards the unity of the three "Masters" in one than toward plurality. Perhaps different theological formulations were current among different bands along the Bay or among different individuals in given bands; or maybe the relationship was vague in the native mind; or possibly the memory of some of my ~~informants~~ may have slipped a cog.

The Supreme Being was consistently conceived of as being somewhere above, – *icpemik*, up above. No hint at all emerged of any relationship of the Supreme Being to the sun or other heavenly body. I failed to inquire explicitly on this point, but I am pretty sure that, were the Supreme Being in any sense solar or lunar, some indication of this would have come out in the many hours of free conversation and of questioning devoted to the subject of the Supreme Being. The York Factory Cree solar concept of the Supreme Being as reported by la Potherie should be interpreted probably as a misconception on his part or as an indication of influences in this respect as in some other respects on York Factory culture from the area west or south thereof.

No mythological or folklore elaboration of the supreme *Manitū* concept appeared. Nor did I find any linking up of *Manitū* with the culture hero and trickster cycle.

The *Manitū* was clearly personal in the minds of my ~~informants~~, and not identified with impersonal supernatural force. In fact nowhere among the Albany River Otchipwe, among the Eastern Cree, or among the Montagnais have I been able thus far to find the word *manitū* used to denote such force in connection with the Supreme Being belief, with conjuring, or with any other phase of magico-religious culture. *Manitū, so* far as I can discover, always denotes a supernatural personal being, *Manitūwē'o*, in the Moose dialect, is used for "he is a 'spirit'". For "he has supernatural [conjuring] power", or "mind power" as distinct from physical strength, they say *sōkadisi'u*. The word *manitū* is, my ~~informants~~ say, not used to denote magical or conjuring power among the coastal Cree, nor, so I was told in 1927, among the Fort Hope Otchipwe of the upper Albany river. [39]

---

[123] For use of "Father" see field data supra from Jimmie Acickic (Atawa-pipkat), John Dick (Moose), Mrs. Morrison (Eastmain), Cf. early Algonkin use of "Our Great Father", in le Jeune, JR (Thwaites): xi, 166, 204-6; Otchipwe use of *now,* "My Father", in Midewiwin rite, apparently referring to Supreme Being, in W.J Hoffman, *The Mide'wiwin*, BAE-R 7, 1891: 212-13; Naskapi *use* of "Thy Father", in Bossé, 214, and Athapaskan use of "Grandfather", in Taché, 9, both quoted in full infra. For early use of "Master of Life" to denote Supreme Being among Cree farther west, cf.: Mackenzie, i: cli, cliii; Franklin: 77, 113; Harmon: 315, 317, – full titles given infra under footnote 13.

There is no clear information as to the appearance of the Supreme Being except from one informant who stated that he was thought to have had a body. There is no question at all of him having had a wife or children. All but one informant stated that he was never seen.

The Supreme Being was conceived of quite clearly as distinct from the powagans or guardian spirits, and also from *Mikenak*, the chief spirit or "spokesman" of the conjuring tent on the west coast who corresponds to Mistā'bēo on the east coast of the Bay or to Mistapīu as the name was recorded by Doctor Strong in the northeastern section of the Labrador peninsula. On the west coast of the Bay, too, the Supreme Being was quite distinct from Atihkwatcahk, the metamorphosed caribou man, who according to one account, that of Jeannette, was a sort of master of the caribou. There was no supreme evil spirit. At least all my informants had never heard of any, and two or three of them were quite emphatic in their denials. The *Matci Manitū* occasionally referred to by informants turned out on fuller inquiry to be either the hungry, cannibalistic *Wihtiko*, or else *Mikenak*.

All informants agreed that the Supreme Being was really the master or "boss" of things in general, including mankind. As to whether he was the maker or creator, informants differed. Two of them, Jeannette and John Dick, considered him the maker. In view of the fact that Jeannette in at least two or three other points in her otherwise very clear account introduced clearly Christian elements and in view of the consistently negative evidence on the point from the other informants, it seems more likely that the Supreme Being was conceived of as master rather than maker; although on this particular point too there may have been differences of opinion and belief among the individual Indians or bands themselves. Information as to whether the first man and woman were made by the Supreme Being pointed rather towards a negative.

The evidence is perfectly clear that the Supreme Being was not of the otiose type. He was distinctly active in his relationship both toward the conjurers and toward the rank [40] and file of the people. There are certain minor contradictions in the evidence as to the relation of the Supreme Being to conjuring and to the conjurers, but in the main the evidence seems strong that it was in the last analysis from the Supreme Being that the conjurer got his power, though this was conceived of as coming to him immediately from the powagan or powagans or from *Mikenak*. Some informants, particularly Patrick Steven, affirmed a quite intimate relationship between *Mikenak* and *Manitū*.

The Supreme Being was emphatically the one who gave the people their food. That he also looked after life and health seems equally clear. It was chiefly through dreams that he informed them what to do to have a successful hunt and to recover from sickness. Taking the evidence by and large, there can be no question that *Manitū* bulked large in the native religious consciousness, but I could not say that theism bulked larger than either of the two other great sections of the whole magico-religious complex, namely, conjuring and hunting observances.

So much for the dynamic relationship of the Supreme Being to man. What active relationship did man have toward the Supreme Being? There were no statues or images of *Manitū* and there was nothing like cursing. If there was any relationship between the respect paid to the bones of animals and the respect paid to the Supreme Being it must have been a tenuous or else an indirect one. To cover meat when it was carried from tent to tent, and not to waste meat, were quite definitely looked upon as required and expected by the Supreme Being. Two informants, Jeannette and John Dick, affirmed that a breach of the socio-moral law would offend the Supreme Being, but this relationship to the socio-moral law is implicitly or explicitly denied by other informants. I suspect Christian influence in these two informants as regards this particular point. It seems very much more likely that the Supreme Being's relationship to the socio-moral law was either extremely indirect and tenuous or else nil.

Prayers for food and for health were made to the Supreme Being, particularly, it would seem, in circumstances of [41] more than ordinary need. Thanksgiving was made after the *Manitū* had granted food or health. The ~~informants~~ who knew of the former use of the three names, Master of Food, of Life, and of Death, were positive that the Indians had nothing to do with the Master of Death.

Throughout most or all of the James Bay area, first-fruits sacrifices and first-fruits observances of a magical, manistic, aniinistic or theistic character are markedly developed, They are carried out when the first animal or bird, such as beaver or goose, of the season is killed, or when a young boy brings down his first game. The more common kind of sacrifice proper is the offering of a bit of grease or meat just before eating. It is this last kind of sacrifice proper that was the typical and exclusive one offered to the Supreme Being, usually with some simple non-formalized mental or vocal prayer, and it took two forms. In the one, the piece of meat or spoonful of grease was thrown into the fire; in the other, the piece of meat was held up toward the sky in the right hand and then put into the holder's mouth and eaten. In either case, after this all present ate the food prepared.

There can be no reasonable doubt but that the custom as such of throwing meat or grease into the fire, – regardless of whether the purpose be magical, manistic, animistic, or theistic, – is aboriginal. I have found the rite, – chiefly with a manistic purpose, – all through the northern Algonquian area; mention of it occurs repeatedly in the older Algonquian sources; and it is, as is well known, of widespread diffusion on the North American continent. In view of these facts, as well as of the field evidence we have given, the aboriginality of the use of the rite among the James Bay Cree as part of the aboriginal theistic or Supreme-Being cult would seem to be reasonably established.

As regards, however, the second form, that of holding up the meat toward the sky, Harvey Smallboy's explicit testimony might suggest that this rite was introduced later, around 1843, by the two men from York Factory. Perhaps this was the case. But I am a little more inclined for the reasons given supra[124] to think that Harvey was mistaken. [42]

So much for the Supreme Being concept and cult as such. It will, we believe, help to a better understanding of both to view them in their relation to the other phases of the magico-religious culture of the James Bay Cree and Montagnais.

The overwhelming mass of the magico-religious beliefs and observances of the Cree and Montagnais of James Bay fall into three great divisions: the theism or Supreme-Being concept and cult which we have just outlined; "conjuring" or shamanistic practices centering largely around the shaking-tent rite, and carried on by professional, semi-professional, or specially qualified conjurers or shamans through the mediation of their guardian spirits; and the numerous hunting observances connected with the killing of game animals and birds and with the disposal of their remains, and carried on by the rank and file of the people.

The conjuring practices as well as the hunting observances appear in the main to have a mixed animistic and magical coloring, with the animistic seemingly more dominant, even in the conjuring practices. In fact it is more upon the supernatural personal helper, – upon the individual's powagan or guardian spirit or upon the chief conjuring spirit, *Mikenak* or *Mistabeo*, – than upon control of anything like impersonal supernatural force that the conjurer seems to rely for producing effects. In most of the hunting observances it is the animal or bird "spirits" that are propitiated or honored. Among the Tête-de-Boule Cree farther to the southeast, supernatural

---

[124] See footnote 5, supra.

chiefs of the main game and fur-bearing animal species are well developed, but I have so far found little trace of such chiefs among the James Bay Cree. The observances appear in the main to be for the animals or birds as such, or at most as somewhat spiritually or animistically conceived. I should be inclined to say, − although judgment in the case may have an element of the subjective in it, − that animistic conceptions are more pronounced than sheer magical ones. On the other hand, apart from conjuring proper and from the respect paid to game animals and birds, animistic beliefs and [43] practices seem appreciably less elaborate than among the Algonquians within or closer to the horticultural belt.[125]

Manistic beliefs and practices are little in evidence, apart from simple food offerings to the dead. The concept of the soul and of the future life was very vague. There seems to have been no idea of reward or punishment in the future life. At most some kind of survival was believed in, as evidenced, for instance, by the common saying that the northern lights are the dead dancing. The dead did not go to the Supreme Being. Among the Cree of the west coast of the Bay there seems to have been relatively little fear of ghosts or of the dead. As one Moose informant remarked to me: "The whites have more fear of ghosts than the Indians have". Such fear seems a little more pronounced among the Montagnais of the east coast.

On the whole, then, of the four broad phases of super-naturalism, − theistic, animistic, manistic, and magical, − theism and animism appear to be the more dominant, with magic, in the sense of control of impersonal supernatural forces, less marked, and with manism present only in a very minor degree.

As to how the three main phases of magico-religious culture among the James Bay Indians bulked relatively in the living native consciousness, it is not easy to say. If I had to risk an estimate, I should be inclined, − with apologies to the statisticians and with no little misgiving as to the objectiveness of the estimate, − on the basis of 100 points to rate the Supreme-Being belief and cult at about 30, conjuring and the shaking-tent complex at about 30, and the hunting observances at about 40.

One final question calls for a brief discussion, namely: To what extent are these three main phases or clusters of beliefs and practices organically related to one another? Broadly viewed, they appear fairly independent one from another. From the field data we have given, there was seemingly a somewhat closer tie-up between conjuring and the Supreme-Being complex, than between the Supreme-Being complex [44] and the hunting observances. One of my best informants, however, Patrick Steven, had obtained from his father an account which welded these three clusters into an organic unity as follows. The three, − the Masters of Food, of Life, and of Death, − constituted only parts or phases or aspects or appellations of the one supreme *Manitū*. *Mikenak*, the chief conjuring-tent spirit was the master of the inferior conjuring beings, the *powagans*, and was himself directly under and responsible to the supreme *Manitū*. As for the hunting observances, it was perhaps (Patrick was not so clear here) the supreme *Manitū* who instigated the respective animals to be angry if the Indians did not properly respect the game that was killed. This looks like a "theological" synthesis of the whole magico-religious culture into a unified system. Whether this synthesis was due to the individual intellect of Patrick's father who was a conjurer and apparently a very able and intelligent one, or whether this linking together of the three clusters in the whole magico-religious culture was more widely held in earlier times, − as from Dr Strong's evidence it seems to be held today in northeastern Labrador, − it is not easy

---

[125] Cf, e.g, Diamond Jenness, *The Ojibwa Indians of Parry Sound: their social and religious life*, Ms, National Museum of Canada, Ottawa.

to decide. Some of my other ~~informants~~ tied together pretty closely the conjuring and the Supreme-Being rites. But as a rule, apart from the custom of covering the meat when it was carried about and from the strict taboo on wasting meat, my other ~~informants~~ reported little if any relationship in the old times between the game or hunting observances and the Supreme-Being cult.

Discussion of Field Evidence

So much for the facts as reported and for such generalizations as appear to follow legitimately therefrom. Three questions obtrude themselves. First, Are the accounts reliable? Second. Have we to do here with Christian influence? Third, Have the James Bay Cree and Montagnais derived their Supreme Being concept and cult from the neighboring Algonquian-speaking peoples with whom they have been in contact, especially on the west coast? We shall discuss each of these questions in turn. [45]

A. ~ Are the ~~Informants~~ Reliable?

That the respective accounts may contain minor errors of detail here and there is more than likely in view of the fact that for some decades past the *Manitū* cult has not been a living one. The contradictions evident in certain details between respective ~~informants~~ may point toward the same conclusion, although these minor contradictions may perhaps be due to other causes, such as vagueness in the pre-Christian native concepts, or individual variability from the absence of any organized priesthood or formalized rites and rituals, or variations (which occur on the Bay in many non-religious culture-traits) from region to region and from band to band.

On the main characteristics, however, of the Supreme Being and his cult, the testimony of the many ~~informants~~ shows quite marked concordance, and the circumstances under which the information was gotten effectually barred collusion. Furthermore, I have found all of these ~~informants~~ extremely truthful and dependable on the non-religious phases of native culture, both contemporary and ancient, and have been able to check up their general reliability on scores of points, in fact on hundreds, both from information gotten independently in both contiguous and distant areas and from the published and manuscript sources on the North. The concordance, moreover, of the west coast, data, as far as they go, with the east coast and northern Labrador data, and this in fair detail, is an additional evidence of reliability, as is also the concordance of our own field data with the published data on the theism of the northern Athapaskans and Algonquians in general and on that of the Cree and Montagnais in particular, which will be cited later.

The reliability of our ~~informants~~ is also indicated by the sources of their information. These sources were their own parents or grandparents, with whom they had frequently conversed on the matter and whose memory reached either well beyond the time of the first coming of the missionaries in the forties or else well back into the time when the old beliefs were still clearly remembered by surviving elders, born and reared in full pre-Christian paganism. There are [46] numerous indications both in our field evidence and in the modern missionary reports that the old beliefs persisted as a living memory from pagan days at least well toward the beginning of the present century and in the case of some of the oldest people almost to the present time. My ~~informants~~ were moreover as a rule most emphatic in stating precisely how and under what circumstances they had learned of the old ways from their parents or grandparents.

It may be added too that when on a point here or there assiduous indirect questioning brought out only negative results, and when as a last resort I used the direct question, – as, for instance, in regard to residence with the *Manitū* in the future life, the crossing of the river to get to the abode of the dead, the possession of a son by the *Manitū*, – the answers were likewise negative. A very specific evidence of the reliability of rny present-day ~~informants~~ on beliefs prevalent just prior to the coming of the first missionary in 1840 is the complete and detailed exactitude of the information as remembered by them on the coming of the two men from York Factory, around 1843 – the details of which will now be given.

In 1932 and again last summer, 1933, considerable information on these two men was gotten from old Simon and Ellen Smallboy, from their son Harvey, from Frank Rickard, and from Charlotte Sutherland. The composite story from these five ~~informants~~ runs as follows. In the time of Harvey's grandfather and when Charlotte's sister was still in the cradle board, two Indians came down the west coast of the Bay from York Factory. One called himself Jesus, and the other called himself *Wasidik* that is "The Light" ["it is lightsome", subjunctive]. The former of the two is supposed to have gone up to heaven and to have seen the *Manitū* and to have come back with a book. These two taught the natives along the coast a hymn in which occur the words "Be happy, the light has come among you", or which at any rate stressed the idea of light. The other of the two, *Wasidik*, did not go to heaven but stayed on earth. These two, besides teaching the people the hymn and some prayers, brought a "book", and also [47] had the Indians observe Sunday and the Sabbath rest. These two men came before the ministers or priests came.

The coming of these two men evidently made a very vivid impression on the people, for it is still keenly remembered and in detail. By checking up the probable ages of my ~~informants~~ and of their informants by dead reckoning. I had concluded, not knowing at the time the exact dates of the coming of the missionaries, that the two men from York Factory must have appeared somewhere around 1850.

A search through the missionary literature on my return home finally resulted in the lucky discovery of a detailed contemporary account of this religious movement from the pen of the Wesleyan missionary, Rev. George Barnley, who was stationed then at Moose Factory. This account, is given in a letter written by him from Moose Factory, September 23, 1843. Practically every detail given above is verified by Barnley. I append here data from his letter:

> "Two hymns (printed probably by Mr Evans, but certainly by some person familiar with evangelical truth and poetic numbers) were in circulation among the Indians at York Factory, and thence found their way to Severn House". The two natives were conjurers. These two withdrew for a time from the society of others and on returning "presented themselves before their countrymen as extraordinary messengers from heaven. The first of the two hymns referred to above commenced with an allusion to light; the second, to our blessed Saviour. Of these circumstances the impostors availed themselves, to augment their influence; one calling himself *Wasetek* 'Light'; the other assuming the sacred name of 'Jesus Christ'. Their recent absence was accounted for by the announcement of certain visits having been made both to the regions of future blessedness, and to those of future woe". The hymns were "evidently the production of an Indian mind in a heathen state". The movement reached down the coast as far as Moose, but did not pass over to the east coast of the Bay. It reached Moose in or about 1843.[126] [48]

---

[126] Wesleyan-Methodist magazine for 1845, London, 1845, v.68, 201-4.

So much for the two accounts, – one contemporary by Barnley and the other carried along purely by oral tradition among the Indians. The detailed exactitude of this oral tradition harking back nearly a hundred years to the very time when Christianity was first being introduced is an added indication, it seems to the present writer, of the reliability of the aboriginal memory regarding the beliefs held immediately prior to the first modern missionary influences around the same time, 1840, although of course not a strict demonstration thereof.

Thus far we have dealt with what we may call the personal criteria of reliability. Let us turn to the cultural criteria, namely, the degree in which the data from James Bay and Labrador check up with the data from the other northern woodland peoples, the Athapaskan-speaking peoples farther northwest, and, particularly, the Algonquian-speaking peoples in the north and elsewhere. A preliminary word of explanation may however be in order for including the northern Athapaskans at all. They are here included on the ground that northern Athapaskan culture and northern Algonquian culture are basically one. This basic unity can be pretty clearly established, the present writer believes, from the published sources, and from his own unpublished field data gathered in the Mackenzie valley and in the eastern Canadian woodland area. We shall review first the northern Athapaskan evidence on Supreme-Being beliefs and cults, and then the Algonquian, to determine in how far these agree or disagree with the data outlined in the preceding pages from James Bay and Labrador.

Our information on northern Athapaskan theism has been briefly summed up by Morice.[127][10] I wish to add here a word on the theism of the Chipewyan, the branch of the Déne who are nearest geographically to the eastern and northern Cree. These Chipewyan data are from Archbishop Tache's [49] very important, but seemingly little known, account of the Chipewyan.

Archbishop Taché wrote his account in 1851, after four or five years spent among the Chipewyan, at the time of the first opening-up of missionary work among them. He had, therefore, ample opportunity to observe them in their pagan state, and his exact and minute account of general Chipewyan culture shows him an exceptionally good observer.

> "Aussi nos Montagnais [that is, Chipewyan, not eastern Montagnais], sans autres lumières que celles de leur raison, son parvenus á la connaissance de Dieu, sans y joindre ce mélange grossier d'absurdités qui captivait les peuples les plus éclaires de l'antiquité . Ils croyaient en un seul Dieu, créateur et conservateur de tout, rémunérateur de la vertu et vengeur du crime, en un Dieu éternel dont les soins providentiels s'étendaient á tout ce qui existe. Seulement, peu faits aux idées purement spirituelles, ils supposaient ce Dieu revêtu d'une forme humaine, dont les proportions gigantesques répondaient á son pouvoir, et dont la délicatesse des organes lui permettait de voir et d'entendre du haut du ciel tout ce qui se faisait et se disait sur la terre." He was called by "les noms de Créateur (*Niottsi*) et de puissant (*yeddariyé*)".
>
> "Il est surprenant qu'avec ces idées sur la divinité, les Tchipeweyans n'eussent aucun culte, ni aucune cérémonie religieuse quelconque. Seulement aux reunions, surtout aux festins, quelqu'un des vieillards exhortait l'asseniblée à reconnaître la libéralité de Dieu, à éviter le mal qui seul peut suspendre le cours

---

[127] [10] AG Morice, "The Canadian Dénés", in *Annual archaeol*. rpt. 1905, Toronto, 1906, 203-4; rt. H. Faraud, *Dix-huit ans chez les sauvages, Voyages et missions de*, ed. Fernand-Michel, Paris, 1866, 356-57.   {See appendix for English translations}

des bienfaits du Tout-Puissant. Suivait une fervente prière pour demander la santé, le succès a la chasse et autres choses nécessaires à la vie présente. On jetait ensuite au feu et on enterrait sous le foyer quelques bouchées des aliments qui devaient être offerts aux conviés. Quelques sacrifices plus considérables avaient aussi lieu, mais si rarenient qu'ils n'étaient, pour ainsi dire, point d'usage. Tel est absolument tout le culte public que cette nation rendait à la divinité. On trouve pourtant quelques traces de jonglerie; mais, outre qu'il est permis de les croire de fabrique étrangère [Cree?], ce [50] n'étaient guère que des prières, accompagnées de plus de bruit que les autres. Les jongleurs avaient, sans doute, la prétention de passer pour des hommes extraordinaires; mais ils ne s'adressaient jamais qu'a Dieu, et ces superstitions n'avaient jamais les résultats fâcheux qu'elles ne présentent que trop souvent chez les peuples voisins. Le culte particulier était assez universel. Quelques personnes adressaient tous le jours à Dieu de ferventes prières, d'autres ne le faisaient que dans les circonstances critiques.

" J'ai entendu raconter plusieurs exemples, qui prouvent combien les prières de ces âmes simples étaient puissantes auprès de Celui qui a dit: 'Demandez, et vous recevrez'. Voici un fait entre plusieurs. J'examinais un jour le main d'un vieillard privé de son pouce; s'étant aperçu de mon attention, il me dit d'un ton de conviction qui me toucha:

'Vois cette main. J'étais un jour à la chasse, en hiver, loin de ma loge. II faisait froid. Je marchais; tout-à-coup j'aperçois des caribous; je les approche, je les tire, mon fusil crève, et m'emporte le pouce. Déjà beaucoup de mon sang n'était plus. En vain, je m'efforçai d'en tarir le source: impossible. Peu à peu je prenais froid. J'essayai d'allumer du feu: impossible. Alors j'eus peur de mourir; mais, me souvenant de Celui que tu nommes Dieu, et que je ne connaissais pas bien, je lui dis: 'Mon graud-père, (Se tssiyè,) on dit que tu peux tout; regarde-mois, et quisque tu es le Puissant, soulage-moi'. Tout-à-coup, plus de sang, ce que me permit de mettre ma mitaine. Je regagnai ma loge, ou j'écrasai de faiblesse en entrant. Je compris alors, ajouta-t-il, profondément ému, je compris quelle est la force du Puissant. Depuis ce moment, j'ai toujours désiré le connaître. C'est pourquoi, ayant appris que tu étais ici, je suis venu de bien loin, pour que tu m'eiiseignes à servir Celui qui m'a sauvé cette fois et qui seul nous fait vivre tous".

The Chipewyans, according to Taché, also believed in a multitude of malicious spirits,

"ennemis de Dieu et des hommes; toujours en guerre avec le premier, sur lequel ils avaient quelquefois l'avantage, ce dont ils ne se servaient que pour nuire à 1'homme. Aussi attribuaient-ils à ces esprits mauvais tous leurs revers, leurs maladies et surtout [51] la mort, quand elle arrivait avant la décrépitude de 1'âge. Ils croyaient que ces esprits n'avaient pris naissance, qu'-après le déluge; qui, de plus, ils avaient une union très-ètroite avec les animaux, ennemis de l'homme ou qui lui inspirent de l'horreur, entre autres les serpents. De là une extrême attention à ne rien dire contre ces animaux, dans la crainte d'exciter leur courroux. Quoique le mot de blasphème se trouve dans leur langue, ce crime si commun parmi les chrétiens était inconnu parmi eux. Ils croyaient que de paroles injurieuses contre la divinité ne pouvaient qu'augmenter leurs peines".[128]

The foregoing is Tache's description in full of Chipewyan religion. There is no mention by him of a supreme evil being. A large number of the points in his general description of Chipewyan culture I have been able to verify independently, during a stay among the Chipewyans in 1931, but I did not get anything on their early theistic cult, being at the time on the trail of other information, namely, that bearing upon the general relationship of northern Algonquian culture to northern Athapaskan.

We may now turn to the Algonquian-speaking peoples. A great deal of the evidence on Algonquian theism has been assembled and discussed by Loewenthal and Schmidt, and hence need not be reviewed here.[129] We shall confine ourselves more to the data on the northern Algonquians not given by them.

The Supreme Being belief among the Otchipwe, the Algonquians closest geographically and culturally to the [52] eastern Cree, is well known.[130] The present writer has also found it very definitely in his own field studies among the Otchipwe of Rainy Lake and of Lake of the Woods, and from Cree ~~informants~~ he has gotten apparently reliable reports of it among the Otchipwe of the middle Albany and upper Atawapiskat Rivers, who are the Otchipwe closest to the Cree of the west shore of James Bay.

The existence of theistic beliefs and cult among the western Cree is reported in a good many of the earlier as well as more recent sources. The Supreme Being is often there called *Kitci Manitū* and Master of Life. A supreme evil being is also recorded, but without such detail

---

[128] Alex. Taché, "Lettre de, à sa mère", dated Isle à la Crosse, Jan. 4, 1851, in *Rapport sur Le missions du diocèse de Québec*, Mars 1853, no. 10, Quebec 1853: 7-10; also in *Annnales de la propagation de la foi*, Lyons 1852: xxiv, 333-36. The *Rapport sur les missions*, just cited, will hereafter in the present paper be cited as RMQ. The Rapport ended with no. 21, March 1874, being continued as *Annales de la propagation de la foi pour la province de Quebec*, Montreal, beginning n.s. I, Feb 1877 (hereafter cited as APFQ).

[129] J. Loewenthal, *Die Religion der Ostalgonkin*, Berlin 1913: passim, esp. 59-90; W Schmidt, *Der Ursprung der Gottesidee*, II Teil, II Band, Muenster i W 1929: 394-872.

[130] The more important data on Otchipwe theism have been extracted at length and discussed by Schmidt, loc. Cit: 475-507. See also; P. Jacobs, *Journal of,* NY 1855: 3-4; John McLean, *Notes of a twenty-five years' service in the Hudson's bay territory*, 2 v., London 1849: repr., Toronto 1932: 160; [G.A. Belcourt], "Mission de la Rivière-rouge", in RMQ, Janvier 1839: no, 1, 12; J. Long, *Voyages and travels of an Indian interpreter and trader,* London, 1791, repr., Chicago 1922: 169, 174; J. Stewart, "Rupert's land Indians in the olden time", in *Annual archaeol. rpt. 1904*, Toronto 1905: 89-90, 95, 98, In his *Net in the Bay,* 2d rev. ed., London 1873: 217, Bishop David Anderson, speaking of the Otchipwe of Martin's Falls, about 300 miles up the Albany River from its mouth, states: "It was painful and depressing to find them almost, entirely ignorant of the nature of God; they scarcely knew, they said, of such a Being, and regarding a future state, they either knew nothing, or would not declare their notions". This would seem to imply that they had at least some concept of a Supreme Being. On the Supreme Being among the Algonkins of Abitihi. See Poiré, "Journal" in RMQ, Janvier 1840, # 2: 51-52; J.N Laverlochere, in RMQ, Avril 1849, # 8: 64-65.

as might enable us to identify him better.[131] [53]

A number of our earlier sources state very definitely that the Cree of the York Factory district, on the west coast of Hudson Bay proper, who were and are very closely allied in culture and language to the James Bay Cree and who were not infrequent visitors to the James Bay area, had a Supreme Being belief and cult. The first of these sources is, however, vague, as Father Marest during the short time he spent in the region had given most of his attention to the whites and had learned, as he tells us, very little of the religion of the Indians. The other sources are much clearer.

Father Gabriel Marest, in his Letter of 1695 or 1696, writes of the Indians of Fort Bourbon (so called under the French; Fort Nelson, York Fort, and York Factory under the English):

"'Ja'i su qu'ils ont des espèces de Sacrifices; ils sont grands jongleurs; ils ont, comme les autres, l'usage de la pipe, qu'ils appellent *calumet;* ils font turner le Soleil, ils font fumer aussi les personnes absentes".[132]

We may suggest that it was quite possibly the use of the calumet-offering and the custom associated therewith of holding the calumet up to the sky that may have given la Potherie the idea that the *Quichemanitou* was the sun. That the York Factory Supreme Being was solar is not mentioned in our other sources.

La Potherie, who was at York Factory in 1697 for a short time and who apparently got a good deal of his information from a Frenchman, [Lieutenant?] Martigni. who had lived fifteen months among the natives, writes as follows of the York Factory district Indians:

"Ils reconnoissent comme ces anciens heretiques [the Manicheans] un bon et un mauvais esprit. Ils apellent le premier le *Quichemanitou*. C'est le Dieu de prosperité. C'est celui dont ils s'imaginent recevoir tous les secours de la vie, qui préside dans tons les effets heureux de la nature. Le *Matchimanitou* au contraire est le Dieu fatal. Ils l'adorent plus par crainte que par amour . .. Ces deux Esprits selon la croyance de la plûpart, sont le Soleil et la Lune. II y a de l'aparence qu'ils reconnoissent le premier pour le Souverain maître de [54] l'Univers: aussi quand ils se trouvent dans quelques afflictions publiques, ils lui font des

---

[131] E. Umfreville, *The present state of Hudson's bay,* London 1790: 189-90; A. Mackenzie. *Voyages* [1789-1793], 2 v., repr. NY 1902: i, pp.cli, cliii, civ, clix; DW Harmon, *Journal of voyages and travels in the inferior of North America* [1800-1819], repr, NY 1922: 62, 315-17; John Franklin, *Narrative oj a journey to the chores of the Polar Sea in the years 1819, 20, 21, and 22,* London 1823: 77, 113; RT Rundle, "Letter" dated Norway House, in *Wesleyan-Methodist mag. for 1841,* London 1841, v.64: 163-64; J. Richardson, *Arctic searching expedition,* NY 1852: 268; L Laflèche, "Lettre", 1855, in RMQ, Mars, 1855 no. 11: 125-27; H Y Hind, *Narrative of the Canadian Red river expedition, 2 v;* London 1860: i, 113; E.R. Young, *By canoe and dog-train among the Cree and Saulteaux Indians,* NY [1890?]: 119-20; same, *Stories from Indian wigwams and northern campfires,* NY 1892: 81; A Skinner, *Polit. organis ... Plains-Cree,* AMNH-AP, vxi, pt.vi, 1914: passim.

[132] G. Marest, *Lettre* [1695 or 1696], in JR (Thwaites), v. 66: 108.   {See translated appendix}

sacrifices". La Potherie mentions the following as sacrifices: smoking the calumet; throwing tobacco or something else to the spirit of the moon when caught in a storm on the water; burning the first animal killed. The *Matchimanitou* referred to can be identified from the description given by la Potherie as the spirit of the shaking-tent rite.[133]

Robson, who spent six years in the Hudson Bay region around York and Churchill in 1733-36 and 1744-47, writing of the York Factory or Fort Churchill Indians or both, says; "They have a religious apprehension of some malevolent and capricious being, whom they are frequently afraid of; for when they eat, they throw a piece of flesh into the fire as a kind of offering to him, and when they go out in their canoes, they cast something ashore to render him propitious".[134]

The Clerk of the California (Charles Swaine, Theodore Swaine Drage, supposed author), who spent the winter of 1746-47 at Fort Nelson (York Factory) and who has given us a rather long and detailed account of the Indians of the region, based upon "what I could attain by my own Observation, and that which I could rely on as Fact, from the Revelations which were made me by others" (Preface, iv), states; They "are not without the Sense of a Deity" "It is a received Opinion amongst the *Indians* in those Parts, that there are two Spirits, one whom they call *Manitou,* to which Spirit, they attribute all the Perfections of the Deity, the other Spirit they call *Vitico,* and that Spirit they imagine to be the Cause of all the Evil and Misfortune that happens to them, and concerns himself much with them. These Juglers pretend to an Intimacy with [55] *Vitico. ...*" Drage then goes on to describe the conjuring tent and its rite, ascribing to *Vitico* seemingly the leading role of spokesman therein. "The *Manatou* had all the Perfections of the Deity ascribed to him, and *Vitico* the other Spirit, supposed the Cause of all Disorder and Mischief". "Nor do the *Indians* make any likeness of *Manatou* or *Vitico,* or have they any Temples or Altars". "Neither do these People worship *Manatou,* but to *Vitico* sometimes they make an Offering; where there is wanted a Removal of a present Evil, or to avert a future one".

"In a time of great Scarcity or Sickness", there was a type of dog sacrifice to *Vitico,* with a prayer for Health, or, as the Case is, more Plenty". "They have a Notion of a personal Appearance of *Vitico* ..., but not of *Manitou."* When drunk, they used to go out of their tents to shoot *Vitico* dead with their guns. They believed in a future life, with rewards and punishments according to socio-moral conduct on earth; but there is no mention of Manitou or other beings being the rewarders or punishers. At death, the person reached a great river, across which the good were transported to the happy life, while the wicked were carried to a rocky barren land by the canoe.[135]

Ellis, who was on the same expedition with Drage and who like him spent the winter of

---

[133] "Bacqueville de la Potherie, *Histoire de I'Amerique septentrionale,* 4 v., Paris 1753: i, 121-25, 129-31. It is probably from Marest and la Potherie that Charlevoix, *Histoire de la nouvelle France,* Paris 1744: iii, 181, got the following regarding the York Factory district Indians: "Ceux, qui les ont phis fréquentés, assurent qu'ils ont, comme ceux du Canada, l'idée d'un bon. & d'un mauivais Genie, que le Soleil est leur grande Divinité".

[134] J. Robson, *An account of six years residence in Hudson's-Bay, from 1733 to 1736, and 1744 to 1747,* London 1752: 48.

[135] Clerk of the California [Charles Swaine, Theodore Swaine Drage, supposed author], *An account of a voyage for the discovery of a north-west passage,* 2 v., London 1748-49: i, 183, 235-36, ii, 40-43.

1746-47 in the York Factory region, has this to say of the Indians living there:

> "They acknowledge a Being of infinite Goodness, whom they stile *Ukkewma,* which in their Language signifies the great Chief; they look upon him as the Author of all the Benefits they enjoy, and speak of him with Reverence. They likewise sing a kind of Hymns in his Praise, and this in a grave solemn Tone, not altogether disagreeable. Yet their Sentiments on this Head are very loose and confused. ... They likewise acknowledge another Being, whom they call *Wittika,* whom they represent as the Instrument of all kinds of Mischief and Evil; and of him they are very [56] much afraid; but however we know of no Methods made use of by them to appease him".[136]

Wales, who spent thirteen months in 1768-69 in the Hudson Bay region, largely around Churchill, wrote as follows of the Indians of the Churchill district: "They acnowledge two Beings; one the author of all good, the other of all evil. The former they call *Ukkemah,* which appellation they give also to their chiefs; and the latter they call *Wittakah.* They pay some sort of adoration to both, though it is difficult to say what. Their opinion of the origin of mankind is, that *Ukkemah* made the first men and women out of the earth, three in number of each; that those, whom we Europeans sprang from, were made from a whiter earth than what their progenitors were, and that there was one pair of still blacker earth than they. They have likewise an imperfect traditional account of the delluge; only they substitute a beaver for the dove".[137]

Umfreville, who resided eight years at York Factory between 1771 and 1782, says of the Indians of the vicinity:

> "Exclusive of these superstitious ideas [he has just been describing 'the Devil' in terms that evidently identifies him with the Wihtiko], the religious sentiments of these people, though confused, are in many respects just. They allow that there is a good Being, and they sometimes sing to him; but not out of fear or adoration, for he is too good, they say, to hurt them. He is called *Kitch-e-man-e-to,* or the Great Chief. They further say, there is an evil Being, who is always plaguing them; they call him *Whit-ti-co.* Of him they are very much in fear, and seldom eat any thing, or drink any brandy, without throwing some into the fire for *Whit-ti-co.* If any misfortune befals them, they sing to him imploring his mercy; and when in health and prosperity do the same, to keep him in good humour. Yet, though obsequious sometimes, at others they are angry with him, especially when in liquor; they then run out of their tents, [57] and fire their guns in order to kill him. They frequently persuade themselves that they see his track in the moss or snow, and he is generally described in the most hideous forms. They believe that both the good and the bad Being have many servants; those of the former inhabiting the air, but those of the latter walking on the earth. They have likewise an opinion that this country was once overflowed; an opinion founded on meeting with many

---

[136] H. Ellis, *A voyage to Hudson's-Bay,* London 1748: 193-20.
[137] W. Wales, "Journal of a voyage, made by order of the Royal society, to Churchill river", in *Philosophical transactions,* for the year 1770, London 1771: lx, 128-29.

sea shells far inland".[138]

David Thompson, who lived among the Cree of Churchill, York, and inland, and among the more western Cree most of the time between 1784 and 1807, is the last of the earlier writers to be cited on the theistic beliefs of the Cree of the York-Church ill district. In his long account of the 'Nahathaway' or Cree culture, he does not distinguish in most points between the York-Churchill and inland Cree, but speaks of both together. His detailed account of their culture was written after six years' residence among the Nahathaway, and may refer more to the woodland Cree inland from the coast around York Factory than to the coastal Cree proper. Thompson is careful to call attention to the fact that his account of the native religion includes only such tribal views as have not been learned from whites, that his knowledge of it was collected from the old men, and that it was gathered, not by direct questioning, but by living and conversing with the natives as one of themselves. He had some speaking knowledge of the language.

"Hell fire", Thompson writes, "they do not believe". "They believe in the self existence of the *Keeche Keeche Manito* (The Great Great Spirit) ... and [believe] that the visible world, with all its inhabitants must have been made by some powerful being; but have not the same idea of his constant omnipresence, omniscience and omnipotence that we have, but [think] that he is so when he pleases, he is the master of life, and all things are at his disposal; he is always kind to the human race, and hates to see the blood of mankind on the ground, and sends heavy rain to wash [58] it away. He leaves the human race to their own conduct, but has placed all other living creatures under the care of Manitos (or inferior Angels) all of whom are responsible to Him; ... [as] the guardians and guides of every genus of Birds and Beasts; each Manito has a separate command and care, as one has the Bison, another the Deer; and thus the whole animal creation is divided amongst them". "They believe in ghosts but as rarely seen, and those only of wicked men, or women". "The Sun and Moon are accounted Divinities and though they do not worship them, always speak of them with great reverence. ... The Earth is also a divinity, and is alive". "The '*Metchee Manito*' or Evil Spirit, they believe to be evil, delighting in making men miserable, and bringing misfortune and sickness on them, and if he had the power would wholly destroy them; he is not the tempter, his whole power is for mischief to, and harrassing of, them, to avert all which they use many ceremonies, and other sacrifices, which consists of such things as they can spare, and sometimes a dog is painted and killed; whatever is given to him is laid on the ground, frequently at the foot of a pine tree". One of Thompson's Indian friends used to speak every morning to "the Great Spirit and the Spirits of the forests, for health to all of them and success in hunting, and to give to his *Poowoggin* where to find the Deer, and to be always kind to them, and to give them straight dreams, that they may live straight". This man was a conjurer who practised the shaking-tent rite. On a later page and in a different connection Thompson writes: "'*Wee tee go*' is the evil Spirit, that devours humankind".[139]

A little sporadic missionary work was apparently carried on around York Factory toward the end of the seventeenth century. No resumption there of missionary work took place until some years after 1820, the date of the Reverend John West's passage through York Factory on his way to the Red River settlement. [59]

On the culture of the Indians of James Bay proper we have almost nothing from 1670-75

---

[138] E. Umfreville, *The present state of Hudson's bay*, London 1790: 42-43, 189-90.
[139] David Thompson's *Narrative of his explorations in western* America, 1784-1812, ed. J.B. Tyrrell, Toronto 1916: 78, 82-85, 90-91, 125, 260.

to 1908. This accounts for the fact that we have almost nothing throughout that intervening period on their religion. Gorst's statement of 1670-75 and Skinner's negative report of 1908-9 were given at the beginning of the present paper; Father Saindon's account under his name in the field evidence. Our only other references, so far as the present writer can discover, are the short and none too clear ones in McLean and Laverlochere.

John McLean gives a detailed account of the massacre in the early winter of 1830-31 at Hannah Bay, at the extreme southern end of James Bay, of the Hudson's Bay Company factor and his family, – an event, we may add, on which oral tradition is still vivid at Moose Factory. McLean got his information on the affair from the Labrador Indians and from "an individual that escaped from the massacre". The ring leader in the attack, an Indian, was a conjurer who had considerable influence among his people. "This man told his fellows that he had a communication from the Great Spirit, who assured him that he would become the greatest man in Hudson's Bay if he only followed the course prescribed to him. which was first, to cut off their own trading post, and then with the spoil they got there to hire other Indians, who should assist in destroying all the other posts of the Company possessed in the country".[140]

Father Laverlochere, writing about the same time as did McLean, states:

"Les tribus indiennes du nord de l'Amerique, celles du moins que j'ai pu visiter, n'ont point de fétichisme. Ils croient qu'il y a un esprit supérieur et bon qui ne peut point faire de mal, et pour cette raison, ils ne s'en mettent nullement en peine; mais ils croient aussi qu'il y a le génie du mal, presque aussi puissant que le premier; qu'il a une multitude de satellites qui se trouvent partout pour faire du mal, et qu'il faut les apaiser et se les rendre favorables en leur sacrifiant quelques restes de tabac, ou un chien que l'on pend par les pieds de derriere, ou quelques [60] entrailles d'un castor".

When Father Laverlochere wrote this, in 1848, he had been each summer since 1845 with the Algonkin Indians of Temiskaming and Abitibi, whose evangelization began in 1836, and had just returned from his second short visit to Moose Factory and his first to Albany.

In his letter of the following year, after his second visit to Albany, he reported that one Albany Indian, a young man nineteen or twenty years old, whom he had just instructed and baptized, said to him:

"Il est vrai que nous sommes bien malheureux dans nos forêts, ensevelis dans la nuit profonde de la magie, nous venons au monde, nous grandissons et puis nous cessons de vivre comme les bêtes des nos forêts. Nous ne savons pas que là-haut dans sa grande lumière le Grand-Esprit veille sur nous". From the whole context it seems reasonably clear that this Indian was referring to native rather than to Christian beliefs.[141]

For the "Montagnais" Indians of the vicinity of Quebec, described by Fathers Charles l'Allemant and Paul le Jeune in the earlier Jesuit Relations, we have only very meager data on

---

[140] J McLean, *loc. cit*: 99-100.
[141] J.N Laverlochere, "Lettre", Dec. 25, 1848, in RMQ, Avril 1849, # 8: 64-65; "Lettre" 1849, ibid, # 9 1851: 92.   {See appendix for English translations}

native theism and on rites that may have been associated with it. From the linguistic data given by Le Jeune, we have good ground for concluding that some at least of these "Montagnais" were Cree-speaking, using an *rR* dialect as do the modern Cree-speaking Tête de Boule of the St. Maurice River and as did until recently the Cree-speaking Kesagami band just south of James Bay.

Father Charles l'Allemant, writing in 1627 of the Indians around Quebec, states:

"Aux festins qu'ils font pour la mort de quelqu'vn ils font la part du defunt aussi bien qu'aux autres, laquelle ils iettent dans le feu". 'Il leur semble que comme eux nous addressons nos Prieres au Soleil. ... Ils n'ont aucun cult diuin, ny aucunes sortes de Prieres. Ils croyent neantmoins qu'il y en a Vn qui a tout fait; mais pourtant ils ne luy rendent aucun honneur. Entr'eux ils ont quelques personnes qui font estat de parler au Diable; [61] ceux là font aussi les Medecins, & guarissent de toute maladie". That they address prayers to the sun may perhaps be an inference from their looking upward when praying.[142]

Father Paul le Jeune writes in his 1633 Relation, of the "Montagnais":

"Il disent qu'il y a vn certain qu'ils nomment *Atahocan,* qui a tout fait: parlant vn jour de Dieu dans vne cabane, ils me demanderent que c'étoit que Dieu, ie leur dis que c'estoit celuy qui pouuoit tout, & qui auoit fait le Ciel & la terre: ils commencerent à se dire les vns aux autres *Atahocan, Atahocan,* c'est *Atahocan.* Ils disent qu'vn nominé Messou repara le monde perdu dans les eaux", referring here to the flood story in which Messou plays the rôle that Wisekwedjak plays among the eastern Cree. On a later occasion, however, when le Jeune questioned two of the Indians, they answered "qu'ils ne sçauoieiit pas qui estoit le premier Autheur du monde, que c'estoit peut-estre Atahocham, mais que cela n'estoit pas certain". "Dans leurs festins, ils iettent par fois quelques cuillerées de gresse dans le feu, prononcant ces parolles *Papeouekou, Papeouekou,* faites nous trouuer à manger, faites nous trouuer à manger; ie crois que cette priere s'addresse à ces Genies, ausquels ils presentent cette gresse comme la chose la meilleure qu'ils ayent au monde". The "Genii" referred to by le Jeune are the *Khichikouai;* at the present time the word *Kijiko* is used by the Tête-de-Boule Cree and the Abitibi Algonkin for guardian spirit or for the being(s) who used to come into the shaking tent during this conjuring rite. *Papewe* is still used in many places in the northern Algonquian area, in the meaning of "good luck!", as when a bit of meat or grease is thrown on the fire. To complete le Jeune's testimony: "Faisans festin d'Orignac, celuy qui luy auoit donné le coup mortel & qui faisoit le festin, apres auoir distribué la chair, ietta de la gresse dans le feu, disant: *papeouekou, papeouekou*".[143] [62]

---

[142] Charles l'Allemant, *Lettre,* 1626, in JR (Thwaites): iv, 200-2.

[143] Paul le Jeune, *Relation ... 1633,* ibid., v, 154; *Relation ... 1634,* ibid: vi, 156, 172-74, 204, 290. Belief in what looks like a Supreme Being, [62] addressed as "Great Father", is elsewhere much more explicitly reported by le Jeune, but apparently of Algonkins who frequented Quebec, in his *Relation of 1637,* ibid: xi, 166, 204-6.   {See appendix}

On the religion of the Montagnais-Naskapi farther north in the Labrador Peninsula we have a number of brief, − all too brief, − earlier statements. Father Henri Nouvel, in the Relation of 1663-64, referring to the Ouchestiguetch, a band living north of the Papinachois country, whom he met and preached to for three days during his pioneer journey into the Labrador hinterland, wrote:

"Ayant esté aduerty que parmy ces Cathecumenes il y en auoit trois, qui auoient ionglé autrefois; ie les appellay en particulier en la Chapelle; & les ayant examinez sur ce qu'ils auoient fait en ionglant, & qu'elles estoi[en]t leurs pensées, ils me dirent qu'ils auoient eu cette pensée, qu'il y auoit vn bon & vn mauuais manitou, qu'ils hayssoient le mauuais, & aymoient le bon; que tout ce qu'ils auoient fait, ce n'auoit esté que pour honorer le bon manitou".[144]

Two-thirds of a century later, Father Pierre Laure, writing in 1730 of the Mistasini Indians, mentions a sacrifice they offered to the dead, but gives nothing clear in his Relation on any Supreme Being or offering to Him: "Rarement entre eux ils boivent ou mangent sans donner avant aux morts une petite portion de leurs mets qu'ils jettent au feu".[145]

In 1808 James McKenzie wrote as follows of the Naskapi, by whom he understood the Indians of interior Labrador as distinct from the "Montagners, or Shore Indians" of the southern coast of the Labrador Peninsula:

"They [the Naskapi] believe in a 'Great Spirit' who made the earth and the Nascapees, and in an inferior deity, who made the different kinds of wild animals, and distributed them among the Indians in proportion to their merits and the fervency of their prayers. This God is, therefore, adored whenever the belly feels concerned. He [63] is not longer than their little finger, is dressed in white and called *Ka-wab-api-shit,* or the White Spirit. They believe also in an evil spirit, who is a busy meddling body, forever planning mischief to counteract the good works of *Ka-wab-api-shit,* on which account they always implore him to have mercy on them, and, since he has not the power, any more than the will, to do them good, at least to do them no harm. As for the 'Great Being', they never worship him, because, being all goodness, he has not the power, and it would be against his nature, to do them any mischief, and will do them all the good he can without being teazed into it." The conjurers "intercede ... with the Good and the Bad Spirit". They pray [apparently to *Ka-wab-api-shit*] as follows; "Great Master of animals among the clouds bless us, and let us continue to make a good hunt as usual". From the context in McKenzie it would look as if *Ka-wab-api-shit* acted as spokesman in the shaking-tent rite.[146]

John McLean was with the Naskapi of the Fort Chimo region from 1837 to 1842. and

---

[144] [Henri Nouvell, "Journal", in H. Lalement, *Relation de ... 1663 & 1664,* ibid: xlix, 66-68.

[145] Pierre Laure, *Mission du Saguenay: relation inédite* [1730], A.E Jones, ed, Montreal 1889: 37.

[146] James McKenzie, "The king's posts 1808", in L.R Masson, *Les bourgeois de la Compagnie du nord-ouest,* 2 v., Quebec 1889-90: ii, 414-15.

had good opportunity to observe them when they were still nearly all pagans. He wrote of their aboriginal religion as follows: "They believe in the existence of a Supreme Being, the Ruler of the universe, and the Author of all good. They believe, also, in the existence of a bad spirit, the author of all evil. Each is believed to be served by a number of subordinate spirits. Sacrifices are offered to each; to the good, by way of supplication and gratitude; to the evil, by way of conciliation and deprecation. Their local genii are also supposed to be possessed of the power of doing good, or inflicting evil, and are likewise propitiated by sacrifices; the 'men of medicine' are viewed in nearly the same light'. The Fort Chimo trading post had been established only seven years previously to McLean's arrival there in 1837.[147]

In the Report of the Special Commissioners appointed by the Government of Canada to investigate Indian affairs occurs the following laconic reference to the religious [64] conditions prevailing among the Naskapi around 1857: "They [the Naskapi] are almost 2500 souls, one thousand of which have embraced Christianity, the others are 'heathens', the missionaries not having succeeded in reaching them all yet. They acknowledge a Superior Being, who they say lives in the sun and moon, and to whom they sacrifice a portion of every thing they kill". It is hard to say what weight is to be given to this statement. The maker of it, David E Price, apparently gives it at second hand.   He was acquainted at first hand with the Montagnais of the upper Saguenay territory. The reported residence "in the sun and moon" is not corroborated by other accounts of the Naskapi.[148]

New Catholic missions among the Naskapi were inaugurated by the Oblate Fathers around the middle of the last century. At the time of Father Charles Arnaud's first visit to them in 1853, they were nearly all still pagan. He wrote as follows of them:

"En général, les sauvages infidèles de ces contrées [upper interior Labrador Peninsula] croient à l'existence de deux divinités qu'ils appellent *Manitous* (esprits); mais cette croyance est si confuse dans leur esprit qu'ils ne peuvent guères en rendre compte. Suivant eux, il y a le bon et le mauvais *Manitou.* Le bon est bon essentiellement. C'est lui qui accorde le succès dans toutes les entreprises; ils n'ont donc rien à en craindre. Mais ils redoutent le mauvais *Manitou,* car c'est a lui qu'ils attribuent tous leurs malheurs. Ils n'ont, cependant, aucune manière propre pour rendre a ce mauvais Manitou ce qu'on dirait un culte, si ce n'est quelques petites pratiques superstitieuses, auxquelles ils attachent beaucoup d'importance, et qui forment tout leur bagage en fait de religion extèrieure".

It is not quite clear from the context whether or not Father Arnaud identifies the above evil manitou with "*Atshem*" [= *Atcen,* another name for *Wihtiko*] whom he [65] describes a little later on as l"e mauvais esprit". The Montagnais or Naskapi who accompanied Arnaud to the Naskapi country were much frightened at a brilliant comet:

---

[147] J. McLean, loc. Cit: 258.

[148] DE Price, "Letter, dated Chicoutimi, 14th Nov., 1857, Appendix no. II to Report of the Special commissioners appointed on the 8th of September, 1856, to investigate Indian affairs in Canada, Appendix (# 21)", to *Journals of the Legislative assembly of the province of Canada*, v. 16, Toronto 1858: n.p.

"Nous avons entendu dire par nos ancêtres que de pareils signes présageaient le colère du Grand Esprit".[149]

A quarter of a century later, Father Zach. Lacasse, also an Oblate, in a long account of Naskapi religious belief and especially of origin myths, reports among other things the following pertinent details:

"Le Naskapis sait qu'il existe un grand Esprit et que celui-ci a un antagoniste, l'esprit du mal qu'il redoute plus que le Grand Esprit. ... Le Grand Esprit avait un fils qui était né de sa tête".

This "fils" was Mesh who figures in the origin myth as a culture hero, about as he did in Le Jeune's account previously cited in the present paper. I may here add parenthetically that a Lake St. John Indian told me several years ago that *Mec* was the same as *Mistabeo*, but I have no confirmation of this identification. To return to Father Lacasse's account. The wolverene fomented a revolt against Mesh and the Great Spirit, The latter thereupon brought on the flood. A little farther on in his account, Father Lacasse quotes his native ~~informant~~: "Le Grand Esprit crea le Naskapis quand il crea les autres hommes". Still farther on: Caribou and man used to dwell together in the same lodge; then the caribou became fearful of man, saying to him, among other things "Tu tueras mon corps, mais mon âme repassera dans le corps d'un autre caribou façonné par *l'ombre* qui plane au-dessus des forêts et qui veille sur la destinée de la nation des caribous". Certain details here and there in Father Lacasse's long account suggest a slight post-Columbian and Christian influence, but in the main the account is clearly aboriginal.[150] Incidentally two of these beings, and perhaps all three − the Great Spirit, Mesh (Mistabeo?), and the caribou-guardian, − correspond fairly closely to those found by Dr Strong and described earlier in the present paper. [66]

Father FX Bossé was told by the oldest of the then living missionaries among the Montagnais and Naskapi, one who had worked over thirty-four years among them, that the Naskapi had replied as follows to this missionary when he urged them not to eat up everything at once but to lay aside food for future lean days:

"Nos pères mangeaient tout ce que leur envoyait Ie Grand Esprit, et nos pères étaient *fins,* nous faisons comme nos pères.... Je tues dix caribous; c'est le Grand-Esprit qui me les envoie parcequ'il voit que j'ai faim; il a un gros coeur pour moi, le Grand Esprit, et il veut que je mange ... je mange tout. Le Grand Esprit rit, et m'engraisse encore mille caribous là-bas, dans les terres des Naskapis. Tu voudrais . .. que je cache le *pemican* que le Grand-Esprit m'envoie? Mais cela insulte le Grand Esprit. Si je meurs cette nuit, après l'avoir fait, je paraîtrai devant la face du Grand-Esprit, son oeil sera fâche, et il me dira tu es un mauvais fils, tu n'as pas eu d'esprit. Tu me traites comme un *matshimanitou. ...* Tu fait pitié à ton Père d'en haut. ... Il n'enverra plus ses caribous dans ton chemin de chasse". There is possibly some Christian influence here, but in general aboriginal

---

[149] Ch, Arnaud, "Lettre", Nov. 10, 1854, in RMQ 1855, # 11: 83-85, 71.
[150] Zach. Lacasse, "Lettre", Nov., 1878, in APFQ, n.s. # 7, Feb 1879: 17-23.

concepts appear dominant.[151]

Finally Turner says of the Ungava Nenenot: "All these minor spirits are under the control of a single great spirit having its dwelling in the sky".[152]

A review of the evidence, fragmentary as this evidence is for many sections of the far-flung Algonquian peoples, makes it reasonably clear that a Supreme Being belief is part of Algonquian culture as far back as our information goes. This would seem to add appreciably to the reliability of the data obtained for the James Bay Cree and Montagnais-Naskapi of the east coast and Labrador. The food sacrifice seems from very early times to have been used. both for the dead and for the superior spirits. Who the commonly reported "evil spirit" was is not clear in all [67] cases. In many cases he quite obviously is the Wihtiko for whom among at least the modern James Bay and Tête-de-Boule Cree, there is plenty of fear but nothing that can be called in any real sense cult. In some other cases it looks as if the "evil spirit" is *Mikenak*, Mistabeo or some other of the beings associated with conjuring and the conjuring tent. It is just possible, however, that there may be a sort of supreme evil spirit, distinct from any of these others, among some sections of the Cree, but it is unlikely that such a belief is at all widespread. I think we can say with all reasonable confidence that such a belief is not found among the James Bay Indians.

To sum up. That there may be certain minor errors of detail in the accounts as recorded from the field by Miss{!?!} Flannery, Dr Strong and the present writer is probable enough, considering the circumstances under which the data had to be gathered. That however the data are substantially accurate seems reasonably established, first, from the qualifications of the ~~informants~~ themselves, and secondly from the conformity of the data for the James Bay and northern Labrador Algonquians with the independently gathered earlier and more recent data from the other Algonquians and from the northern Athapaskans.

B. ~ Has There Been Christian Influence?

Is the theism which we have found among these northern Algonquians of James Bay and Labrador due to the importation of Christian teachings by white explorers, traders, or missionaries? Before we attempt to answer this question directly it may be well to give a summary sketch of exploration, trading, and missionary work on the Bay.

There was practically no face-to-face contact between whites and natives in the Bay up to 1668. Hudson and his men in 1610-11 had only a fleeting glimpse of the natives. James in 1631-32 apparently saw none at all. In 1668 the first trading post on the Bay, that at Rupert House, in the extreme southeastern section, was founded by Groseilliers. This post was taken over by the Hudson's Bay Company in 1670. Since this date, traders, those of the Hudson's Bay [68] Company especially, have been on James Bay uninterruptedly up till the present day.[153]

---

[151] Zach. Lacasse, "Lettre", Nov., 1878, in APFQ, n.s. # 7, Feb 1879: 17-23.

[152] LM Turner, *Ethnology of the Ungava district, Hudson Bay territory*, BAE-R #11 1984: 273.

[153] A good summary of the early history of exploration in the James and Hudson's bay region may be found in S.E Dawson, *The Saint Lawrence basin and its borderlands*, London 1905: ch. xxii. Longer popular account in A.C Laut, *The 'Adventurers of England' on Hudson bay*, Toronto 1914; more detailed in same writer's *The conquest of the great northwest*, NY 1908. Cf. also E. Voorhis, *Historic forts and trading posts of the French regime and of the English fur trading companies*, Ottawa 1930: 4-6 and s. vv. in

The first missionary to penetrate to the Bay was Father Charles Albanel. He came overland by way of Mistasini, reaching Rupert House in 1672 and spending five days at a point twenty leagues up the coast from Rupert House. At this point he met some of the Indians, and during his very brief stay there instructed the natives and baptized sixty-two of them, children and adults. On his second trip to Rupert in 1674 he was made prisoner by the English, probably without having had opportunity to do any appreciable evangelizing. A little further sporadic missionary work was carried on by his Jesuit confreres during some of the following years, especially at Albany on the west coast between 1686 and 1693, and at York Factory on Hudson Bay proper up to 1696. For nearly a century and a half thereafter, until 1840, no missionary of any denomination visited James Bay, so far as our records show.[154] [69]

The modern missionary period on James Bay began in 1840, with the arrival at Moose Factory of the Wesleyan missionary, the Reverend George Barnley. Here he made his headquarters for seven or eight years, paying longer or shorter visits to Albany on the west coast and to Rupert House on the east coast. All of the reports on his work lead us to conclude that, although he baptized a good many of the natives, their indoctrination and Christianization was at best very superficial. At present there appears to be hardly any traditional memory of his work, – this sharply contrasting with the still vivid memory of the two native "missionaries" from York Factory. One ~~informant~~ did recall his name, pronouncing it as if it were spelt in English "Byly". The absence of *rR* in the Moose dialect and the unwonted consonantal cluster *rnl* seem to account for this distortion of his name.[155]

The real Christianization of the James Bay natives began with the arrival a few years later

---

[154] Alphabetical list of forts. Oldmixon, loc. cit, has an invaluable account of the history of James Bay around 1670.

On the early Catholic missions on James Bay, at York Factory, and in some adjacent areas, from 1672, the date of Father Albanel's first journey to James Bay, to 1696, when Father Marest was taken prisoner by the English at York Factory, see: JR (Thwaites): i, 17, xiv, 287, xli, 257, lvi, 148-217, lviii, 296, lix, 306-7, lxiv, 260-67, lxvi, 77; Ivanhoe Caron, ed., *Journal de l'expedition du chevalier [Pierre] de Troyes à la bate d'Hudson, en 1686,* Beauceville 1918: 8, 12-13, 16, 43-44, 90; C. de Rochemonteix, ed., [Intendant Antoine Baudot, not Father Silvy], *Relation par lettres de Amerique septentrionalle,* Paris 1904: viii-ix, xiv-xvi, xxxi-lxiii, 109-11; same, *Les Jésuites et le Nouvelle-France au XVIIe siècle,* 3 v., Paris 1895-96: ii: 371-76, iii: 269-84. The James Bay Catholic missions came to an end with the murder of Father Dalmas at Albany in 1693; the Hudson Bay ones, with the imprisonment of Father Marest at and deportation from York Factory in 1696. From 1693 and 1696 until 1847 no Catholic missionary to my knowledge reached either James or Hudson Bay.

[155] On the Wesleyan missions in James Bay, the best published sources are: Letters from George Barnley, in *Wesleyan-Methodist magazine* for 1841, v. 64: 166-69 (169-71); for 1843, v. 66: 82-83; for 1845, v. 68: 201-4. Other data on James Bay and western Cree Wesleyan missions, ibid., esp: v. 63: 358; v. 64: 159-65, 172-73; v. 65: 884-85; v. 66: 73-83; v. 68: 204-7; v. 72: 892-94. Shorter summaries of James Bay and other early Wesleyan missions to the Cree in: W. Moister, *A history of Wesleyan missions,* 2d rev. ed, London, 1871: 84-86; G.H. Cornish, *Cyclopaedia of Methodism in Canada,* Toronto 1881 i: 349-51; G.G Findlay and W.W Holdsworth, *The history of the Wesleyan Methodist missionary society,* i, London 1921: 465-76 passim.

of the Oblate Fathers and of the Church of England missionaries. Father J.N Laverlochere and A.M Garin were the first Oblates to come, reaching Moose in 1847, and the former visiting both Moose and Albany in 1848. In 1851 there came to Moose as resident lay missionary, Mr John Horden, afterwards Bishop Horden, who was ordained at Moose in 1852 and consecrated bishop of Moosonee in 1872. Within less than a decade after the coming of the Catholic and Anglican missionaries, nearly all the Indians on either coast became Christians, remaining so to the present.[156] [70]

Since the dawn of the modern missionary period around the middle of the last century, Christian theism and Christian doctrines and practices in general have deeply penetrated into Indian life. Much, however, of the older magico-religious culture, particularly the older conjuring complex and hunting observances, remained well intact far beyond the middle of the last century, and a very considerable proportion of it is at least partly functional even today. All or nearly all of what is no longer functional is still vividly remembered by the older people. Through their help it is possible to reconstruct practically the whole of the native magico-religious culture as it thrived around 1840 and earlier. And this culture as reconstructed is unmistakably Indian, with very few traces of European magical and religious conceptions and observances. As an instance of European infiltration may be cited the belief, told to me at Fort George in 1932, – although seemingly absent elsewhere on the Bay, – that a child born with a caul will never die of drowning or meet death on the water. But, all in all, such infiltrations appear quite rare and exceptional, and even where they occur the Indians more commonly know that they are of white introduction. In general, as regards non-theistic magico-religious culture, the James Bay Indians show rather marked tenacity of their own culture and impermeability to that of the Europeans.

As regards, however, theistic concepts and practices, Christian influence has been profound since 1840. Of the theism that may for the moment be assumed as aboriginal, [71] most has been swamped out or swallowed up, although meat is still covered when it is carried abroad and the feeling against, wasting meat is still, it seems, as strong as of old. Some Christian influence, though of a minor nature, has also pretty clearly colored in some respects the accounts of what our ~~informants~~ believed to be pre-Christian theism. For instance, the form of address, "Our Father in heaven", reported by Mrs Morrison, certainly sounds post-Christian. It is quite likely, too, that the linking of the *Manitū* to the socio-moral order by two of our ~~informants~~, Jeannette and John Dick, betrays Christian influence. But apart from these and perhaps some other and minor details, the general concept of the Supreme Being and of the observances associated therewith, as reported by our ~~informants~~, seem with all reasonable clearness to be

---

[156] On the modern Catholic missions in James Bay, see files of RMQ, especially the following letters of Oblate Fathers: Laverlochere, Letter of [70] 1848, in # 8 1849: 34-68; of 1849 no. 9 1851: 67-99; of 1850, ibid: 99-104; Paillier, of 1851, # 10 1853: 79-87; Garin, of 1853, ibid: 135-40; of 1853, # 11: 1855, 4-17; of 1855, # 12 1857: 1-16; Déléage, of 1858, # 13, 1859: 131-41; of 1859, # 14, 1861: 174-92; Nédclec, of 1871, # 20. 1872: 70-78. See for more recent history, J.E. Saindon, *En missionnant*, Ottawa 1928. On the missions of the Church of England in James Bay, *see:* David Anderson, "Letter", dated Aug. 10, 1852 from Moose Factory, in *Church missionary intelligencer* 1852: iii: 281-84; same, *The net in the Bay,* 2d rev. ed., London 1873 (first ed. written in 1853); A.R Buckland, *John Harden, missionary bishop,* 7th ed, London 1900. Cf. also on early Wesleyan and Anglican missions in northern area, S Tucker, *The rainbow in the north,* 4th ed, London 1856.   {See appendix for English translations}

aboriginal, not post-Christian, and for the following reasons.

First of all, the whole concept with its associated observances has a strong aboriginal flavor. The Supreme Being is decidedly more of a master than of a maker. The Supreme Being as maker was quite unknown to most of our informants, whereas the idea of mastery was emphasized by all of them. The names for the Supreme Being, excepting the appellations "Wooden-shoe Wearer" and perhaps "Our Father", have a decidedly native ring. The three names, "Master of Food", "Master of Life", and "Master of Death", are again quite Indian, or certainly not distinctively Christian, and the second of these three names, "Master of Life", or as we got it. "Thou who hast mastery over life", is one that has not to my knowledge been reported recently from Algonquian peoples but one that appears over and over again in the earlier evidence before there could have been any reasonable ground whatever for suspecting Christian influence.

Further, the function of dream-sending attributed to the Supreme Being, and the dynamic relationship of the Supreme Being to the conjuring complex, appear as typically aboriginal, certainly not as Christian. The present-day Christian Indian of James Bay is much more apt to look upon the conjuring rites as the work of the "devil". Again, [72] the practice of covering the meat when carrying it abroad and the strict taboo on wasting meat, in both cases lest the Supreme Being be offended, seem decidedly Indian, as does also the first-fruits offering of food, whether by holding it up or especially by throwing it in the fire. Aboriginal, too, appears the very vague idea of the future life, a vagueness that almost amounts to the denial thereof.

All in all, the concept of the Supreme Being and the practices associated therewith distinctly conform to Indian and non-Christian patterns rather than to Christian ones.

Secondly, there is a consistent absence of distinctive Christian beliefs and practices in the complex as revealed by the field data, and our older Indian informants as a rule drew a sharp line of demarcation between what in their present Christian belief was pre-Christian and what was not. They were emphatic on points such as the following. The Supreme Being had no son; that He has "we first learned when the missionaries came". The Supreme Being was not called *Kitci'manitū* or *Kice'manitū,* as He is now. He was not, as far as most of the informants had heard, in pre-Christian days the maker or creator. Souls did not go to him at death. No idea of future reward or punishment, of heaven or hell, existed. Little or nothing was known of the first man and woman. There was no trace of the Christian doctrine of the fall and of original sin. The relation of the Supreme Being to the socio-moral code was weak or nil. There was no devil in the traditional Christian sense.

If the theism we were able to record had been in whole or in large part the result of earlier trader or missionary teaching, it is almost inevitable that some one or other of the distinctive Christian teachings such as these would have found their way into the theistic complex in the native mind. But actually they are all consistently absent, nor could I find any indication whatever of such, in spite of the most persistent inquiries made for the express purpose of determining if and in how far Christian influence had been at work. In view of the long contact, since 1668, of the Indians of the Bay with the whites, I had rather [73] expected to find evidences of considerable Christian infiltration, and I was surprised to find so little trace of it. It would be odd, to say the least, that of the whole range of Christian teaching and practice only its basic theism should have been adopted and borrowed.

Thirdly, not only the general concept of a Supreme Being but also a number of significant details in the concept itself and in the associated observances are independently matched and confirmed by the data reported by older and earlier observers from times when Christian influence could not have been operative at all or to any appreciable extent. These earlier data, which we have already given, show similar pre-Christian theistic concepts and observances among the James Bay Cree,[157][40] the York Factory Cree, the inland and western Cree, and the Cree around Quebec; among the Montagnais of the Quebec region and of the hinterland up from the lower St. Lawrence and into interior and northern Labrador; among the Otchipwe, Algonkins, and other Algonquians; and among the culturally related northern Athapaskans. It would be strange, too, that the concept should be found among all or practically all the other Algonquian peoples and be absent from just one section of the Cree and Montagnais. Finally, while widespread diffusion is far from being a reliable index to age or aboriginality, such widespread and continuous diffusion as this among peoples related by culture or by language or by both, many of whom have not been in contact with one another since pre-Columbian days would appear to add some weight at least to the other evidence for age and aboriginality.

Fourthly, our James Bay Cree ~~informants~~ derived their information on the earlier theism, not from a vague remote tradition, but from their own parents or grandparents, and the memories of these parents and grandparents reached [74] well back into at least the period prior to the reopening of mission work around the middle of the last century. These parents and grandparents could be expected to know well what was pre-missionary as distinct from what was post-missionary, and, our ~~informants~~ emphasized, had made clear the distinctions to our ~~informants~~, their children and grandchildren. Our ~~informants~~ were most explicit themelves in distinguishing between beliefs that existed before the coming of the nineteenth century missionaries and those that came in with these missionaries, even down to such details as the one given by old Charlotte, that "cursing started when Christianity started". The distinctions they made, – as, for example, between theistic mastery only before the missionaries and theistic creation after, between a non-socio-moral Supreme Being before and a socio-moral one after, between no divine sonship before and a divine sonship after, – all agree with what we know from other sources as regards both native Indian beliefs and Christian ones. That such oral tradition harking back nearly a century could be exact is further confirmed by the exactitude of the closely related oral tradition of the coming of the two men from York Factory which checks up so strikingly with Barnley's contemporary account of this event, an event that occurred just at the time when the modern missionary period first began.

One final point calls for a word of explanation. How could it happen that the Indians of the Bay could be exposed so long – from 1668 up to 1840 – to white influence and yet have taken on so little of European religious culture? The fact can, we believe, be explained with reasonable satisfactoriness.

As for the traders, throughout most of the north country they were concerned exclusively or almost exclusively with one thing, the business of trading a limited range of the white man's products for the Indian's furs. They did not go in much for mixing religion with business. They were after skins, not souls. An occasional trader, like David Thompson, did a little amateur Christian indoctrination at odd moments, but he and the few of his type of whom we [75] have record were decided exceptions. In fact, as a rule, so far at least as the men of the Hudson's Bay Company were concerned, the average employee had little opportunity to teach the natives the Christian religion, even had he wished to do so. In the olden days, as contrasting with more

---

[157] Thomas Gorst's account, in Oldmixon, cited at beginning of present paper. The Indians around Rupert House today speak a Montagnais dialect, but in Gorst's day, 1670-75, to judge from the short vocabulary he gives, the Indians there must have been Cree, and they used an r dialect, as did the nearby Kesagami Lake Indians until very recently when their dialect ceased to be spoken.

recent ones, "they [the Company's 'servants'] were shut up in the forts, as sailors are shut up in a ship, scarcely ever venturing out in winter, and hardly ever holding converse with a savage in his wild state. .. This choice and habit of seclusion grew into a rule with the Company's employees. ... It was the discipline of the quarter-deck". "The whole of the actual trading of the Factory was in the hands of two officials known as traders. None other of the Company's servants at any fort were permitted to have direct intercourse with the Indians, save in exceptional circumstances". "There was neither clergyman or divine worship".[158] Such is the general story of the north country in the early days. There is no evidence that James Bay was an exceptional area.

As for the early missions between 1672 and 1693, they were at best sporadic, and must have necessarily been superficial in their effects. Father Albanel, for instance, spent in all only five days in instructing the natives of the coast close to what is now Eastmain. Something of Christian teaching may also about this time have filtered into the east or southeast coast of the Bay from the missions of the Saguenay. Some further missionary influence was exercised around Albany on the west coast between 1686 and 1693. This about completes the story. From 1693 to 1840 no missionaries at all visited the Bay. Had any appreciable amount of teaching survived the long interval of nearly a century and a half, one or other of the distinctly Catholic tenets or practises should have survived, and some word about them would almost certainly be found in the fairly lengthy original accounts of the first nineteenth century Wesleyan, Catholic and Church of England missionaries. But no mention of such occurs. There had been plenty of time for the little that had been learned to be forgotten. [76]

<h3 style="text-align:center">C. ~ Has There Been Otchipwe or Algonkin Influence?</h3>

One of my Albany ~~informants~~, old Jeannette, believed that the word *Manitū* was of recent Otchipwe origin. This is pretty clearly an error on her part, as is evident from the early occurrence of the word for the Supreme Being among the James Bay, York Factory, and other Cree. The Abitibi Algonkins used to come down to the Bay, as is recorded by Oldmixon, when the whites first visited at Moose shortly after the founding of Rupert House, and they did so until comparatively recent decades. At Albany and Atawapiskat on the west coast there was for long years considerable mingling of Otchipwe and Cree in trade and marriage. The possibility therefore of an Otchipwe or Algonkin origin for the theism of the west coast of the Bay cannot be ruled out in advance.

As regards the Algonkins, not much need be said. except that while it is theoretically possible that they imported theism to the natives of the Bay, it seems actually very improbable, to say the least, in view of the distribution of the theistic complex among the distant Cree and Montagnais who were, unlike the Cree of Moose Factory, far remote from the Algonkins.

As regards the Otchipwe, more can be said. There has certainly been close association from times far back between the inland Otchipwe of the upper Albany and Atawapiskat rivers and the coastal Cree nearer the mouths of these rivers, and the theism of the Otchipwe is well developed. However, actually, in spite of this close association, the Cree appear to have absorbed very little in the main from their Otchipwe neighbors, either in magico-religious matters or in other phases of culture. The common Otchipwe belief, for instance, that the soul after death must cross a river on an oscillating log was quite unknown to any of my ~~informants~~. Nor were any of them familiar with any of the typical characteristics of the Midewiwin, such as

---

[158] B Willson, *The Great Company,* Toronto 1899: 176, 170, 177, cf. 308-9.

resuscita-tion or the use of the *migis* shell. The name *Mikenak* for the spokesman of the shaking-tent rite is about the only outstanding evidence of Otchipwe influence to be found in the James Bay magico-religious system; my attention was first called to this linguistic point by Dr Truman Michelson. [77]

Skinner reported the existence of more than one class of conjurer on the Bay, and the former prevalence of a sib system at least at Albany,[159] both of which cultural features, especially the latter, might suggest Otchipwe influence. The most meticulous inquiries on these points in 1927, 1932, and 1933, made among even the oldest and best informed Indians, elicited quite positive denials of the former prevalence of either of these cultural features among the west coast Cree. As a last resort, I explained to my ~~informants~~ in fairly minute detail the sib system as well as the different kinds and degrees of medicine men as found among the Otchipwe, but even such direct questioning brought from all ~~informants~~ a consistent and emphatic negative. One or two of the ~~informants~~ knew something of the sib system prevailing among the inland Otchipwe, but were positive that nothing of the kind had existed among the Cree nearer the Bay. Some had heard of the term *wābano* for conjurer, but held that it was merely another name for *mitēo*, ("conjurer") and all maintained that there had never been but one kind of *mitēo*. None had ever heard of such a typical Otchipwe name for the shaking-tent rite as *tcisakiwin*. All the evidence I have been able to gather seems to point to the conclusion that the sib system and Midewiwin elements reported by Skinner as found among the Albany Cree were in reality, not part of coastal Cree culture, but of the culture of inland Otchipwe resident at or visiting Albany or of Otchipwe descendants among the Cree there.

There appears then to be no evidence for assuming basic Otchipwe influence among the Cree of the west coast, and consequently no good ground for assuming that the Supreme Being complex of the west coast Cree has come to them from the contiguous inland Otchipwe. There is still less likelihood that Otchipwe influence has had anything to do with the theism as found by Miss Flannery at Eastmain and by Dr Strong and the earlier authorities cited on the inland Labrador peninsula. The early theism of the York Factory Cree, who, so far as I can discover, were not in close contact at all with Otchipwe, makes more improbable still [78] an assumption of an Otchipwe origin for the James Bay Cree theism.

The field data, presented in the present paper and the discussion and interpretation thereof, leave much to be desired. The "reconstruction" in the field had to be carried out under the handicap of many practical difficulties and limitations. The writer hopes that it will be possible for him to return to the Bay in the summer of 1934 and to gather further information, particularly from the east coast of the Bay and from the more northern section of the west coast. The east coast appears to offer the better chance for a fuller check-up.

---

[159] A Skinner, *Eastern Cree,* AMNH-AP, v. ix 1911: 56, 60.

Monotheism Among ~~Primitive~~ Peoples
by
Paul Radin

Ethnographical Museum Basel Switzerland
1954

Preface

The little essay here reprinted represents the "Arthur Davis Memorial Lecture" delivered before the *Jewish Historical Society* in 1924. It has long since been out of print and unavailable. It is being republished on the insistence of friends and colleagues, possibly because it was one of the first treatments of the subject by a professional ethnologist.

Since it was written an enormous literature has accumulated on the subject. Much of this literature has been summarized by two distinguished scholars: by Pater W Schmidt in his *Der Ursprung der Gottesidee,* of which eleven volumes had appeared before his death early this year and by R Pettazzoni in his articles «Allwissende Höchste Wesen bei primitivsten Völkern» in *Archiv fur Rel. Wiss.;* Vol. XXIX, 1931: 108-129 and 209-243 and his «La Formation du Monothéisme» in *Revue de l"Université de Bruxelles*, March-April, 1950. Cf. also his early work *Dio,* Vol. I (Rome 1922).

In the thirty years since the appearance of this essay my own views have changed to a certain extent, as can be seen in my *~~Primitive~~ Religion*, Chapter XII, "Monolatry and Monotheism" (New York 1937) and *Die Religiöse Erfahrung der Naturvölker* (Zurich 1951): 106-119. About the existence of some form of monotheism among practically all ~~primitive~~ peoples there can be little doubt. The only point in question is whether we find a pure monotheism and not some form of monolatry or henotheism and whether it is the belief of a comparatively small number of individuals, a special group, or of the tribe as such. In determining this it is important to remember that many of our best works on the subject come from priests and missionaries who naturally and understandably begin with certain preconceptions which often make their data and their conclusions somewhat biased. On the whole, I feel that pure monotheism in the late Hebraic, Christian and [4] Mohammedan sense of the term is rare. It is clearly encountered in certain parts of Africa, especially West Africa, and in Polynesia. Its occurrence in aboriginal America and Australia, it seems to me, is more than doubtful. As an essentially philosophic belief entertained by a few deeply religious individuals and connected with origin myths it may, however, appear everywhere.

Apart from a few minor changes the essay appears exactly as it was printed in 1924.

Lugano, 1954   Paul Radin

I

To most men monotheism is intimately bound up with the Hebrew Scriptures and with those religions manifestly built upon its foundation – Judaism, Christianity and Mohammedanism. Because of the definite association with these three great historic faiths of the last three thousand years, and of the integral part it plays in those civilizations which, rightly or wrongly, we regard in many ways as representing the highest cultural expressions to which man has hitherto attained, monotheism has come to have a very specific meaning and has been given a special evaluation. To the average man it signifies the belief in an uncreated. Supreme Deity, wholly beneficent, omnipotent, omniscient and omnipresent: it demands the complete exclusion of all other gods. The world in its most minute details is regarded as His work, as having been created out of nothing in response to His wish. To presuppose the existence of anything prior to Him is to deny His most salient attribute. He it is who intervenes in the affairs of man, and any assumption that He can act through the intermediation of other deities is idolatry by implication, even though he has expressly given these deities their forms, their attributes and their powers. It is never pure monotheism.

It is perhaps only natural that with so sharp and clear-cut a definition of the Deity there should have arisen the feeling that such a monotheism represents the highest attainable type of religious expression. Nations without it, however high their contributions to the world's progress in other directions may be, are looked upon unconsciously as inferior. Yet it would be unfair to state that it was merely this vague and unconscious estimate that lay at the basis of man's evaluation of the significance of monotheism. A cursory glance at the history of religious thought of the so-called ~~primitive~~ peoples or at the religious evolution of civilized nations before the [6] advent of Christianity – the Jews alone excepted – did seem to indicate the existence of a number of distinct phases through which religion had progressively passed. The earliest stage, it seemed, was to be found among ~~primitive~~ peoples. There we find a religion characterized by a faith in innumerable, often indefinite, spirits, a belief in the general animation of nature: animism in short. All the great historical religions show, it is now generally admitted, definite indications of having passed through such a period.

This seemed to be followed by a second and much later stage in which the worship of definite, mainly anthropomorphic deities prevailed ; the polytheism of the ancient Egyptians, Babylonians, Greeks and Romans. We encounter a distinct and possibly special phase in the religion of the ancient Persians where, as is well known, two great principles existed – the principle of Good and the principle of Evil. Ultimately we reach the last period, monotheism, and from this there has been no noticeable relapse. This was in brief what the history of all religions seemed to indicate.

It is the prevalent view to-day that where animism or polytheism prevails monotheism is excluded, and where monotheism prevails animism and polytheism are in the main absent; that as we pass from animism to polytheism, from dualism to monotheism, we are proceeding from a belief in a multiplicity of spirits devoid of special attributes, to a belief first in two deities and then to a belief in a single god – a god endowed with the highest ethical attributes. The evolution of religion thus manifests, it would seem, a definite tendency toward an integration of our mental and emotional life, a tendency toward the development of an exalted and positive ethical ideal. Both, it can be claimed, imply progress, one in the realm of the intellect and the other in that of morality. It is not astonishing therefore that even to many non-religious individuals pure monotheism should consequently connote the highest form of religious experience. And yet it is perhaps not amiss to point out that in a development such as that just outlined we are basing our evolution on factors that, in large measure, are essentially non-religious.

Be this as it may, certainly no one would seriously deny that it is the intellectual and ethical estimate of pure monotheism that has coloured the attitude of most people toward non-monotheistic and non-ethical faiths, and no fact could perhaps have demonstrated this so clearly as the reception accorded to the famous book written by that most courageous of thinkers, Andrew Lang. In 1898, he published "The Making of Religion", in which he claimed that the [7] evolutionary school in ethnology was hopelessly wrong in one of its fundamental assumptions, that namely a belief in a Supreme Deity did not now and never had existed among so-called ~~primitive~~ tribes. He contended that ethnologists, misled by certain preconceptions, had misinterpreted those indications pointing in such a direction, crediting to Christian influences those definite instances where the facts could not possibly be denied. But he went much farther. He contended that the fairly elevated conception of a Supreme Deity found among such simple tribes as the aborigines of Australia could only be understood by assuming that the traces of monotheism there encountered, represented a definite degeneration of an older and purer faith partially contaminated to-day by animistic beliefs. In other words, monotheism had preceded animism and a purer faith had secondarily been contaminated by the superstitious accretions of a later degenerate time. As was the case in so many of Lang's theories or intuitions, if you wish, he was only partially right.

It might have been surmised that such a theory would have been hailed with delight by the layman. Yet this was not the case. The layman indeed seemed to feel a certain resentment at having mere "savages" anticipate a supposedly exalted religious faith. That the professional ethnologist and ethnological theorist should have scouted the idea is natural enough, considering the ascendancy of the evolutionary theory at the time. To a certain extent, too, the specific instances selected by Lang and his manner of argumentation were partly responsible for the unfavourable reception of his thesis. We all know how his delight and skill in controversy often led him to defend uncritically selected facts and inherently weak positions. Yet it was not this, of course, that influenced the attitude of professional ethnologists. To have admitted among ~~primitive~~ peoples the existence of monotheism in any form would have been equivalent to abandoning their whole doctrine of evolutionary stages. And this they were not prepared to do, nor did the facts at the time definitely warrant it. No one, for instance, would have contended that the vast majority of the members of those tribes among whom the belief in a Supreme Deity had been found shared this belief, except perhaps in the vaguest degree, and it seemed apparent that even the few to whom it was in appearance an active faith found no difficulty in worshipping other deities as well. It might in fact have been said that actual worship was the precise thing the Supreme Deity did not receive. So attenuated and functionless a concept, [8] known to a selected few in each community, could assuredly, the critics insisted, be best explained as due to Christian influence.

Twenty-five years have elapsed since Lang wrote his book and his intuitive insight has been abundantly corroborated. The ethnologists were quite wrong. Accurate data obtained by trained specialists have replaced his rather vague examples. That many ~~primitive~~ peoples have a belief in a Supreme Creator no one to-day seriously denies. For the notion however as held by Lang, that it represents a degeneration from a higher and purer faith, there is not the slightest justification; nor is there any adequate reason for believing that the specific forms which it has assumed, the "contaminations" to which it has been subjected, or the inconsistencies in which it has been involved, have ever been different.

It was one of Lang's great merits that he recognized some of the salient features of this belief in a Supreme Deity of the aborigines. Such a deity had no cults; prayers were only infrequently directed to him and he rarely intervened directly in the affairs of mankind. As we shall see, these statements are only partially true and, at best, hold for only the first of the two general groups into which creative deities can be divided. The second group embraces those whom Lang regarded as contaminated with later animistic accretions, where the Supreme Deity is represented as only partially a creator, and where he has become fused with mythological heroes − with the sun or the moon, with animals, or with anthropomorphic and, occasionally, indefinite spirits. The main character with which he became most frequently amalgamated was one who is the dominant actor in the mythologies of practically all ~~primitive~~ peoples. He is known in ethnological literature as the Transformer, Culture-hero, Trickster. The first term owes its origin to the fact that it is his role to transform the world into its present shape and to bestow upon mankind all the various elements of culture. We thus have two concepts: the Supreme Deity, Creator of all things, beneficent and ethical, unapproachable directly and taking but little interest in the world after he has created it; and the Transformer, the establisher of the present order of things, utterly non-ethical, only incidentally and inconsistently beneficent, approachable, and directly intervening in a very human way in the affairs of the world.

These two figures represent two contrasting and antithetic modes of thought; two completely opposed temperaments continually in conflict. All that has been called contamination and degeneration is but the projection of the image of the Transformer upon that of a [9] Supreme Creator and vice versa. Indeed, it is only thus that certain inconsistencies in the portrayal of either can be understood. If, as we shall see, it is true that the Transformer has introduced certain human-heroic, occasionally but extremely rarely, even gross features into the otherwise elevated concept of the supreme deity, it is equally true that wherever the belief in a supreme deity has prevailed he has in large measure been purged of his non-moral character and become invested with many of the attributes of a purposive and benevolent creator. But I am anticipating. It will be best to give a number of concrete examples, first, of a creator who in varying degree partakes of the attributes of a Transformer and Culture-hero;[160] and secondly, of a creator quite freed from such accretions.

II

Among the Crow Indians of Montana[161] the Sun is the Supreme Deity, but he has in the minds of many become so definitely merged with the Transformer, in this particular instance the Coyote, that the two cannot be kept apart. "Long ago", so the myth runs, "there was no earth, only water. The only creatures in the world were the ducks and old man (Sun, Coyote). He came down to meet the ducks and said to them, 'My brothers, there is earth below us. It is not good for us to be alone'." He thereupon makes them dive and one of them reappears with some mud in its webbed feet. Out of this he creates the earth and when he has made it he exclaims, "Now that we have made the earth there are others who wish to be animate." Immediately a wolf is heard howling in the east. In this manner everything in the world is created.

---

[160] For an excellent discussion of the conditions found in aboriginal Australia, cf. the famous work of W Schmidt, *Der Ursprung der Gottesidee* 1912.

[161] RH Lowie, *Myths and Traditions of the Crow Indians,* Anthropological Papers of the American Museum of Natural History, New York, vol. XXV, part I: 14ff.

Not a very exalted type of creator you will justly exclaim. But he is a creator none the less in two essential respects: first, in that practically nothing exists until he creates it; and secondly, in that all his creative acts are the results of his expressed will and that they are beneficient. Let me point out one other fact – the new ethical re-evaluation of the Sun-Coyote. In the cycle connected with him as a Transformer he possesses hardly one redeeming feature. He is obscene, a fool, a coward and utterly lacking in self-control. Yet the [10] moment he becomes associated with the creative deity all this disappears.

Let us take another example. Among the Thompson River Indians of British Columbia[162]1 the concept of a creator is still vague, but the creator himself is definitely dissociated from the Coyote. "Having finished his work on earth and having put all things to rights, the time came that the Coyote should meet the Old Man. ... When he met him he did not know that he was the 'Great Chief or 'Mystery', because he did not appear to be different from any other old man. The Coyote thought, 'This old man does not know who I am. I will astonish him. He knows nothing of my great powers.'... After saluting each other the Old Man derided Coyote as a person possessed of small powers: the latter consequently felt annoyed and began to boast of the many wonders he had performed. ... 'If you are he (Coyote) and so powerful as you say, remove that river and make it run yonder.' This the Coyote did. 'Bring it back'. The Coyote did so. ... 'Place that high mountain on the plain.' The Coyote did so. 'Replace it where it was'; but this the Coyote could not do because the Old Man, being the superior in magic of the two, willed otherwise. The Old Man then asked Coyote why he could not replace it and the latter answered, 'I don't know. I suppose you are greater than I in magic, and make my efforts fruitless.' The Old Man then made the mountain go back to its place. ..."
After declaring himself as the Great Chief, the Old Man addresses Coyote as follows: "Now you have been a long time on earth; and since the world, mostly through your instrumentality, has been put right, you have nothing more to do. Soon I am going to leave the earth. You will not return again until I myself do so. You shall then accompany me and we will change things in the world, and bring back the dead to the land of the living. ..."

Often enough we are told very little about the creation of the world itself and we first meet the creator in a fully-formed world of his own. His task then becomes that of creating the present universe, This is the case, for instance, with an interesting figure of the Wintun Indians of Northern California[163]2 called Olelbis, "he who dwells on high." "The first that we know of Olelbis", the natives claim, "is that he was in Olepanti. Whether he lived in another place is not known, but in the beginning he was in Olepanti, the highest place. [11] He was there before there was anyone here on earth and two old women were alway with him." What interests us in Olelbis is that, although presumably only a creator of the universe in a very partial sense and although he subsequently creates the world in which we live, human beings, etc., and behaves very much as a normal culture-hero, he possesses no traces whatsoever of the attributes generally associated "with such an individual. He is a highly ethical, beneficent deity concerned only with the welfare of mankind.

If we turn to the famous Supreme Beings of the Australian aborigines the picture again changes. They are generally, though not always, complete creators, but it is their culture-hero and transformer aspects that dominate. They are, for instance, married and have children. Yet in

---

[162] J Teit, *Traditions of the Thompson River Indians of British Columbia*, Memoirs of the American Folklore Society, Boston 1900: 48.

[163] J Curtin, *Creation Myths of Primitive America,* London 1899: 3ff.

spite of all this they differ from the transformer in one important respect, in being highly ethical and beneficent.

Strictly speaking, the example to which I shall now turn does not belong to the above type at all. But as the Supreme Deity in this case has been affected by the dominant faith of the people, namely ancestor-worship, it seems best to include it here. I refer to the very marked monotheism of the Amazulus of South Africa[164] as described by Bishop Callaway. "*Unkulunkulu*", so their creation-account runs, "is no longer known (i.e no memory of him exists). It is he who was the first being; he broke off in the beginning (i.e. sprang from something). We do not know his wife and the ancients do not tell us that he had a wife ... *Unkulunkulu* gave men the spirits of the dead; he gave them doctors for treating disease, and diviners. ... The old men say *Unkulunkulu* is (i.e. was a reality); he made the first men, the ancients of long ago."

There are a number of suggestive features about this *Unkulunkulu*. The name itself means the "old-old one" and his other desinations imply priority and potential source of existence. But what is his relation to mankind? There the versions differ, some regarding him as having created men, others as having begotten them. It is likewise quite difficult to decide often whether he is regarded as the direct ancestor of man or as a true creator. What has happened seems clear. The Amazulus are ancestor-worshippers, worship the spirits of the departed, and this has influenced their conception of the Supreme Being to the extent of transforming him into the mythical ancestor of his race. Something of the irresponsible Transformer still clings to him at times as the following story indicates. [12] He sends a chameleon to say, "Let not men die", but the chameleon lingers along the road and he then dispatches a lizard to say, "Let men die". Thus it is that death came into the world. But such traits are unimportant. When indeed it is recalled that the spirit of the deceased ancestor is predominantly evil and has to be propitiated, the fact that the partial transformation of *Unkulunkula* into an ancestor has in no way affected his ethical and benevolent activities, lends additional corroboration to the well-nigh universal moral nature of the Supreme Being among ~~primitive~~ peoples. Whatever else may happen his ethical nature apparently can in no way be contaminated.

As we pointed out previously all these creators have some of the features of the Transformer, and yet it seems obvious that they cannot be explained as gradual developments from the latter. They are manifestly quite independent and if consequently we And a Supreme Deity with the attributes of a culture-hero, this is to be regarded as secondary, as an accretion which I cannot help feeling represents an attempt to bring him nearer to man. It failed, we may surmise, because of the strength of other religious currents and because of the absence of a cult in his honour.

In the second class of supreme deities, that group where we find only a faint admixture of the attributes of the Transformer, all doubt as to the deity's creative role and complete lack of intimate relation with mankind is removed. Intermediate divinities carry out his commands and it is to them that man must pray. These two new-factors have led to a strengthening of his former traits. His character becomes correspondingly ennobled and to his ethical attributes are added omnipotence and omniscience. Yet as he becomes further removed from men, though reverence and awe may increase, he becomes of less interest to the ordinary individual, for the latter is naturally concerned only with those deities associated with his daily needs, i.e. with the minor gods. The Supreme Being thus develops into what has been admirably described as an

---

[164] Bishop Callaway, *The Religious System of the Amasylu*, Natal 1870: 1ff.

otiose deity, one resting on his laurels after the creation of the world and leaving it entirely to its own devices-Such an otiose deity is found, for instance, among the Wichita of Texas.[165] "In the times of the beginning there was no sun, no stars nor anything else as it is now. Time passed on. *Man-never-known-on-earth* was the only man that existed, and he it was who created all things. [13] When the earth was created it was composed of land and water, but they were not yet separated. The land was floating on the water and darkness was everywhere. After the earth was formed, *Man-never-known-on-earth* made a woman whose name was *Bright-shining-woman*. After the man and woman were made they dreamed that things were made for them and when they awoke they had the things of which they had dreamed. Thus they received everything they needed. ... Still they were in darkness not knowing what was better than darkness."

Here we have most emphatically an otiose deity. Apart from the creation of the earth and man he bestows, so to speak, only the potentiality of things. It is this first man who causes the sun and moon to appear and who creates day and night, but only in obedience to an impulse, be it remembered, which *Man-never-known-on-earth* has implanted within him. "The man that creates things is about to improve our condition", he is informed later on. "Villages shall spring up and more people will exist, and you will have power to teach the people how to do things before unknown to them." Throughout the story of creation this divine impulse is expressed by a voice directing the activities of the hero.

At times fortunately the creation is described at greater length. Thus among the Uitoto of Colombia,[166] South America, we find the following poetic account: "In the beginning there was nothing but mere appearance, nothing really existed. It was a phantasm, an illusion that our father touched; something mysterious it was that he grasped. Nothing existed. Through the agency of a dream our father, *He-who-is-appearance-only*, *Nainema*, pressed the phantasm to his breast and then was sunk in thought.

"Not even a tree existed that might have supported this phantasm and only through his breath did *Nainema* hold this illusion attached to the thread of a dream. He tried to discover what was at the bottom of it, but he found nothing. 'I have attached that which was non-existent', he said. There was nothing.

"Then our father tried again and investigated the bottom of this something and his fingers sought the empty phantasm. He tied the emptiness to the dream-thread and pressed the magical glue-substance upon it. Thus by means of his dream did he hold it like the fluff of raw cotton. [14]

"He seized the bottom of the phantasm and stamped upon it repeatedly, allowing himself finally to rest upon the earth of which he had dreamt.

"The earth-phantasm was now his. Then he spat out saliva repeatedly so that the forests might arise. He lay upon the earth and set the covering of heaven above it. He drew from the earth the blue and white heavens and placed them above."

The creation of all the various animals and plants then follows. We hear no more of him thereafter.

What are we to make of this wonderful bit of imagery? Surely there can be little doubt but that it represents an attempt to solve the riddle of creation by postulating something that existed before the beginning, and our ~~primitive~~ philosopher and theologian has quite logically

---

[165] GA Dorsey, *The Mythology of the Wichita*, Washington 1904: 25ff.

[166] KT Preuss, *Religion und Mythologie der Uitoto*, Göttingen 1921, vol. i: 166-168. Cf also KT Preuss, *Die höchste Gottheit bei den Kulturarmen Völkern*, in *Psychologische Forschung*, vol. ii: 173-186.

assumed that the appearance of" things preceded their actual existence. In the evolution of reality, according to him, three stages may be said to exist: nothing, the appearance of reality, reality. It is an admirable solution of the much vexed question of how a creator can create something out of nothing. There are other solutions conceivable and one of them is found among these very people; namely the creation of the world out of the one thing that existed, the body of the creator himself.

But the speculation of the Uitoto monotheist has gone much farther than this. In one myth we are told that, "When in the beginning of things nothing existed, our father created words and gave us these words from the Juka-tree. *Nofugeri* and our ancestors brought these words to the earth. After he had brought these words to the earth in consequence to a dream, our ancestors gave us the words that our father had created."

In another instance the formulation is even more specific: 'In the beginning the word gave origin to our father."

These are, of course, all interpretations of the religious man. The non-religious man, the realist, has had comparatively little influence upon the figure of the creator except in one important respect, namely in the strenuous efforts he has made to equate him with the ancestor of man, for the Uitoto, in a sense, are ancestor-worshippers. But even he never went to the point of representing these ancestors as directly begotten of the creator as we saw the Amazulu in part do.

Not far from the above-mentioned tribe we find the Kagaba,[167] among whom we encounter a female Supreme Deity and a profession of faith that should satisfy even the most exacting monotheist. [15]

"The mother of our songs, the mother of all our seed, bore us in the beginning of things and so she is the mother of all types of men, the mother of all nations. She is the mother of the thunder, the mother of the streams, the mother of trees and of all things. She is the mother of the world and of the older brothers, the stone-people. She is the mother of the fruits of the earth and of all things. She is the mother of our younger brothers, the French and the strangers. She is the mother of our dance paraphernalia, of all our temples and she is the only mother we possess. She alone is the mother of the fire and the Sun and the Milky Way. ,.. She is the mother of the rain and the only mother we possess. And she has left us a token in all the temples ... a token in the form of songs and dances."

She has no cult, and no prayers are really directed to her, but when the fields are sown and the priests chant their incantations the Kagaba say, "And then we think of the one and only mother of the growing things, of the mother of all things." One prayer was recorded. "Our mother of the growing fields, our mother of the streams, will have pity upon us. For to whom do we belong? Whose seeds are we? To our mother alone do we belong."

Here we have pure pantheism and the recorder of the above data may perhaps be quite right when he insists that we can hardly expect an origin myth, for the All-Mother is obviously nature personified. I am not quite so convinced of this, but it is a fact that no origin myth has been recorded.

If there are traces, however faint they may be, of a direct intervention of the All-Mother of the Kagaba in the ordinary affairs of man, there are absolutely none in the cases now to be cited, the Tirawa of the Pawnee[1681] of Oklahoma and the Earthmaker of the HoChunk

---

[167] *Ibid, Psychologfsehe Forscbung*, vol. ii: 167-173.

[168] GA Dorsey, *Traditions of the Skidi Pawnee,* Boston 1904, and AC Fletcher, *The Hako, a Pawnee Ceremony* in Twenty-second Annual Report, Bureau of American Ethnology,

Winnebago[169] of Wisconsin.

In the Pawnee pantheon Tirawa reigned supreme. To him the lesser gods, both of the heavens and of the earth, as well as the people themselves acknowledged authority. Tirawa rules from his position beyond the clouds and has both created and governs the universe by means of commands executed by lesser gods who are subject to him.[170] [16]

The two temperaments which we see clashing incessantly in the interpretation of the Supreme Deity, that of the permanently devout man and the idealist, and that of the intermittently devout, the practical man, the realist, are transparently reflected among the Pawnee. The supremacy of Tirawa is never questioned by the latter, but something of his role as creator of all things is taken from him. The sun, moon and the stars are not mentioned as specifically formed by him. They are merely given their proper places and functions, i.e. Tirawa, somewhat like the Culture-heroes, transforms things. The following is assuredly the account of the realist: "In the beginning was *Tirawahut* (the Universe-and-Everything-Inside); and chief in *Tirawahut* was *Tirawa*, the all-powerful, and his spouse was *Atira* (Vault-of-the-sky). Around them sat the gods in council. Then *Tirawa* told them where they should stand. And at this time the heavens did not touch the earth.

"*Tirawa* spoke to the gods, and said: 'Each of you gods I am to station in the heavens; and each of you shall receive certain powers from me, for I am about to create people who shall be like myself. They shall be under my care. I will give them your land to live upon, and with your assistance they shall be cared for. You, sun, shall stand in the east. You shall give light and warmth to all beings and to earth.' 'You, moon, shall stand in the west to give light when darkness comes.' 'You, evening star, shall stand in the west. You shall be known as Mother of all things; for through you all things shall be created. ' "[171]

It is the same realist who in the following litany converts him merely into the most potent of gods: −

<table>
<tr><td align="center">I</td><td align="center">II</td></tr>
<tr><td>We heed as unto thee we call!</td><td>We heed as unto thee we call;</td></tr>
<tr><td>Oh send to us thy potent aid!</td><td>Oh send to us thy potent aid!</td></tr>
<tr><td>Help us, oh, holy place above!</td><td>Help us, Hotoru, giver of breath![172]</td></tr>
</table>

And it is unquestionably the idealist who speaks in the following. It is a final profession of faith.

I

I know not if the voice of man can reach the sky;
I know not if the mighty one will hear as I pray;
I know not if the gifts I ask will all granted be;
I know not if the word of old we truly can hear;
I know not what will come to pass in our future days;

Washington 1911.
[169] P Radin, *The Winnebago Indians* in Thirty seventh Annual Report, Bureau of American Ethnology, Washington 1923: 277-316.
[170] G A Dorsey, *Traditions of the Skidi Pawnee*: xviii-xix.
[171] *Ibid*: 3-4.
[172] AC Fletcher, *ibid*: 286.

I hope that only good will come, my children, to you. [17]

II

I now know that the voice of man can reach to the sky;
I now know that the mighty one has heard as I prayed;
I now know that the gifts I asked have all granted been;
I now know that the word of old we truly have heard;
I now know that Tirawa hearkens unto man's prayer;
I know that only good has come, my children, to you.[173]

There is no doubt whatsoever in the minds of the Pawnee that Tirawa reigns supreme and that the minor gods are his ministers only. In one of their prayers he is invoked in the following manner:

Father, unto thee we cry!
Father thou of gods and men;
Father thou of all we hear;
Father thou of all we see −
Father unto thee we cry![174]

His unapproachability and the realization that only through his ministers, the lesser gods, can man be brought into relation with him is forcibly brought out in such an invocation as this: −

Father, thou above, father of the gods,
They who can come near and touch us,
Do thou bid them bring us help.
Help we need. Father, hear us![175]

In the account of origins given by the Uitoto we saw the problem of the creation of the world out of nothing solved in a very ingenious manner. But no attempt was there made to create the creator. Yet this is precisely what the Ho-Chunk Winnebago of Wisconsin[176] essayed.

"What it was our father lay on when he came to consciousness we do not know. He moved his right arm and then his left arm, his right leg and then his left leg. He began to think of what he should do and finally he began to cry and tears began to flow from his eyes and fall down below him. After awhile he looked down below him and saw something bright. The bright objects were his tears that had flowed below and formed the present waters.... Earthmaker began to think again. He thought: 'It is thus. If I wish anything it will become as I wish, just as my tears have become seas.' Thus he thought. So he wished for light and it became light. Then he thought:

'It is as I supposed; the things that I have wished for have come into existence as I

---

[173] *Ibid*: 343 ff.

[174] *Ibid*: 314.

[175] *Ibid*: 314.

[176] P Radin, *ibid*: 212-213.

desired.' Then he again thought and wished for the earth and this earth came into existence. Earthmaker looked on the earth and he liked it but it was not quiet. ... (After the earth had [18] become quiet) he thought again of how things came into existence Just as he desired. Then he first began to talk. He said, "As things are just as I wish them I shall make one being like myself." So he took a piece of earth and made it like himself. Then he talked to what he had created but it did not answer. He looked upon it and he saw that it had no mind or thought. So he looked upon it again and saw that it had no tongue. Then ha made it a tongue. Then he talked to it again but it did not answer. So he looked upon it again and saw that it had no soul. So he made it a soul. He talked to it again and it very nearly said something. But it did not make itself intelligible. So Earthmaker breathed into its mouth and talked to it and it answered."

Here we have a theory not so different after all from that of the Uitoto. The creator is represented as being born and coming into consciousness. Water is formed from his tears. But this does not take place as the result of a conscious wish. It is only after he has recognized the water and inferred that it had originated from his tears that he realizes his powers and begins to create at first gropingly and then confidently and intelligently.

Earthmaker, like the *Tirawa* of the Pawnee, never holds direct communion with men. He acts only through his intermediaries, the deities and the Culture-heroes he has created. At times, however, a daring realist will attempt to establish such a direct communion. I know of one instance where a man argued that if Earthmaker had created all the deities from whom we derive our powers, and if it is Earthmaker who bestowed them upon the deities, then he himself must possess even greater powers. Why not then supplicate Earth-maker directly; see him face to face, as one does the spirits? The man gives up everything – happiness, the goods of the world, lastly his own child, and finally he hears a voice from above saying, "My son, for your sake I shall come to earth." The man turns in the direction of the voice, perceives a ray of light extending from the heavens to his camp and a voice again speaking: "Only thus can you see me my son. What you ask of me, to see me face to face, I cannot grant."[177] So not even the realist can alter him profoundly; he is a deity unapproachable and invisible.

In one of the cults, practically a feast to all the gods and a plea for victory in war, a further attempt has been made to convert him into a god of the general type: – [19]

"Hearken, Earthmaker, our rather, I am about to offer you tobacco. My ancestor concentrated his thoughts upon you. The blessings you bestowed upon him .,. those I ask of you directly (i.e. and not through the customary intermediation of other spirits). Also that I may have no troubles in life."

Or we get an even more definite attempt at transformation into a cult-deity: –

"Hearken, Father who dwells above, all things you have created. Yet if we were to offer you some tobacco you would thankfully accept it you said. I am about to offer you a handful of tobacco and a buckskin for moccasins and a white-haired animal to be cooked so that you may have a holy feast. ... If you accept

---

[177] *Ibid*: 291-293.

them, the first thing I ask of you will be the honour of killing an enemy in full sight of the people, of leading war-paths. ..."[178]

Yet if there is one thing upon which practically every Winnebago would agree it is that Earthmaker is under no conditions ever associated with war. What we have here is not merely an attempt to make him a cult-deity but an example of swaggering so very common among ~~primitive~~ people.

The most difficult of all the concepts of the Supreme Deity to understand is that found among the Dakota.[179] A very remarkable account was secured from them which purported to be the secret instructions for a priest (shaman). In this priestly doctrine it is definitely asserted that the Great Mystery, the Supernatural Being called *Wakan Tanka*, cannot be comprehended by mankind. *Wakan Tanka* behaves like a definite individuality, may be pleased or displeased, propitiated or placated and its aid may be secured by appropriate sacrifice. This Great Mystery communicates with mankind through various individuals and in various ways. The chosen medium is the shaman. The following are the doctrines which only the shamans know, according to Mr. Walker, the recorder of these facts: – [180]

> Wakan Tanka is one, yet it is many who are
> Wakan Tanka Waste, the Benevolent Gods:
> Wakan Tanka Sica, the Malevolent Gods.

The Benevolent Gods are of two kinds, the Gods and the Gods' Kindred, the former divided into the Superior and the Associate [20] Gods, the latter into the Subordinate Gods and the God-like. Each of these four classes consists of four individuals, the individuals of the Superior Gods being the Sun, Sky, Earth, Rock; of the Associate Gods, Moon, Wind, the Feminine, the Winged God; of the Subordinate, the Buffalo, Bear, Four Winds, Whirlwind; of the godlike, the spirit, ghost, spirit-like, the imparted Supernatural Potency.

We now come to the most remarkable part of this mystic theology. *Wakan Tanka*, the Great Mystery, has four essences to be regarded as one-the Chief God, the Great Spirit, the Creator and the Executive. The Chief God has four individuals (Sun, Moon, Buffalo, Spirit) that are as one; the Great Spirit four individuals (Sky, Wind, Bear, Ghost) that are as one; the Creator-god, four individuals (Earth Feminine, Four-Winds, Spirit-like) that are as one, and lastly, the Executive God, four individuals (Rock, Winged, Whirlwind, Potency) that are as one. This mysticism is carried through in every detail. So, for example, all these individualities, apart from the four winds, had no beginning, though some came before others and some bear the relation of parent and offspring. The Dakota ~~informant~~ added, "This is *Akan* (mysterious), for no one of mankind can comprehend it. They will have no end." Another ~~informant~~ in answer to a direct statement that he had named eight deities and yet claimed that they were but one, replied, "Yes. The sun and moon are the same, the sky and the wind are the same, the Rock and the Winged one are the same, the Earth and the Beautiful woman are the same. These eight are only

---

[178] *Ibid*: 447, 455.

[179] J.R Walker, *The Sun Dance and other Ceremonies of the Oglala Division of the Teton Dakota,* in Anthropological Papers of the American Museum of Natural History, vol. xvi, part II .

[180] *Ibid*: 78-92.

one. The shamans know how this is but the people do not know. It is a mystery." This same man stated that he frequently prayed to *Wakan Tanka* and that if the prayer was about things of great importance it was carried to the Sun; if about health or strength, to the Sky; if about implements, to the Rock; if about food or clothing and such things, to the earth.

Clearly this is explicit monotheism avowedly mystical. The deities as intermediaries have disappeared; they are merely aspects of the Great Mystery. "When *Wakan Tanka* wishes one of mankind to do something he makes his wishes known either in a vision or through a shaman", one of Mr. Walker's ~~informants~~ stated. This same individual was quite definite as to the oneness of *Wakan Tanka*. "The shamans address him as *Tobtobki*n, which in their language means four times four. He is like sixteen different persons; but each person is *kan* (mysterious). Therefore they are all the same as one."[181] [21]

Such is the creed of the priests. No pretence is made that it holds for the people. Among them the sixteen aspects of godhead are sixteen distinct deities, although the shamanistic terminology has penetrated to them too. In a myth about the wind it is stated, *Wi* (the Sun) was chosen because he was *Wakan Tanka* and his wife Moon and the Sky and the Rock were all chosen for the same reason. Yet apparently they all appeared as distinct deities. Nor, for that matter, need we suppose that all the shamans, in spite of their creed, were not sometimes more polytheistic than monotheistic. It seems a rather suspicious circumstance that one of the shamans in answer to certain interrogations stated: "Rock is the oldest. He is the grandfather of all things. Earth is the next oldest. She is the grandmother of all things. Sky comes next. He gives life and motion to all things. Then follows the Sun. *He is above all things and above all Wakan Tanka*."

But the inconsistencies are really unimportant. The significant fact remains that such a mystical Supreme Essence was postulated and actually became the official creed of all shamans.

This last example has introduced us to certain mystical elements, and although it may be somewhat beside the point, I cannot refrain from giving another instance of a very special nature in which mysticism is carried still one step farther.

Among the HoChunk Winnebago Indians[182] an interesting religious revival has recently taken place based largely on a religion borrowed from their southern neighbours and which included certain marked Christian features. The older Winnebago concept of Earthmaker, as set forth previously, has in this new faith been equated with the Christian Deity. Yet the main element in this new syncretism has, however, nothing to do with Christianity. It is the worship of the peyote (a small cactus found in northern Mexico), which when eaten, either in the natural state or in a concoction brewed from it, produces certain narcotic effects. It was after partaking of the peyote rather copiously that a certain individual developed the following theology which he dictated to me in HoChunk Winnebago: – [183]

"Then again I prayed to Earthmaker. ... As I prayed I was aware of something above me and there he was! Earthmaker to whom I was praying, he it was. That which is called the soul, that is it, that [22] is what one calls Earthmaker. Now this is what I felt and saw. All of us sitting there, we had all together one spirit and I was their spirit or soul. Whatever they thought of I immediately knew. I did not have to speak to them and get an answer to know what their

---

[181] *Ibid*: 152-159.

[182] P Radin, *The Peyote Cult of the Winnebago Indians*, Journal of Religious Psychology 1914: 1-22.

[183] P Radin, *The Autobiography of a Winnebago Indian*, University of California Publications in American Archaeology and Ethnology, Berkeley 1920 vol. xvi: 441-442.

thoughts had been. Then I thought of a certain place far away, and immediately I was there; I was my thought.... All those that heed Earth-maker must be thus, I thought. I would not need any more food, for was I not my spirit? Nor would I have any more use of my body, ... My corporeal affairs are over."

III

We have now briefly enumerated some of the main types of monotheism to be encountered among ~~primitive~~ peoples. But monotheism itself presents a number of phases. A recent classification of its history divides it into three stages; into monolatry, i.e, a belief in a Supreme Being but the persistence of the worship of other deities at the same time; implicit monotheism, i.e, a belief in a Supreme Deity yet no definite denial of the existence of other gods, and lastly explicit monotheism, a belief in a Supreme Deity and a denial of the existence of other gods.[184] If this were true, it might at first glance follow that we would have to deny the existence among any ~~primitive~~ peoples of anything except monolatry. But it might be asked, is it really the mere fact of the worship of other gods or spirits or Culture-heroes that constitutes the fundamental difference between explicit monotheism and monolatry? What of those cases where lesser gods have been created by a Supreme Deity; where all their powers have been derived from him; where they are merely his intercessors? Are we to interpret every act of worship not directly addressed to a Supreme Deity but to his divinely appointed intermediaries as contrary to the spirit of monotheism? I am afraid that we should then soon find ourselves confronted with great difficulties. I cannot enter into the theological aspects of this question here. For us it is the historical aspects of this question that are of prime importance, and to some of these we must now turn. How, it may be asked, are we to imagine the intermediary role of certain deities and Culture-heroes to have developed and what relation does the Supreme Being bear to the other deities? [23]

Everyone acquainted with the religion and mythology of ~~primitive~~ peoples is well aware of the fact that the same deities and Culture-heroes who figure as the ministers of a Supreme Deity are also known in an entirely different connection where no such relation is involved. The Winnebago, for instance, have four Culture-heroes and in many versions of their exploits there is not the slightest indication of their having been created by Earthmaker. The account of their creation by him seems obviously secondary. The same is true in regard to a deity who is regarded as the chief of the evil spirits. In many Winnebago myths, in fact in all those not concerned with the problem of the origin of man, it is explicitly stated that the chief of the evil spirits is equal in power and importance to the great, good spirit. In one of the ritualistic origin myths, on the other hand, he is explained away as the Deity's first inadequate attempt at creation. Having been cast aside as unsatisfactory, he imitates Earthmaker but only succeeds in creating evil. Many more myths of this type could be adduced all pointing in the same direction and all tending to demonstrate that the religious systematization is secondary. The intermediary role occupied by many deities and Culture-heroes is clearly the reflection of this unifying influence of the concept of a Supreme Creator.

The second of our problems is more difficult. Can we not indeed satisfactorily explain the concept of a Supreme Deity by regarding him as representing the successive transformations of some particular deity or of some individual spirit? May he not, for instance, represent the

---

[184] C. Buchanan Gray, *Hebrew Monotheism* (Oxford Society of Historical Theology, Abstract of Proceedings for the Year 1922-23).

triumph of the god of some particular cult? Evolutionists have generally answered this question in the affirmative. They would insist in fact that the Winnebago are an excellent case in point. First we have a belief in a number of deities all of equal importance; one then becomes identified with the chief of the evil spirits, and the other with the chief of the good spirits. Gradually but never completely the latter then displaces the former. Such an interpretation is quite reasonable. Yet one factor, it seems to me, has always been forgotten in such an analysis. Why should these transformations all take place synchronously or, if you will, why should they occur in the simplest as well as in the more complex civilizations; and why should they always be connected with the elaborations of religious cults? Why in fact should the unification of religious concepts always go hand in hand with the marked development of a high ethical ideal? Why, for example, should a coarse, selfish, stupid figure in mythology suddenly become an [24] ethical, intelligent and benevolent being when associated with a creator?

The ethical re-evaluation of the Transformer of the myths has never been adequately stressed. A far more fundamental question is involved here, namely how to account for the tendency toward unification in religious beliefs. For this a number of explanations have at different times been advanced. The most important are those which represent it as a reflection of certain forms of social organization, the influence, for instance, of a markedly centralized government or of highly elaborate and unified cults. But it can easily be shown that no correlation whatsoever exists between the existence of a belief in an ethical Supreme Creator and such integrated social units. Some tribes with such a unified social and ceremonial organization possess it, many, indeed the vast majority, do not. But even if we were to grant that such social units had had a perceptible influence upon the wider adoption of a belief of this kind, and I am inclined to regard this as likely, we are no nearer to a real solution.

IV

If, as most ethnologists and unbiased students would now admit, the possibility of interpreting monotheism as part of a general intellectual and ethical progress must be abandoned and if social causations hardly touch the fundamental problem involved, only two alternatives remain open to us. We may either regard such a belief as innate in the theological sense or as the expression of a certain temperament. The first lies quite outside my province. To explain what I mean by the second and how it effects our problem I must permit myself a slight digression.

It is a matter of common experience that in any randomly selected group of individuals we may expect to find, on the whole, the same distribution of temperament and ability. Such a view, I know, has certain terrors because of national and class prejudices, but I do not think it can be really seriously questioned. Certainly not for temperament. But, you might ask, is this true for ~~primitive~~ peoples? Is not their mentality, is not their whole emotional nature utterly different from our own? Most laymen, all sociologists and many ethnological theorists are of that opinion. Nothing in reality is wider from the mark. Perhaps I need hardly insist upon this after the examples of logical and speculative thinking I have given you. [25] ~~Primitive~~ people, as a matter of fact, are quite as logical as ourselves and have perhaps an even truer sense of reality. There is not the slightest indication of the existence of any fundamental difference in their emotional nature as compared with ours. I think we may, in fact, confidently assume that the same distribution of ability and temperament holds for them that holds for us. Indeed I think there is ample reason for believing, granted that chance mating has existed since man's first appearance on earth, that the distribution of ability and temperament never has been appreciably different. What has differed is the size of populations with its corollary of a larger proportion of men of a certain type of ability and temperament. We must bear this in mind in estimating the culture of ~~primitive~~ peoples. At the discovery of America, for instance, it is extremely doubtful whether there were more than 1,250,000 individuals north of the Rio Grande River.

If therefore we are right in assuming the same more or less fixed distribution of ability and temperament in every group of approximately the same size, it would follow that no type has ever been totally absent. I feel quite convinced that the idealist and the materialist, the dreamer and the realist, the introspective and the non-introspective man have always been with us. And the same would hold for the different grades of religious temperament, the devoutly religious, the intermittently, the indifferently religious man. If individuals with specific temperaments, for instance the religious-aesthetic, have always existed we should expect to find them expressing themselves in much the same way at all times. And this, it seems to me, is exactly what we do find. The pagan polytheistic religions are replete with instances of men − poets, philosophers, priests − who have given utterance to definitely monotheistic beliefs. It is the characteristic of such individuals, I contend, always to picture the world as a unified whole, always to postulate some First Cause. No evolution from animism to monotheism was ever necessary in their case. What was required were individuals of a certain psychological type. Alongside of them and vastly in the majority have always been found others with a temperament fundamentally distinct, to whom the world has never appeared as a unified whole and who have never evinced any marked curiosity as to its origin.

Such too is the situation among ~~primitive~~ peoples. If anything the opposition of the two types is much clearer. All the monotheists, it is my claim, have sprung from the ranks of the eminently religious individuals. It is in the ritualistic version of the Winnebago Origin [26] Myth for example, that Earthmaker is depicted as a Supreme Deity who definitely creates the other deities and the Culture-heroes; it is in the ritualistic version of the Culture-hero cycle again that a non-moral, buffoon-like hero, whose acts are only incidentally beneficial to mankind, is transformed into an ethical, intelligent, beneficent creator. No other explanation for the characteristics of the Supreme Deities, as I have attempted to sketch them, is indeed conceivable except upon the assumption that they reflect a definite type of temperament, examples of which we know actually exist in every ~~primitive~~ group. Such people are admittedly few in number, for the overwhelming mass belong to the indifferently religious group, are materialists, realists, to whom a god, be he Supreme Deity or not, is simply to be regarded as a source of power. If men of this type accept such a god, he is immediately equated with the more concrete deities who enter into direct relations with man and as a result contamination ensues. It is thus that that particular type of Creator arose, where a marked admixture of attributes belonging to the Culture-hero and Transformer was manifest.

On such an hypothesis a really satisfactory explanation of the existence and of the dominant traits of the monotheism among ~~primitive~~ peoples can be given. Monotheism would then have to be taken as fundamentally an intellectual-religious expression of a very special type of temperament and emotion. Hence the absence of cults, for instance, the unapproachability of the Supreme Being, his vagueness of outline and his essential lack of function. Whatever dynamic force he possessed for the community is that with which the realists invested him. In so doing they frequently converted him into a cult-deity, into a creator of gods; made him but one among many. This is merely monolatry if you wish, but this in no way detracts from the possibility that the faith of the religious man himself may have been different, may have been essentially explicit monotheism. Yet, even if we should not care to press this claim, the existence of monolatry and implicit monotheism must constitute a definite challenge to the views still current as to the development of the concept of a Supreme Creator.

The view still held both by the ethnological theorist and the student of comparative religion is frankly evolutionary. Only recently in a remarkably lucid address by the late Dr. Buchanan Gray three stages in the development of Hebrew monotheism are assumed; the earliest extending perhaps even beyond the Exile, in which the Jews were divided into two groups one constituting [27] apparently the large majority, worshipping Jahveh and other deities at the same time, and the other worshipping only Jahveh but yet not denying the efficacy of other gods for the people. The second is represented by the belief of the prophets of the third century and after, where Jahveh is thought of as controlling the destinies of all nations but where, at the same time, it is not definitely asserted that no other gods exist. The last stage, that of Deutero-Isaiah, gives us the definite formulation that there is no God but one. Dr Gray goes on to say, "The existence of this third type of belief in Israel cannot be definitely traced back beyond the sixth century. Implicit monotheism might, according to the judgment passed on the age and meaning of certain passages, be traced perhaps somewhat earlier than the eighth century; but wherever and so soon as we find the first type of belief, monotheism, whether implicit or explicit, is excluded."[185]

This is quite definitely in line with the orthodox evolutionary theory. The cardinal error is and always has been the assumption that every element in culture must have had an evolution and one generally comparable to that which exists in the animal world. But it is precisely in its application to culture, to thought and to temperament that the evolutionary theory even in its heyday proved so unsatisfactory and even harmful. It requires no long preparatory stages for an individual with inborn artistic abilities to draw figures both correctly and with a remarkable feeling for line; and there is no reason whatsoever for supposing that certain concepts require a long period to evolve. What, concretely speaking, did Dr. Gray imagine had happened in Israel between the first and the third stages of monotheism? Apparently an increase in intelligence and in the capacity for abstract thought. This is but the old unconscious assumption that progress must make equal strides along the whole line. The general acceptance of explicit monotheism at one stage (if indeed there ever has been or could be such a general acceptance), and its apparent absence in the two earlier stages is taken to mean that it did not exist before. The existence of two varying attitudes toward God at one and the same time, as in the previously cited case of Hebrew monolatry, is regarded as somehow implying that explicit monotheism was absent. Dr. Gray himself partially realized the force of this criticism, for he says further on: "We may admit the possibility in the abstract that even [28] before the eighth century there may have been individual Hebrew monotheists of whom no trace has survived; but the religion of the people as a whole – of the teachers, prophets, priests, as well as the mass of the people – was not monotheistic."[186] To Dr Gray the existence of such a monotheist was a bare possibility because at bottom he could not think of explicit or implicit monotheism except as the result of a gradual evolution and, I surmise, because he would have seen no way in which to explain it if it had actually been found.

Another theologian and historian of religion, the very stimulating Archbishop of Upsala, Dr. Soderblom,[187] is also definitely evolutionistic in his interpretation. Instead of simply

---

[185] C Buchanan Gray, *Hebrew Monotheism* (Oxford Society of Historical Theology, Abstract of Proceedings for the Year 1922-23).

[186] *Ibid*: 8-13.

[187] N Söderblom, *Das Werden des Goffesglaubens* (German translation 1916).

beginning with animism or pre-animism, however, he begins with three factors: Animism, the belief in supernatural power, i.e. *mana,* and the belief in Culture-hero creators (*Urheber*). He does not deny the existence of the All-Father or Creator concept but assumes it as something shadowy and vague among ~~primitive~~ peoples and in his opinion utterly distinct from real monotheism in any form. He, like so many people, can explain the marked resemblances of so many Supreme Creators with the Culture-heroes in but one way, namely that the latter have largely contributed toward the formation of the former. To explain the third, i.e, the mystical aspect, he has recourse to the *Mana* concept. This in itself is exceedingly suggestive especially if we take the belief in Culture-heroes and the *Mana* concept as being in the nature of psychological tendencies, but unfortunately Dr Söderblom does not confine himself to this aspect of the question but predicates an evolutionary development for both concepts. For, like the most orthodox of evolutionists, he cannot bring himself to believe that the mentality of ~~primitive~~ people is not essentially different in kind from our own. He has been led astray, if I may say so, by the data he selected. He practically bases his analysis on the somewhat antiquated instances found in Lang, i.e on the ridiculously inadequate and unsatisfactory material from Australia and the vague statements found in early accounts of the American Indians. But the real criticism of his position is that just indicated, that to him explicit and implicit monotheism must represent the last phases of a long and gradual development.

Explicit monotheism, it is true, is rare among ~~primitive~~ peoples, but it is possibly not quite so uncommon as the literal reading of the [29] facts might seem to indicate. Knowing the tremendous part symbolism plays in the interpreatation of religious phenomena, particularly the Godhead in our own civilizations, what right have we to assume that it played an inferior role in avowedly similar temperaments among ~~primitive~~ peoples especially when it is universally admitted that symbolism permeates every aspect of ~~primitive~~ man's culture? What the facts really are it is admittedly difficult to ascertain, but from my own experience I am inclined to assume that a limited number of explicit monotheists are to be found in every ~~primitive~~ tribe that has at all developed the concept of a Supreme Creator. And if this is true we can safely assume that they existed in Israel even at a time when the mass of the people were monolatrists.

The problem, in short, that confronts us is not as has always been erroneously assumed, the origin of monotheism. That is one which I should say even antedates Neanderthal man. The historical problem connected with monotheism, implicit and explicit, is as I see it, not how monotheism arose but what made it the prevailing and exclusive official religion of a particular people. This we must assume to have been largely in the nature of an historical accident. The Jews and Mohammedans, the adherents of the purest form of monotheism known to-day, are certainly not innately gifted in this regard. It is true that the factors concerned in the complete credal triumph of monotheism in Judaism, Christianity and Mohammedanism have never been satisfactorily explained, but they are emphatically of an individual historical and psychological nature. For myself, I am inclined to believe that the spread of monotheism is far more definitely a reflection of certain facts of a general sociological order than has hitherto been recognized. Certainly it has obviously not been the triumph of the unifying principle over the disruptive, of abstract over concrete thought. Yet, on the other hand, there must be something subtly appealing in monotheism, for wherever it is found a definite influence is seen to be exercised over the thought of those who are stubborn polytheists and animists. Nowhere Indeed has It ever been completely submerged once it has made its appearance, no matter how great the mass of foreign accretions piled upon it.

I am afraid that the thesis I have advanced will seem to many exaggerated, quite contrary to all the ideas customarily associated with ~~primitive~~ peoples. Most of us have been brought up in the tenets of orthodox ethnology, and this was largely an enthusiastic and quite uncritical attempt to apply the Darwinian theory of [30] evolution to the facts of social experience. Many ethnologists, sociologists and psychologists still persist in this endeavour. No progress will ever be achieved, however, until scholars rid themselves, once and for all, of the curious notion that everything possesses an evolutionary history; until they realize that certain ideas and certain concepts are as ultimate for man as a social being as specific physiological reactions are for him as a biological entity. Both doubtless have a history; but in the one case its roots lie in pre-social man and in the other in the lower organisms. It must be explicitly recognized that in temperament and in capacity for logical and symbolical thought, there is no difference between civilized and ~~primitive~~ man. A difference exists – and one that profoundly colours ~~primitive~~ man's mental and possibly his emotional life; but that is to be explained by the nature of the knowledge the latter possessed, by the limited distribution of individuals of certain specific temperaments and abilities and all that this implied in cultural elaboration. In no way, however, does this affect the question of the existence among ~~primitive~~ people of monotheism in all its different varieties. Such a belief, I cannot too often repeat, is dependent not upon the extent of knowledge nor upon the elaboration of a certain type of knowledge, but solely upon the existence of a special kind of temperament. When once this has been grasped, much of the amazement and incredulity one inevitably experiences at the clear-cut monotheism of so many ~~primitive~~ peoples will vanish and we shall recognize it for what it is – the purposive functioning of an inherent type of thought and emotion.

Chapter I

~~Primitive~~ Religions

by Frank G Speck

BEFORE undertaking the study, brief as it may be, of ~~primitive~~ religions, or more exactly, the religions of ~~primitive~~ man, we must accept the broadest conceivable definition of the term, one which defines religion as that which expresses in life the relationship between man and the supernatural realm. We need a definition of this broad character if we intend to analyze and discuss the various types of philosophy, the rites of worship and the beliefs expressing the interactivity between man and the supernatural beings, which play such an important part in the mental life of so-called savages. We shall proceed then, recognizing the idea that the fetish worship of the West Coast African negroes, the universalism of the Algonquian and Iroquois Indians, the demonism of the Eskimo, the ancestor worship of the South African Zulu. as well as that of the Chinese, are as much the manifestations of religion in the real sense as are the phenomena of the more advanced types – what we may term Messianic types because of the importance of the semi-divine revealer personage in them. Some idea may be gained of the astonishing diversity of the field when one realizes that, for instance, in North America alone one encounters several hundred different native languages and most of these are the avenues of expression for as [10] many varieties of religious belief and practice, while again in Africa, Australia, Oceania and Asia, types of religion are about as numerous as the tribes themselves. Is it any wonder, then, that until present-day methods of analysis, classification and definition are introduced into the study of ~~primitive~~ religions the attitude of the student is as yet that of the pioneer classifier of data in a new science?

In dealing with a subject so bewilderingly diffuse, I propose to systematize by presenting first some discussion of ~~primitive~~ philosophy and mythology, then to touch upon the present status of the doctrines of animism, naturism, totemism, fetishism, the taboo, and ~~primitive~~ ethics as religious phenomena, then to give a discussion of the culture-hero concept with a concrete original illustration of the same from a ~~primitive~~ tribe in America. It is rather unfortunate, considering our limitations, that before passing to a concrete presentation of what ~~primitive~~ religion actually is, we shall have to give attention to fallacious concepts regarding the life of ~~primitive~~ man in general. Unfortunately again, he who speaks of the philosophical concepts of the so-called savage must adopt an apologetic attitude by proving, if indeed he can, that the savage has any philosophy at all.

How surprising then it must seem to the uninformed to become aware for the first time, that in the conception of savage mankind the idea of evolution in nature, for instance, is an exceedingly old one. Quoting material presented by Dr Kroeber, we find in Polynesian mythology, as an illustration, that a series of origins by birth is an explanation of cosmic features.[188] In Samoan, fire and water married and begat earth, rocks and trees. In Hawaiian mythology a protracted period of primeval night gave birth to eight periods which were literally [11] born from each other. In the first, appeared worms, corals, shells, seaweed, kelp and grass; in the second, insects and birds; in the third, trees. Jelly fish, fishes and whales; in the fourth, turtles and cultivable plants; in the fifth, *pigs* and human arts; in the sixth, mice and porpoises; in

---

[188] AL Kroeber, Inheritance by Magic, *American Anthropologist,* vol. 18 # 1 (1916).

the seventh, visions, sound, thoughts and sayings; in the eighth, man. Among the California Indians, Solitude and Emptiness appeared first in the cosmic series; Being and Existence then found themselves there.

In American Indian mythologies, almost universally, the germ of the evolutionary scheme is apparent in the frequent reference to pre-existing times when men were animals and became transformed, through accidental stages, into their present-day form. One might safely say, indeed, that the idea of an out-and-out creation of matter is rather inconsistent with American Indian nature philosophy. The idea of a natural unfolding of stages of life is certainly the dominant one here. In fact, the human mind appears to have employed only two idea processes In explaining to itself the origin of the world, the idea of evolution and the idea of creation. Both are presumably derived from analogies of concrete events witnessed in nature: the process of birth and organic growth and the process of construction by human hands. So in the mythology of many savage peoples, the evolutionary idea of growth has equalled in strength that of absolute creation, and we have the apparent paradox that the savage is more scientific in his way of thinking about origins than is the civilized philosopher of more recent times. It required, as it seems, the influence of a Semitic people to turn the modern world's thought into thinking of creational origin. The ~~primitive~~ pattern of thought persists even into the more ~~advanced~~ religions, for there is a striking quasi-scientific tone in early Japanese Shinto mythology, in early Greek cosmogony, in the narratives [12] of the Australian aborigines, while even the Hindu concept of transmigration embodies a similar explanatory thought.

The ethnologist is moreover often obliged to claim dignified consideration for his field of research by bringing forth data showing how the concept of the magical. even the immaculate conception and birth of a culture hero, or of a mythical world-transformer, is an age-old concept in the ~~primitive~~ world, how the fulfilment of an altruistic mission during his life, and his final departure, with the promise of an ultimate return, all figure as episodes in the career of a mythical personage whose attributes may, in part, even be compared with those of Christ, Moses, Hercules, Achilles, Balder, and also, in places, with those of Barbarossa and Arthur of the Round Table. What could be more bewildering to the student than to find, for instance, in a typically indigenous set of American Indian myths, many elements which are cognate in substance with the episode of the disobedience of Eve, the world Flood, the Ark, and the like.

Not from the mythology of one American tribe, but from the traditions of many could be quoted specimen versions in which a disobedient virgin gives birth by magical impregnation to a being who at an early age develops the characteristics of a miracle-worker. Then, and after, in the same mythical hero-cycle, occur episodes which parallel in a crude but significant fashion the episodes of the more modern Messianic versions, if we may refer to the versions of Christianity and Hinduism in this category. We have the manifestation of altruism on the part of the hero personage in behalf of human beings, the destruction of existing monsters and personified evils, the transformation of objects in Nature by means of miraculous power, and, finally, most significantly, the departure of the hero to another world, after leaving his promise to return again in some future time of need to [13] benefit his people. Can anyone fail to stand and marvel before an array of evidence of this sort, testifying to the antiquity of the concept of the supernatural deliverer in, the realm of ~~primitive~~ thought! We need not indeed halt our comparisons with these correlations. To every student of American Indian mythology instances of the occurrence in America of the following roughly assembled list of classical and old Testament mythical motives are very familiar. We have parallels for the narrative of Joshua stopping the course of the sun, Jonah and the whale, Lot's wife, the Potiphar story, Cain and Abel (or the murder between twins personifying good and evil), and the Flood. To cite a few instances from the classical field one might also mention correspondences in America with such tales as the animal foster-mother (Romulus and Remus), Pandora, Achilles, Orpheus, Prometheus (not only fire being obtained by theft in American mythology, but the sun, summer and tobacco among the tales of the eastern tribes), the world fire, Atlantis or Medea, and the Magic Flight, Phaeton, the Symplegades, and many more for which quotations might be cited from published American collections. Besides these, could be mentioned a number of correspondences with familiar European nursery tales, such as Jack and the Bean Stalk, the Abandoned Children, Big Claus and Little Claus, the Werwolf, the race between the hare and the tortoise, Loki, in Scandinavian, Tom Thumb, and the Roc. It is difficult to resist the temptation of discussing at this point whether, like Graebner and Ratzel, we may interpret the occurrence of these parallels as being due to an early process of culture diffusion or whether like Spencer, Tylor, Lubbock, Frazier and Lang, we are to repose confidence in the familiar theories of 'independent origin' and 'fundamental mental unity'. So much for what time permits us to mention regarding ~~primitive~~ man's philosophy of nature. [14]

~~Savage~~ religion is, to proceed to another topic, no less rich in forms of worship than in ideas of philosophy. Through a maze of practices in idolatry, human, animal and object sacrifice, cannibalism, invocation, expiation and bribery, we gain an insight into the attitude of worship of the savage, which might lead us, as it has some others, into the feeling that the worship of ~~primitive~~ man is the outgrowth of the emotion of fear. While fear is unquestionably an element in the religious activity of ~~primitive~~ man at large, I feel that it would be unfair to exclude from consideration instances evidencing higher feelings, such as those of gratitude, of reverence and affection for supernatural beings, occurring in the worship of some ~~primitive~~ peoples. ~~Savage~~ worship is at bottom characterized by emotions, so far as we know them, remarkably like those underlying modern worship. In the ~~primitive~~ tribe we find, moreover, the worshippers varying in the intensity of their devotional activities. Some are deeply religious most of the time, others are intermittently religious, and still others are indifferently religious. It is undoubtedly true, however, that, if we may assume the sense of an average feeling in respect to religion, the savage is in the long run rather more religious than the civilized man, for the former realizes his greater dependence upon the attitude which the supernatural beings maintain toward him than does the latter who has his sense of spiritual independence magnified by the knowledge of his mechanical powers.

The rites and forms of worship of ~~primitive~~ man often exhibit an elaborate and complex religious consciousness. Through prayers, through sacrifices, through emulatory dances and ritualized ceremonies, influence is sought with the supernatural beings. The rites of worship of ~~primitive~~ groups have often been regarded by speculators as activities to be classed in the very lowest nascent stages of human culture. While many of them [15] may be simple and irrational in concept, historically they must be as ancient and in many cases as much the product of specialized development as the modern types of religion. Cannibalism, for instance, might be casually thought, at first blush, to be a nascent activity. An investigation of cannibalism in the region of fetish worship in Central Africa shows on the contrary that this rite is the result of a long process, its inception capable of being traced back through acts of sacrifice to a starting point in the concept of expiation. Cannibal tribes frequently have derived their craving for human flesh through an earlier custom of eating, with ceremonial motives, the sacrifices intended for deities. In some of the most highly developed ritualistic regions of Africa such sacrifices consist of human beings. The connection here is obvious. Sacrifice in itself may be in accord with a deeply religious consciousness since it provides gifts, acceptable in proportion to their importance, to the supernatural beings. Cannibalism then may in some regions be viewed as an evolved rite.

In the ~~primitive~~ world ceremonies of a religious character play a part in most of the current events of life. Pre-natal and birth rites, ceremonial procedures at the period of adolescence, at initiation into certain secret organizations, at the occasions of marriage, death and burial, characterize the passage of life among savages from before the cradle until after the grave. Assuredly the savage impresses us as an essentially very religious creature in so far as his ceremonial obligations toward the beings of the supernatural world are concerned. The great play of fancy in such ceremonies, bringing into life symbolism in art, music and dancing, overshadows the crudities of superstition and the acts which would be considered profane and obscene in civilized communities.

It is not within the legitimate scope of this paper to deal extensively with the various theories of the origin of [16] religion, for although ~~primitive~~ religions may be said to be religions of an early type, there is nothing to warrant the critical student in going so far as to fall into the pitfall of assuming that even the crudest religions with which we are acquainted through ethnology are in any sense near to any truly original form of religious life. They are a comparatively late and advanced product of religious growth, with a complexity corresponding to that of Egyptian, early Semitic or Indian religion, which is developmental instead of primary. Having exonerated ourselves then from the thankless burden of dealing with religious origins, we may relieve our minds by attempting the legitimate and more profitable task of discussing the leading concepts which characterize the religions of ~~primitive~~ tribes, all of whom, in this age of the globe, have ascended to their own variously evolved states of being.

Animism

If any one concept could be regarded as fundamental to both ~~primitive~~ belief and religious practice it would seem to be that of animism. Animism is perhaps the most elementary and universal concept in ~~primitive~~ religious life. The term, while it does not necessarily define ~~primitive~~ religion in general, does at least temporarily characterize it. It is, as Tylor asserted many years ago,[189] the groundwork of the philosophy of religion from that of savages up to that of civilized man. The doctrine of animism as a concept of spirits may, to be sure, afford only a bare and meagre definition of religion at its minimum, but where the root is the branches will generally be produced. Tylor defines animism as including the belief in souls and in a future state, in controlling deities and subordinate spirits: these doctrines practically resulting in some kind of active worship. [17]

Tylor and Jevons derived the animistic concept from the transitional character of beliefs regarding the soul (made conscious to the ~~primitive~~ mind through dreams), and those concerning supernatural spirits. The doctrine is based upon an assumption of ~~primitive~~ man's inability to distinguish the animate from the inanimate. Spencer modifies Tylor's original concept by denying the latter assumption, showing, by certain examples, that since animals can distinguish the animate from the inanimate it is an injustice to attribute a lower stage of discriminating intelligence to man. Durkhetm again treats animism critically and recasts Tylor's and Spencer's later views by creating two categories of thought, *naturism,* which "addresses itself to the phenomena of nature, either the great cosmic forces, such as winds, rivers, stars or the sky, etc., or else the objects of various sorts which cover the surface of the earth, such as plants, animals, rocks, etc.," and *animism,* "which has spiritual beings as its object, spirits, souls, geniuses,

---

[189] EB Tylor, ~~*Primitive*~~ *Culture*, London (1903) vol. I.

demons, divinities, properly so-called, animated and conscious agents like men ... ordinarily not visible to human eyes." For some thinkers animism is the earlier phase of thought, naturism being a derived secondary form, and for others " the nature cult was the point of departure for religious evolution." So it appears, in regard to animism itself, as elementary and fundamental as the concept is as an original starting" point for religious thought, that the several points of view concerning both its definition and its place in religious growth render the position of one who attempts to deal dogmatically with the animistic doctrine open to criticism until the contested questions have been settled.

Later researches, however, show animism to be more than the older conception embraced, that it is based on the concept of magical power believed to be inherent in the phenomena of nature whether animate or inanimate. A more recent characterization of animism has been given [18] by Doctor Boas. He[190] says: "The fundamental concept bearing on the religious life of the individual is the belief in the existence of magic power, which may influence the life of man and which in turn might be influenced by human activity. In this sense magic power must be understood as the wonderful qualities which are believed to exist in objects, animals, men, spirits and deities and which are superior to the natural qualities of man. This idea of magic power is one of the fundamental concepts which occur among all Indian tribes. It is what is called *manito* by the Algonquian tribes; *wakanda* by the Siouan tribes, *orenda* by the Iroquois." By acquiring varying degrees of this supernatural force the various deities believed in by the American Indians are thought to derive their power. Objects in nature which are conceived also to be imbued with some of this spiritual force also come to be classified, by the same means, as incipient deities. This stage, called the pre-animistic stage, in which rites are addressed to impersonal forces has been classed by some religious theorists as one of the earliest phases of human religion. Human beings who through the possession of magic power become able to impress their fellows with their ability to work miracles in healing disease or in controlling the action of spirits are likewise regarded as possessing some of this supernatural force. Hence, we find in all ~~primitive~~ groups individuals to whom are attributed supernatural powers who are known as medicine men, magicians, witch-doctors or, more technically, as Shamans. Shamanism then may be said to be a practise based on the use of supernatural force.

Totemism

Totemism has, like animism, figured prominently in the classification of elementary religious concepts. A [19] better understanding of the great diversity of totemic phenomena in various parts of the world has left students today in a more critical frame of mind, with a less definite feeling as to what totemism really is than they had a decade ago. Tylor, Morgan, Hill-Tout, Robertson Smith, Haddon, Frazer, Lang, McLennan and Durkheim have within the last thirty years elaborated various explanatory theories which, on account of their attempted universal application, have been superseded in more recent years by those of Boas, Goldenweiser, Rivers, and other philosophers whose method has been more inductive.

Goldenweiser, allowing for the cases, which are encountered frequently, where the religious side of the totemic complex is nothing, ventures the definition: "Totemism is the tendency of definite social units (bound together through descent) to become associated with

---

[190] Article 'Religion', *Handbook of the American Indians,* Bulletin # 30, Bureau of American Ethnology.

objects and symbols of emotional value."[191]

Totemism implies the association of so many cultural traits which are not strictly concerned with religion that it never embraces the whole of religion, even when, as in the case of Polynesia, it has developed into a type of religion. For instance, in various regions of the globe we find the concept more characteristically based on the association of social units with belief in descent, taboo, dramatization of myths, ceremonies to multiply the totemic animal, with prerogatives in the ownership of myths, songs, dances, family crests, and the like. Most commonly associated with totemism, however, is exogamy. This is the prohibition of marriage within certain social divisions whose members regard themselves as relatives through maternal or paternal descent, as the case may be, from a common ancestor generally of the animal or plant kingdom. The explanation of this identity of social group and animal has been attempted by theorists in [20] several ways. For instance, Haddon believed that totemism originated from the idea that groups of people developed out of an earlier stage of their life when certain animals were hunted for food, into an attitude of reverence toward the creature and so came to abstain from killing or eating it. Frazer in a later work suggested that the institution originated in an economic arrangement by which the various clans contributed to each other's support by refraining from killing certain animals in order to multiply each other's game supply, and consequently developing a certain religious attitude toward the animal so protected. And there are other theories.

The concept is much too varied to accept any of these theories, none of which reconstructs any absolutely satisfactory universal theory of origin. The best recent authorities show that totemism must have started from many different origins in different regions and developed certain comparable characteristics through a process of convergence. It would be unwise, even if it were possible in this paper, to discuss further the question of the origin of totemism, and it seems inadvisable to prolong a discussion of the religious side of so complex and subjective a concept.

Fetishism

The belief that all things in Nature are animate and that they possess volition, immortality and other mysterious attributes has developed in the mind of ~~primitive~~ man an attitude of reverence and worship which students of religion denote by the term fetishism, a derivative from the Portuguese *feitico*, a charm, sorcery. Fetishism is the doctrine that objects, either natural or artificial, possess an essential magical power which converts them into creatures capable of responding to acts of influence such as invocation, sacrifice, flattery, bribery, supplication, imitative magic and the like. Accordingly, various objects in Nature, which appeal to the imagination of [21] superstitious human beings either by their curious appearance. it may be through dreams or visions, or through supposedly supernatural associations, become regarded as abodes of such *animic*. Such objects are cherished as material helpers, guides or protectors, or are held in fear as malevolent forces which have to be appeased by the various means of cajolery which man since time immemorial has known and practiced to deceive supernatural beings in his own favor. Fetishes may be acquired by individuals, by groups, or by nations for the promotion of their welfare. Fetishes may be small portable objects of every imaginable sort, or they may occur as artificial objects made with every device of ingenuity and art that man is capable of

---

[191] AA Goldenweiser, Totemism, an Analytical Study, *Journal of American Folk-Lore*, vol. 23, # 88 (1916): 275.

employing. In the former class we learn of such fetishes as bones, stones, fossils, feathers, sticks plain or decorated, hair, roots, berries, seeds, parts of animals and human beings, in fact anything, no matter how insignificant in itself, which has in the owner's mind at least some symbolic connection with occult power. Such minor fetishes are frequently known as charms, amulets, talismans, and luck-pieces. And indeed we of to-day have not entirely outgrown their use. Fetishes are often large and elaborate artifacts, representations or images which have become generally known as idols. The phenomenon of idolatry or image worship is thus a close associate of fetishism and so, also, is sacrifice. Africa is generally regarded as the region of the globe where fetishism has been most elaborately developed. Here it constitutes the greater part of religion, its devotees being organized into many fetish cults whose power is often of a political as well as of a religious nature.[192]

Taboo

Another manifestation of the ~~primitive~~ religious complex is taboo, a word of Polynesian origin. The term is [22] applied to an interdiction belonging to or placed upon a person, place, day, name, act, thought or any conceivable thing and idea which is thereby rendered sacred. In the case of objects, communication with the tabooed thing is forbidden under ordinary circumstances to all except a few persons having special privileges. Taboo may have a negative and a positive side; the former, denoting religious prohibition, is the more conspicuous in ~~primitive~~ life. In either aspect the term may be applied to definite periods of the life of the individual in connection with important events. It operates by governing the regulations observed by boys and girls at puberty; by parents before and after the birth of a child (*couvade*); by relatives after the decease of a person; by hunters and fishermen in their occupations; by shamans, doctors, or magicians desiring power to cure the sick, to prophesy or to conjure; and by novices about to enter secret societies. Such are only a few of the instances where taboo operates. The typical negative prohibitions which every student first associates with the taboo proper, however, consist in abstinence from hunting, fishing, war, women, sleep, certain kinds of work, and so forth, but especially in refraining from eating certain foods. The latter prohibition may be applied permanently in the life of an individual or a group in regard to the totemic animal, and it often applies similarly to the killing of certain animals. In ~~primitive~~ society the taboo of name mention and the taboo of intercourse are very common. The prohibition frequently covers the mention of the name of the dead, the mention of one's own name, the right of addressing the mother-in-law directly or vice versa, and the prohibition of intercourse between fathers-in-law and daughters-in-law as well.

Thus it may be seen that taboo is an important aspect of the phenomena of religion, influencing ~~primitive~~ ethical and social behaviour in general to an extent that makes as [23] it in some regions as broad a concept as that of religion itself. In Polynesia, particularly, the taboo was largely a method of government and the fear of retribution from supernatural sources was the direct cause of obedience to it.

~~Primitive~~ Ethics

Thus far in our discussion it must have been apparent to all that the question of the moral

---

[192] RH Nassau, *Fetishism in West Africa*, NY 1904.

influence of religion upon ~~primitive~~ life has been left unmentioned. The reason for this is that we are dealing with ~~primitive~~, not with civilized religions. The ethical characteristics of ~~primitive~~ man's religion are indeed as diverse in their types as are the ethnical types themselves. If, however, we separate, by a somewhat arbitrary line of division, the sphere of ~~primitive~~ life from that of civilized life, we find that in the ~~primitive~~ world relationship with the supernatural beings does not seem to involve the consideration of morals in the least.   In the religious systems prevailing throughout ~~primitive~~ America, Asia, Africa, and Australia there occur very few signs to indicate a belief in retribution during the soul's future life, for the deeds done in this life. As ubiquitous as the belief in a heaven of some sort may be in the ~~primitive~~ world at large, the absence of the concept of reward and punishment for behavior during life leaves the matter of ethical control entirely outside the pale of religion. Custom is thus left to control community as well as individual behavior. One could indeed define most ~~primitive~~ types of religion as being ceremonial systems of non-ethical philosophy and worship. This is a very thorough-going differential feature. It throws into glaring contrast the ~~primitive~~ as against the more advanced Messianic types of religion, and again leaves us to struggle with a theory as to whether the Messiah concept would have been produced independently by a process of gradual thought [24] evolution or whether it is to be accounted for by the hypothesis of supernatural revelation.

We do indeed find instances in the ~~primitive~~ world of the concept of sin, but sin Is in such cases merely the violation of a taboo or an arbitrary custom, finding its settlement in an immediate reaction by the community or by the performance of a ceremony of expiation intended to placate the supernatural force which has been offended. It is only among the Eskimo that any ceremonial atonement comparable to that of modern religions is required for a sin, and atonement there curiously enough is obtained by confession addressed to an anthropomorphic goddess {Sedna}, the Mistress of the Sea Mammals. In the case of these people there exist a number of arbitrary restrictions the transgression and subsequent concealment of which constitute sin. Such restrictions concern food and work. It is, for example, a transgression to perform certain work after a seal has been killed, or after a death has occurred; no work on caribou skin is allowed until sea ice has formed, and none on seal skins after the sea ice has commenced to melt. An elaborate code of social punishment also exists in ~~primitive~~ Africa where a highly organized system of legislation is, and has been for ages, in operation, though as a social-economic not a religious element of culture. Here again is something of a paradox in the fact that the savage is a creature of social self-control more strictly than is the civilized man who requires belief in a religious code threatening eternal punishment or reward for the maintenance of his good behavior.

There remains, accordingly, the impression in the mind of every thinker who studies the relationship between ethics and religion, that a tremendous gap lies between the ~~primitive~~ and the modern types of religion. Even allowing for great diversities in ~~primitive~~ tribal religions it may be generally asserted as true that the ~~primitive~~ [25] types are characteristically not ethical, since their systems do not embody ethical codes. Apparently this is due to the fact that the savage's conception of the superior beings rates them as too important, too egoistic to be concerned at all with what good or bad men may do to each other. This lack of association between religion and the control of behavior in life is so marked that we may generally regard the gap as the dividing line between the ~~primitive~~ and the advanced. Classifying the ~~primitive~~ types as non-ethical, non-retributive systems of philosophy we might attempt to account for the reason why the modern creeds instigated by Messianic personages, such as Moses, Christ, Mohammed or Buddha, bring the doctrines of religion to bear upon life as a moral power. Coordinating results in these speculations, it would seem that where ~~primitive~~ religions are strictly non-ethical the Messiah concept is also lacking. Should one attempt to claim that the culture hero or transformer might in the process of time have developed into a Messiah-personage, he would have to confront the difficulty of explaining why field investigations among" savages have failed to disclose evidences to show where culture heroes, shamans or semi-supernatural figures have metamorphosed directly into such Messiah-personages. The chief function of the Messiah being, as we have seen, to preach the doctrine of ethics as a part of religion, we cannot point to cases where a culture hero or mythical transformer does appear in any such capacity. The problem still remains, however, whether or not this conclusion may be due to lack of information from certain regions of the ~~primitive~~ world and whether future research will bring forth material showing how the ~~primitive~~ concept could develop into the concept of a Messiah. We must be content as yet with investigating the field to secure material covering the gaps of our knowledge [26] before we can hope to draw safe conclusions on a problem so greatly involving the comprehension of ~~primitive~~ man's history, as well as an understanding of his mind.

Culture Hero

The culture hero or transformer concept, which has already been frequently mentioned, is another concept as fundamental in the ~~primitive~~ world as that of animism. Particularly in America, where we have critical and abundant material collected from many regions, can the culture hero character be studied with advantage, so we shall use this field for drawing some concrete illustrations. The story of the so-called culture hero who gave the world its present shape, killing obnoxious monsters, giving man the arts and industries of his culture, is one of the most widely distributed myth-cycles on the continent. The culture hero or transformer, if we choose to call him such, appears first in a period when men are not differentiated from animals. With the appearance of the hero a new historic era is ushered in and we have the story of how men are given their culture and separated from their animal kindred. The transformer teaches men how to kill animals, to make fire and to clothe themselves, posing as a benevolent helper of mankind. But the same culture hero often appears in other groups of tales as a sly, low-principled trickster, even a marplot who vaingloriously thinks himself superior to all other beings whom he tries to deceive. Again, in the words of Boas,[193] "he appears as the victim of his own wiles who is often punished for his malevolence by the superiority of his intended victims. No method of warfare is too mean for him. No trick is too low to be resorted to provided it helps him to reach his selfish end. Often the end sought for is entirely unworthy of the hero who [27] shows such lofty altruism at other times in his career, for his chief aim in his baser moods is the acquisition of richcs and women."

It seems difficult to harmonize two such different aspects of the culture hero myth. Some investigators have tried to show that a gradual deterioration from a purer, earlier form of the myth explains how the more vulgar tales come in as additions to the old cycle of myths. An explanation, however, which does not necessarily involve the idea of literary degeneration 'would seem to be natural, an explanation by which the speculator would account for the dual aspect of the culture hero concept by some process of evolution. To my mind we may seek for such an explanation by regarding the base and vulgar aspects of the culture-hero stories as accretions which have grown up around the central figure of mythology, like stories clustering

---

[193] Introduction to "Traditions of the Thompson River Indians," James Teit, *Memoirs of the American Folk-Lore Society* 1900.

around a point of attraction. In many of the tales where the culture hero frames his actions for the benefit of mankind be is not prompted by altruistic motives but only by the desire to satisfy his own needs. Nevertheless, these tales are often interpreted as indications of an altruistic intention on the part of the hero. The latter attitude, however, does not obscure the purely egotistical motives which the hero possesses, because many of the changes which he accomplishes for the benefit of mankind are only incidentally beneficial. The less the altruistic idea is developed the less "will be the consciousness of a discrepancy between the tales representing the transformer as a benefactor and as a trickster. The higher it is developed the greater will be the discrepancy between these two groups of tales. Accordingly, we find that where the altruistic idea is emphasized the tales of the trickster are separated from the transformer tales and ascribed to another secondary hero. The personage of the hero character is then split into several parts, the one representing the high-principled [28] hero, the other retaining the basic features of the trickster cycle. The higher the civilization of the tribe, naturally the sharper the line seems to be drawn between the culture hero and the trickster.

Since there is a certain advantage in being able to refer to a specific case on this point, I should like to summarize from material gathered by myself, with which I am consequently more familiar, namely, the characteristics of the culture-hero tale as it is related by one of the tribes of the lower St Lawrence region, the Penobscot Indians of northern Maine.[194] Bearing upon the discussion just presented the points to be noted here are, the commingling of altruism with selfishness, and secondly the importance of mere accident in determining the character of transformations in nature. To the Penobscot mind, it would seem, the incongruity of the various parts of the transformer myth has not been very striking, although there is a tendency manifested in this direction, in the separation of the myths Into a primary and a secondary, profane, group by the native narrators.

The culture hero, in the tales of the tribes of this region, bears the name of *Gluskábe* which, literally translated. means 'The Man of Deceit,' 'The Liar'. The term, however, is not applied in a derogatory sense for it implies 'one who overcomes his opponents by strategy'. The sections following under separate numbers are abstracts of independent recitations in the order as given, forming the culture-hero cycle of myths.

Summary of the Penobscot Version of the
Culture-Hero (Gluskábe) Cycle.

I. Gluskabe's Childhood. He lives with grandmother, Woodchuck. He develops into a prodigious hunter as a [29] child. His grandmother prophesies a great future for him as the benefactor of posterity.

2. Gluskábe deceives the Game Animals. He induces them to enter his game bag by lying to them, prophesying the end of the world. His grandmother disapproves. Gluskábe releases the animals from the game close.

3. Gluskábe traps all the fish by a similar hoax. His grandmother reprimands him, and Gluskábe releases the fish.

4. Gluskábe employs a stone canoe. He seeks the home of the Wind Bird.

---

[194] *The* summary presented here is arranged from part of a collection of phonetically recorded texts with translations submitted by the writer several years ago to the Anthropological Division of the Geological Survey of Canada.

His hair is blown off by the force of the wind. He deceives the Wind Bird, and cripples him. The waters then become too calm, Gluskábe is obliged to cure and restore Wind Bird, who properly regulates the winds of the world thereafter.

5. Gluskábe seeks Grasshopper, the retainer of the world's tobacco. He steals his tobacco and seeds, bestows it abroad for mankind, and punishes Grasshopper by giving him only a temporary supply.

6. Gluskábe travels among the lakes and rivers of the north, reducing their dangers for the safety of posterity.

7. Gluskábe discovers people suffering from thirst. He seeks the monster *Aglebému* who withholds the world's water, and kills him. Then from the released water originates the Penobscot River, and the dying people, plunging into the flood, are transformed into various fish and amphibians. From these originate the present day family totemic groups.

8. Gluskábe pursues a monster cannibal moose. Squatty-woman (*Pukdjinskwess*) attempts to hinder him. He escapes her. Their snowshoe footprints become imprinted in the rock. Gluskábe kills the moose. He transforms the moose's intestines, and his own dog into stone, and also his kettle, which is now Mt Kineo.

9. Gluskábe goes in search of the Winter Deity. He is overcome and frozen by Winter. [30]

10. Gluskábe's grandmother, during his absence, is plagued by Foxes. Gluskábe returns, and punishes them.

11. Gluskábe seeks the source of Summer. He hides his eye leaving it in the care of the Chickadee. He encounters his father and his malevolent brothers. He undergoes a smoking test, and a gaming test, and wins both.

12. Gluskábe approaches the dancers who guard the Summer Fluid. He transforms two girls into toads. He steals the Summer Fluid, and escapes his pursuers by a ruse. He recovers an eye from Owl, who has stolen his. He then proceeds to the home of the Winter Deity with the Summer Fluid, and overcomes him by the heat.

13. Gluskábe finishes his earthly mission. With his randmother he departs to the immortal realm where they work, preparing weapons for the future world war, to aid posterity.

The following three episodes are told in detached form as supplements to the story of the hero's career. They are correctly felt, in the minds of the native myth narrators, to be incongruous with the character of the main transformer episodes.

14. Gluskábe fails to stop a Baby crying. He is defeated by the Baby in a filth-eating contest.

15. Gluskábe aids his uncle Turtle to secure women. Turtle projects part of himself beneath the river: this portion is swallowed by a fish. Gluskábe recovers it for him.

16. Gluskábe aids Turtle to marry the daughter of *Kellu,* a bird chief. At

the wedding-feast Turtle violates Gluskábe's rules and is scorched in the fire, whence originates the Turtle's shell. Turtle tries vengeance on Gluskábe. Gluskábe in payment causes Turtle to stab himself.

It seems advisable, in connection with tales like the preceding, since the question often arises among students [31] of ~~primitive~~ religion, to mention a common fallacy which has come into vogue in literature concerning the supposed belief of an anthropomorphic supreme deity among the American Indians. The Indians are often cited as illustrating the case of a ~~primitive~~ people paying reverence to a Great Spirit as a creator and controller of the world. No such monotheistic concept, however, does exist in aboriginal Indian religious beliefs in general, until the concept has been taught the natives by the missionaries. The zeal of the latter has often led them to "read in" their own ideas into their records, with the result that the great supernatural force, and oftentimes the mythical culture-hero figures, like the one just dealt with, have been misconstrued through the bias of the investigator. We should not overlook the fact, however, that the missionaries have correctly understood the situation when they have claimed that the ~~primitive~~ Americans possessed a consciousness of the life after death. The soul of the individual, in American mythology, is generally supposed to travel to a spirit land resembling ours. The journey thither is believed to be beset with many lurking dangers to be overcome by the soul. In some mythologies a slippery log has to be crossed, in others terrific precipices must be skirted, while in others we learn of colliding clouds which are to be avoided. The success of the soul in this journey depends largely upon good fortune, sometimes upon the strength of experience gained by having led a respectable life on earth, and sometimes upon the performance of mortuary rites by the surviving relatives. As describing the realm of departed spirits, the term "Happy Hunting Ground" seems to have been fairly well chosen. Life there is believed to be one of happiness and repletion.

The treatment of so complex a realm of thought has really no natural ending, as the student will learn for [32] himself if he undertakes to penetrate the literature of it. An arbitrary ending has to be made somewhere. There is, moreover, no single textbook to be used with implicit confidence as a *guide*. So until the time comes when scholars in the field of ~~primitive~~ religions, through intensive methods similar to those employed in classical and Semitic research, produce an adequate text and reference work, the few who stand before the panorama of the savage world can, I fear, do little more than surrender to the spectacle of its possibilities.

Bibliography

The beginner in this subject is recommended to consult WI Thomas, *Source Book for Social Origins* (University of Chicago Press), Part VI (Magic, Religion, Myth). An extensive bibliography of ~~primitive~~ religions is given here. RB Tylor, *~~Primitive~~ Culture,* Vol. 2, is valuable for general material and E Durkheim, *The Elementary Forms of the Religious Life,* translated from the French by JW Swain, is useful for the more theoretical treatment of the whole field.

Speck

Each Religion which has influenced the World's History is treated in this volume by a Specialist

RELIGIONS
OF THE
PAST AND PRESENT
Edited by DR J.A MONTGOMERY
Professor of Hebrew, University of Pennsylvania

UNIVERSITY OF PENNSYLVANIA LECTURES

The authors are members of the Department of the History of Religions at the University of Pennsylvania, a Department of remarkable strength and variety.

CONTENTS AND CONTRIBUTORS

PRIMITIVE RELIGION ... FRANK G SPECK, PH.D
THE EGYPTIAN RELIGION ... W MAX MÜLLER, PH.D
THE RELIGION OF BABYLONIA AND ASSYRIA ... MORRIS JASTROW, JR., PH.D., LL.D
THE HEBREW RELIGION ... JAMES A MONTGOMERY, PH.D, S.T.D
THE RELIGION OF THE VEDA ... FRANKLIN EDGERTON, PH.D
BUDDHISM ... FRANKLIN EDGERTON, PHD
BRAHMANISM AND HINDUISM ... FRANKLIN EDGERTON, PH.D
ZOROASTRIANTSM ... ROLAND G KENT, PH.D
MOHAMMEDANISM ... MORRIS JASTROW, JR, PH.D, LL.D
THE RELIGION OF GREECE ... WALTER WOODBURN HYDE, PH.D.
THE RELIGION OF THE ROMANS ... GEORGE DEPUE HADZSITS, PH.D.
THE RELIGION OF THE TEUTONS ... AMANDUS JOHNSON, PH.D.
EARLY CHRISTIANITY ... WILLIAM ROMAINE NEWBOLD, PH.D.
MEDIEVAL CHRISTIANITY ... ARTHUR C HOWLAND, PH.D.

§ J.B LIPPINCOTT COMPANY
Publishers
Philadelphia

Shawnee Female Deity

Introduction

DURING field work among the Shawnee m 1933 and 1934,[195] it was found that mention of a female deity was forever on the lips of ~~informants~~[196] from all three bands of Shaw' nee in Oklahoma. She was commonly called Our Grandmother (*kohkomhθena*),[197] not less commonly referred to as a creator in general or more specifically as a creator of people or of the universe and everything contained in it, including the earth; she was known to have personal names which were infrequently used. Only in respect to knowledge of her personal name is Our Grandmother in the least esoteric. She is accepted and understood by "the folk" in great detail.

Her personality, her associates, her creations and revelations are described in mythologic accounts which are on the whole not contradictory but none the less show numerous differences in detail. Still, variants here are no more numerous than variants in other departments of Shawnee mythology. As a mythological character, Our Grandmother is the dominant member of a small pantheon, a Supreme Deity.

To a greater or less extent, she establishes, observes, or participates in every aspect of Shawnee religion upon which information was secured. Other religious forces, many of them personified, are potent, but as a holy figure, Our Grandmother is unquestionably supreme. Early cultural differences between the various political divisions (*čalakaθa, mekoče, kišpoko, θwikila,* and *pekowi*) are reflected at the present time in three separate bands in Oklahoma: the Absentee Shawnee living between the towns of Norman and Shawnee, the Cherokee Shawnee near White Oak, and the Eastern Shawnee near Miami. It is remarkable that these three bands, and ultimately perhaps the original political divisions, show a consistently unified attitude towards Our Grandmother. She enjoys only nominal association in parts of Shawnee religion which concern the individual *qua* individual: quest of the guardian spirit and witchcraft, for examples; she is firmly integrated in those parts of religion which are communal in expression or interest,

---

[195] Acknowledgments for financial assistance must be made to the Indiana Fellowship at Yale University (1933) and to the American Council of Learned Societies (1934) A basic Shawnee ethnography is being prepared by Erminie Voegelin who put at my disposal her copious field notes. Dr Truman Michelson, of the Bureau of American Ethnology, generously allowed us to read his Shawnee field notes, MS 2719, 1911, and MS 1711, 1916.

[196] ~~Informants~~ who are credited with specific viewpoints in this paper are indicated by their initials: Mary Williams (MW), 25 years old, Billie Williams (BW), 64 years, James Clark (JC), 50 years, Jennie Cegar (jc) 70 years, Thomas Wildcat Alford (TWA), 74 years, all of the Absentee Shawnee; Frank Daugherty (FD), 75 years, of the Cherokee Shawnee; Nancy Sky (NS), 62 years, who comes from the Black Bob band, now extinct, but spent most other life with the Eastern Shawnee.

[197] Shawnee texts are being prepared for publication. In order to avoid duplication, only a few strategic Shawnee words are given in this paper. These words are written in the phonemic orthography described in *Shawnee Phonemes* (Language 11: 23-27 1935). It should be noted that the glottalic phoneme, here written *h*, is phonetically a glottal stop before consonants and a fricative before vowels.

as for example concern with the future of the group, i.e, prophecy, and with ceremonial dances. [4]

The Creator's Personality

Information is to be had concerning the Creator's appearance, her personal names, her language, her dwelling place, and her associates. The extensions of the Creator's personality, especially her dwelling place and associates, are of infinitely greater importance in Shawnee religion than the more intimate details concerning her person.

In the innumerable references to Our Grandmother, little concerning her appearance save the implication that she is an anthropomorphic female being is vouchsafed. Indirect evidence would suggest that she has grey hair, for one of the hairs from her head is found on some newly born babies. Her immense size may be judged from the fact that in the Orpheus tale she can pick up adult men and hide them in cracks in the lodgepole of her house (MW). Opinions as to her appearance vary, however. She is also said to be a little woman with white hair and good teeth (NS). Again, she is described as having separated teeth (JC). Perhaps because she can change her appearance, no particular shape or size is felt to be especially characteristic for her. That she wears short skirts may be seen when she is re' fleeted in the full moon. In the Rescue of Corn tale, she is painted with round spots on her cheeks and her hair is parted down the middle by Shawnee attendants.

Her personal name is most frequently given as *paapooθkwe*, which is said to mean "cloud." Compare the inanimate noun *paapooθkwaki*, cloud, *paapooθkwakiiwal*i, clouds, and the inanimate intransitive verb *pooθkwatwi*, it is cloudy, *pooθkwahki*, subordinate mode. Other names ascribed to her are *šikalaapihši* and *liiθiikapihši*. Both have the characteristic feminine ending -*hši*, but are otherwise not clearly analyzable. Jones[198] gives the name of "the Great Spirit" or "Good manitu" as *weshellequa* and quotes Captain McKee as pronouncing *Coashellequaa*. Neither of these names is recognized at the present time. The stem *maneto* is employed after the stem *mači*, bad, to describe the devil (*mačimaneto*); the stem *maneto* is also used before animal names to indicate that the animal in question is supernatural, usually in an unpleasant sense. When used by itself, not in compound with other stems, maneto means snake or serpent, and is rarely applied to the Creator. TWA says that formerly Our Grandmother's personal name was kept a secret and known only to a few people. JC says her names were generally known. She was called *paapooθkwe* in the 1934 fall Bread Dance.

Formerly certain Shawnee doctors who attended children had knowledge of a special non-Shawnee language, thought of as a private dialect of Our Grandmother and known by children under four years of age but unlearned as soon as Shawnee was learned. When these doctors died, opportunities to secure specimens of this language were lost. The Shawnee are aware that their Sauk neighbors still have doctors who are able to converse with babies, and the presence of such doctors is reported for the Prairie Potawatomi and Menomini,[199] [5] and possibly for the Fox.[200] Shawnee mythology contains no reference to the Creator's language. Our

---

[198] David Jones, *A Journal of Two Visits Made to Some Nations of Indians on the West Side of the Ohio, in the Years 1772 and 1773* (reprinted for J. Sabin, New York, 1865), 62.

[199] Alanson B Skinner, *The Mascoutens or Prairie Potawatomi Indians*: Part III, *Mythology and Folklore* (Bulletin, Public Museum, Milwaukee, vol. 6, no. 3: 327-411, 1917), 380.

[200] Truman Michelson, *Autobiography of a Fox Woman* (Annual Report, Bureau of American Ethnology, 40: 291-349, 1918-19): 343, footnote 29.

Grandmother certainly speaks Shawnee, and by implication other languages as well; the spirits of the dead seem to continue speaking their native language, for they are tribally segregated.

Knowledge or Our Grandmother's present dwelling place is gained most convincingly from the accounts of living Shawnee who have made the journey there and back again, a not uncommon Journey for modern prophets. The reports of those who made this journey are obviously influenced by the description in the Orpheus tale which differs from those who have made personal observations in emphasising the spaciousness of the dwelling. When the four mortal visitors in the Orpheus tale arrive at the door of the typical Algonkin bark house in which Our Grandmother lives, they find her sitting on a sleeping scaffold weaving a basket (*škimota*, a term not applied to any earthly basket). Her Silly Boys enter and criticize her housekeeping, remarking that they detect a very evil smell, an allusion to their pretence at being cannibals. They are of course aware of the visitors whom they attempt to frighten. When Our Grandmother tires other Silly Boys, she picks up a poker and hits them on their legs. Then she prepares a meal in the usual Shawnee manner, building a fire and cooking, using pottery dishes and bark platters and plates, and wooden spoons; but she prepares her food in a little "inexhaustible food supply" clay pot. Her visitors are surprised when they find that they cannot eat all of the food contained m the little pot, which is emptied only after she has eaten.

Variants of the Orpheus tale differ not so much in the description of the dwelling place itself as in details concerning its approach. In an Eastern Shawnee variant, it is merely stated that an ocean is crossed, but much land was also traversed because several pair of mocassins were worn out on the journey. In an Absentee Shawnee variant, the visitors go to a western region beyond the end of the earth, crossing four oceans, passage over the last one being possible only as the rhythmically rising and falling sky ascends and leaves an open gap. While the Journey seems to be on a horizontal plane, the visitors find themselves in a higher region with Our Grandmother because she shows them a "sky-window" through which she looks down on her earthly children to determine whether they are obedient, and because on their return journey the visitors take a short route back to earth, being lowered through the sky-window in a basket and passing through a region located between earth and heaven m which birds and others live. This suggests "levels of heaven" of which the Fox have four[201] and the Delaware twelve.[202] In this sense, the Shawnee Creator does not live on the very highest level of heaven, however, because the sun, the same sun which passes over the [6] earth and not a brighter light as among the Delaware,[203] passes over the land to which the Shawnee dead go.

The Shawnee land of the dead is simply described as the place where the Creator stays or lives, and is said to resemble the earth in every way. Only sporadic details are given. Thus, even though Our Grandmother does not take sweat baths, she has a sweat lodge for doctoring visitors. The souls of the virtuous dead are segregated by tribes, which are further subdivided into kin groups. An especially pleasant place of constant dancing and feasting is reserved for the souls of warrior men and women. The souls of the dead must theoretically be equated to the souls of the unborn to allow for rebirth, but sometimes the latter are spoken of as a separate group. From whatever group it comes, a soul goes to earth and jumps through the mother's vagina and into the

---

[201] *Idem,* 135-36, 139.

[202] Frank G Speck, A *Study of the Delaware Indian Big House Ceremony* (Publications, Pennsylvania Historical Commission, ~~2 vols~~, Harrisburg, Pa., 1931), 2: 175, 177.

[203] M.R Harrington, *Religion and Ceremonies of the Lenape* (Indian Notes and Monographs, New York, 1921): 53-54.

body of the child through the fontanelle just before birth.

An Eastern Shawnee variant would have it that babies live rather on the little stars of the Milky Way before they are born. Constellations in general are residences or personifications of mythologic figures who are sometimes accompanied by mortals. Cumulus cloud formations show Our Grandmother's grandson playing and making various ephemeral animals for the amusement of people on earth. Heavenly bodies are spoken of as though they were in a sense suburbs of the Creator's proper residence. The moon, for example, would seem to be close enough to be a "shade" or shadow for Our Grandmother, presumably as a mirror in which she is reflected, and so ceremonies are held at full moon when she may be seen, bending over a pot, cooking.

The souls of the dead and (or) the unborn are temporary, or at least more or less recent, associates of Our Grandmother. Her permanent associates include her grandson whose personal name is Rounded-side (*haapočkilaweeθa*) according to the Absentee Shawnee and Cloudy Boy (*paapooθičskilawehθiiθa*) according to the Cherokee Shawnee, her little dog, and in the Orpheus tale at least her Silly Boys who are giants if their feet, which make tracks five feet long, are in proportion to the rest of their body. Sometimes a little bantam rooster is added to this list (NS), and the devil is sometimes present, not as an Indian but as a white man; in one description he is said to be a cloven-hoofed Hebrew. Cyclone Man (also described as a woman) was mentioned both as living with Our Grandmother and with his colleague, West Wind.

The Shawnee pantheon includes also deities which dwell on various levels in the universe, which is thought of as an amygdaloid figure containing the earth at its broad base and the home of the Creator near its apex, just below the sun. There appears to be some feeling for a level of heaven above the Creator, but its resident is absent in the current mythology. The levels below the Creator (including the observable heavenly bodies, invisible regions of the winds, floating islands, stations for birds, etc, and the earth with regions within the earth) are almost densely populated with mythological figures and minor deities. [7] These have a certain power of their own but in their adventures are never quite free from the controlling influence of the Creator. An example in point is the tale, Rescue of Corn Person (translation from the variant of MW):

> A long time ago two old women were being lived with by one man. Once when it was day time he alone, the man, stayed home. Finally it was late in the afternoon but still those with whom he was staying had not come, so he thought to cook for himself; after waiting awhile he went to find and gather roasting ears of corn.
>
> When he came over there, he would begin to take roasting ears off the stalk. Perhaps he was lucky he came, for in that place corn is growing which is of curious shape. The thing which he found looked like a woman's vagina. Now he said that he heard about her; the man always heard, he said, "There is a saying that the Corn Person, our mother, is a woman; if it is really true that she is called this name, she will be embarrassed now when I have intercourse with her." Then he pulled ouc his penis; he stuck that in the place where the corn was cracked.
>
> After he had intercourse with her, then from there he went back to the house. Now the Corn Person went away along through the night. Now the old woman who stays there arose early in the morning; right now she went to the corn crib when she arose. When she arrived over there, there wasn't any corn.

An account follows of how the rescuer had to cross four oceans as in the Orpheus tale, for Corn Person fled to Our Grandmother who created her. Corn Person was persuaded to return to earth only when the rescuer argued that it was Our Grandmother's intention that she should benefit the Shawnee on earth.

It happens sometimes that the Shawnee take what would seem to be an unfair advantage of their knowledge of Our Grandmother's instructions to the personified forces of nature. The Creator told the winds that they must treat Indian women as though they were their own sisters, and not stare at the women when they were naked; she also told the women that they must respect the winds. This injunction is not always followed by women who sometimes pull their skirts up to their waist when it is cloudy, thus frightening the wind' borne clouds back in embarrassment.

Another and functionally distinct type of associate which Our Grandmother created is the witness, an intermediary between Shawnee who are praying for assistance and the ultimate source of all assistance, the Creator. The term for witness, *teepweewe*, means also truth, being a nominalized form of the verb *teepwe*, it is true. No Shawnee individual would care to give a categorically limited list of witnesses. Rather, the notion seems to be that if anything has been used as a witness, then it is a witness. But a feeling for relative importance prevails: tobacco is the leader of the witnesses; fire, water, and eagle are of" first rate importance. Other witnesses are in a sense subsidiary.

We find among the Fox mention of two ""reporters" which are similar to the Shawnee concept of witnesses. It will be noted that both the Fox and the Shawnee accord fire a major role among their witnesses; the sky is secondary in Fox, correcting fire's report in case the latter makes any mistakes, while in Shawnee the sky is a subsidiary witness. The [8] dog might be considered a witness both for the Fox and Shawnee with some reservations. The Shawnee have many more witnesses than the Fox.[204]

Tobacco functions as a witness in two ways. Upon minor occasions a pinch of tobacco is put on the ground; for major events, as the Bread Dance, prayer for rain, or preparations for a hunting trip, tobacco is burned, never smoked. The smoke from the burning tobacco is compared to a telephone connecting the people's words to Our Grandmother. The same is true of the smoke from tobacco smoked in council.

The smoke from fire likewise serves to transmit the people's prayers to the Creator, but fire has an additional function to warn Cyclone Man that Our Grandmother's children are living near the fire.

Eagle feathers are used as a witness at ceremonial dances. Eagle does not breed with any other kind of bird, but remains faithful to his own species; accordingly, his feathers serve as a faithful witness.

Certain witnesses are better suited to one sex than the other. Tobacco and fire are more especially men's witnesses, while water is sometimes felt to be particularily {ok} suitable as a woman's witness.

Subsidiary witnesses include Thunderbirds, sacred bundles, cedar in peyote meetings, the four winds equated with the four directions, the stars, the sky, all uncultivated plants used as

---

[204] Truman Michelson, *Contributions to Fox Ethnology* (Bulletin, Bureau of American Ethnology, 85, 1927): 85, 109-110, 127, 145, 146; *Notes on the Buffalo-Head Dance of the Thunder Gens of the Fox Indians* (*idem*, 87, 1928): 4, 19, 29, 47, 51; *Observations on the Thunder Dance of the Bear Gens of the Fox Indians* (*idem*, 89, 1929): 33-37, 47, 51-53; *Contributions to Fox Ethnology II* (idem, 95, 1930): 49, 175; *Notes on the Fox Wâoanōwiweni* (*idem*, 105, 1932): 127, 129.

medicinal herbs. Certain of these have special powers and are spoken of as Our Grandmother's partners; they may be directly appealed to. Thus, Thunderbirds are prayed to for rain. Each of the forty-eight stars in the American flag has a Shawnee name. The Indians accepted the stars as witnesses to their treaty of peace with the whites. Subsequently, when the whites were going to fight, the stars came down to advise the Indians.

Creations and Revelations

Creations can be divided into four periods, from an external analytic point of view. The first period concerns the time before Our Grandmother, for which one obscure reference to an otiose deity who originated Our Grandmother is made (JC). This single reference, cautiously offered by an excellent informant as a remark made by his father which he did not quite understand or remember, may reflect an earlier period of Shawnee mythology or may merely reflect a confused bit of mythology from a neighboring tribe. It was during this first period, at any rate, that the Creator descended from the void above and created the basis of the earth, a turtle, the earth to rest upon the turtle, bodies of water to rest upon the earth, and successively other observable features of heaven and earth. Most of the cosmic creations were performed while the Creator and her grandson and little dog were living on the recently completed earth. Some variants note the presence of the devil. People are [9] taken for granted rather than specified. The earthly residence of a presumably small group before the flood marks the second period. During this period Our Grandmother permits her grandson, and in some variants the devil, unwholesome license. The third period is the time after the flood when Our Grandmother was still on this earth. The fourth period extends to the present time and is marked by the residence of Our Grandmother above the earth, from which place she dispenses medicine and other benefits to mortal visitors.

During the first three periods. Our Grandmother originates nothing bad, only beneficial things. Evil origins and happenings are ascribed to her grandson and constant companion, Rounded-side, or to another grandson introduced in some variants, the devil, over whom she has little control; also, the Creator herself occasionally bungles in her creations. But once she retires to her present residence, her creations or rather instructions are without the least suggestion of bungling. Her grandson, Rounded-Side, no longer originates catastrophes, but innocently plays with cumulus cloud formations. When the devil punishes, he does so under her auspices. She tolerates the nonsense of her Silly Boys, but without question has firm control over them. But she herself is less given to continuing the creation of good things. Rather she guards jealously her accomplished work, boasts about her power in a way calculated to arouse awe, plays the role of policewoman rather than benevolent deity, and on occasion metes out punishment.

The flood is precipitated by Rounded-side (translation from an Eastern Shawnee variant by NS):

> Long ago there were people right here, the one who created us, Our Grandmother, and the little boy, Rounded-side, her grandson. "Don't do this, you must always go this way," she told him but that little boy would think, "What's that tabu for, I wonder." (In an Absentee Shawnee variant, the prohibition is specifically against going west.)
> Now that boy runs off. Now he goes this way. Finally he found him. He went in the house. There he is inside, a big man having a big stomach.
> Now that boy is there. Finally late in the evening he went home. Now he

goes back again. He mocks the hoot owl.

Now he moves fast. He runs. He moves fast. Now he has a knife in his hand. Now he sticks him, he sticks him in his stomach. (The boy cuts a transparent fish monster in the Absentee Shawnee variant.)
Now that water is spilling out. Now the boy runs outside and he is being chased by that water. Now he runs home. He moves fast. He comes running up there to his grandmother.

Now they run away from the water. They climb on a tree. (In the Absentee variant they escape in a boat.) All the people are drowned.

Now that one, Our Grandmother, is worrying. Finally she calls that crawfish. Finally he comes. He brings earth in his hand. (In the Absentee variant, Turtle and Water Lizard dive unsuccessfully before Crawfish dives and brings up mud.) Now Our Grandmother takes the earth. He brings earth again, and a little bit more again. Now she calls that buzzard. Now he comes. He, the buzzard, comes. The buzzard rubs it on his wings. "You must dry the earth," she tells him. Now that buzzard goes away. He goes and dries it. He goes and flys. [10]

Oh, now the earth is dry all over. Now when it got dry, then the water goes below. However, the old folk are all dead. (In a Cherokee Shawnee variant, the Creator deliberately instigates a flood to destroy the people whom she made in the first creation because they are too large, too strong, too destructive.)

There follows an account of creation in the post-flood period, which agrees with other variants insofar as the origin of the present day Shawnee are accounted for.

~~Informants~~ are well aware of the innumerable differences in accounts dealing with this period, a state of affairs which is calmly accepted. "That's the way it is. Different people say that the Shawnee were created in different ways" (jc). Differences are, however, chiefly concerned with the order of creation of the political divisions. It seems probable that each political division formerly had its own origin tale. The following paraphrase is from the variant of MW.

Curiously enough, Our Grandmother did not create the Shawnee first, but began with the Delaware. When she completed a Delaware man and woman, she put them on the east side of a fire which she had kindled. Then she created one Shawnee division, in the form of an old man and old woman. After this she created a young couple who were expected to have children who would constitute three of the Shawnee divisions. Here, apparently, her interest in creating people ceased. On the way home her grandson, Rounded-side, aroused her suspicions when he wanted to hunt deer. She warned him not to return to tease the couple she had created and left to "play together" (copulate). Her grandson immediately returned to the couple, created the *pekowi* and *kišpoko* divisions, and insulted the young woman whom Our Grandmother had created. The young couple were unable to have intercourse for. two years because Our Grandmother misplaced their genitals when creating them. (The Creator's blundering, in an Eastern Shawnee variant, consisted in misplacing arms and backbone.) During the first year they fashioned dolls out of black mud and later threw the dolls away across the ocean. From these playthings of the young couple negroes originated. To the negroes Our Grandmother gave a language and a way to live. She seems to have had no objection to others creating people. Indeed, it was in her presence that her grandson created all the remaining Indian tribes so that the *kišpoko* division would never become lonesome, i.e., have plenty of enemies to fight. Once people were created, by herself or others, she was deeply concerned for their future welfare. She repaired the blundering she was guilty of in creating her first young couple, and they had twin boys from whom the remaining political divisions are derived.

In some such way, Shawnee people are accounted for, but the problem of providing a plan of living for these people still remained. The Creator asks her grandson, "What are you going to give *pekowi* to make a living from and keep healthy on? What will *kišpoko* have to make a living from?" and seems to regard this task as both more difficult and more interesting than that of creating the people. She accomplishes this task in the main single-handed, and while her grandson gives to the *pekowi* divisions "wheat and other kinds of herbs" and to the *kišpoko* alien tribes to fight, it is apparent that in so doing he is merely understudying the Creator's role.

Our Grandmother gave a sacred bundle to the first political division which she created; this bundle was then given into the custody of other divisions and was finally divided among the divisions. Opinion also has it that each division was originally given a separate bundle. Other members of the Creator's pantheon involved are the Thunderbirds and her grandson. The latter [11] gave the *kišpoko* division its bundle which originally contained feathers from the Thunderbirds. Perhaps the small wooden figure of a boy in the bundle of the *θwikila* division is a representation of Our Grandmother's grandson.

During the post-flood creations, Our Grandmother brought all the divisions together on this side of the ocean. It would seem that some or most of the divisions were originally created on this side, but at least *mekoče* and *čalakaθa* (in one variant only the latter) had to be brought over. Perhaps because the political divisions were then assembled together, other benefits which the Creator dispensed in the post-flood period are generally spoken of as lessons for the Shawnee as a whole. She taught them how to take care of themselves, how to live, to conduct ceremonial dances, how to raise corn and hunt, what kind of houses to build, and their laws. The Shawnee laws (*kwteletiiwena*) are noteworthy for their extreme length and comprehensiveness of subject matter. The laws for men are taught to boys, the laws for women to girls. A text has been secured of the former which is largely given in the first person, as though Our Grandmother herself were talking.

After the Creator retired to her present residence – how and when are not vouchsafed to us – she continued to dispense benefits to the Shawnee, supplementing her creations in the post-flood period. She habitually gives visitors to her home instructions to take with them when they return to earth. To the visitors in the Orpheus tale she brings plants which were also growing on earth and gives instructions in the use of these plants in doctoring so that their remedial effects may be taken advantage of on earth. At the same time she teaches her visitors the sacred ways of making fire. She also arouses in the minds other visitors a healthy respect for her own powers by constantly answering their thoughts before they are expressed. One visitor thinks to himself that Our Grand' mother is unaware of their presence at her door; again, he suspects that she knows what he *is* thinking about. To these thoughts Our Grandmother replies in a way which frightens her visitors.

"You don't have to tell me that you are here; I know that you are. I knew when you started on your journey; I knew when you thought of coming here before you held your council.... Yes, I always know what you're thinking."

She replies to the surprise which her visitors express at her ability to finish all the food in the "inexhaustible food-supply" receptacle with a statement which is still believed, "Well, I'm the Creator. And I can do anything; that's why I can eat all the food. You are only children."

Our Grandmother nowadays receives but one type of visitor, men and women who have prophetic inclinations. Her communications to these modern visitors consist chiefly in ad' vice not to deviate from her established ways, and in explanations of the future. Potentially, however, she may still create new ceremonies by instructing her visitors in what to do when they return to earth. In this way, according to an Absentee Shawnee variant, the Buffalo Head Dance of the Cherokee Shawnee was recently originated; but the Cherokee Shawnee themselves have a different version of its origin. An old woman who visited Our Grandmother recently brought to the Absentee Shawnee additional rites to be associated with the *kišpoko* sacred bundle; a male visitor brought instructions for the performance of the Men's Dance.

No complete account of Our Grandmother's creations is given in any one place. As the various periods of creation are treated in the mythology, typical creations are mentioned, [12] as has been noted. The nearest approach to a comprehensive list of creations occurs in the Shawnee laws. As specific items of nature or culture are described, their origin is generally attributed to Our Grandmother. From these various sources, it is clear that Our Grandmother's creations are always beneficial to the Shawnee directly and to mankind in general. The presence of harmful people and animals in the world today is explained away in one way or another.

Witches or people who wield a maleficent power over others exist without sanction of the Creator; indeed, they are as cordially disliked by Our Grandmother as by the Shawnee. Hence, Our Grandmother would not approve of a sweat lodge doctor or any other powerful Shawnee helping a witch who is ill.

The chief witching substance is a piece of the indestructible snake flesh which was secured from the original monster *maneto*. Our Grandmother, inconsistently enough, created *maneto* in the concrete sense of snakes of various sorts. The inconsistency is resolved in the explanation that when *maneto* (snakes) were created, our Grandmother told them to hold a council every year and explain her rules to their young and not to bother mankind; subsequently, the *maneto* (snakes) became disobedient.

Rodents and insects in general Our Grandmother did not create, but she did create harmless things like lizards which do not bite or cause damage by chewing. Lizards are not in a class with harmful things like mosquitoes and rats, which must be attributed to the consumed bones of witches' dust, sometimes said to be blown on by the devil.

Cyclone Man commands respect not because of any capacity for good he possesses, but because he often withholds disasters he could inflict. Being a creation of Our Grandmother, be is not regarded as distinctly evil, but visitations from him are certainly not desired. Oliver

Spencer[205] gives a pertinent description of a Shawnee's behavior during a hurricane which lay bare a wide swath in the nearby forest and which terrified young Spencer.

The Indians were perfectly calm ... gazing with a delighted sort of wonder and frequently expressing their admiration at more vivid bolts or heavier peals, with the customary exclamation, wawhaugh! waugh!

Creator's Participation in Religion

Shawnee religious observations make ubiquitous reference to the Creator. The annual ceremonial dances are said to be performed to worship Our Grandmother and thereby pre' serve mankind and the world. Other ceremonies have perhaps less ambitious intentions or imply a more direct, single purpose, but even so Our Grandmother is at least mentioned. Even if a ceremony is not primarily devoted to her, she will punish its neglect. In addition to her constant observation of the Shawnee from above, she makes certain appearances on earth to inspect or participate in ceremonies at closer range. More than that, she already knows what sort of behavior to expect, and she will in special circumstances communicate her foreknowledge to others. And finally, she is recognised as an important factor in the [13] efficacy of essentially independent religious forces, as sacred bundles, magical practises, and guardian spirits.

The annual ceremonial dances provide the chief vehicle for worshipping Our Grandmother. These ceremonies differ in their preliminary preparations, in their performances, and in their immediate objectives, but share in their particular parts a direct, lengthy prayer to the Creator. It is the spring and fall Bread Dances, .the former having as its immediate objective a plea for plentiful crops, the latter for plentiful hunting, which require the most elaborate preparations for the culminating feast. Twelve specially selected men hunt for game which twelve women cook. All ceremonies include a feast, however. The Cherokee Shawnee Green Corn Dance is actually quite a different ceremony from the Absentee Shawnee Men's Dance, but the two are sometimes equated because both occur at the height of summer when the first crops ripen and are acknowledged with thanks. Formerly the Doll dance, associated with false faces, served in annual worship of the Creator. Each political division had a doll which the Absentee Shawnee called *paaθkaka*, a term reserved by the Cherokee Shawnee for false face. The Doll Dances were discontinued before the Civil War, but a Seneca version of the False Face ceremony was subsequently reintroduced to the Eastern Shawnee for a short time. The Buffalo Head Dance forms an addendum to the Green Corn Dance of the Cherokee Shawnee. It is not given by the other Shawnee bands and is exceptional in being the only annual ceremonial dance which Our Grandmother did not create; it has, nevertheless, taken on the general pattern and spirit of the divinely created dances. It was originally a war dance given to Tecumseh (*circa* 1800) by his guardian spirit, a buffalo. Those who perform it nowadays, all kin of Tecumseh, are conscious of its secular origin but say that their purpose in performing it is to worship Our Grandmother. Prayer to the Creator is especially for plants which buffalo, now nonexistent, find nourishing. The ceremony is paradoxical in many ways and is interesting in this connection as demonstrating implicitly the extent to which the annual ceremonial dances are felt to be occasions for worshipping the Creator.

Variety in prayers to the Creator is determined more by differences in interest of the

---

[205] C.M Spencer, *Indian Captivity* (New York 1852): 51.

individual praying than by the different ceremonies. The words of the prayer are only slightly changed for different ceremonies. Approximately the same emphases are given in all prayers. When a famous old orator, now deceased, unduly emphasised his personal interest in abstinence from whiskey, he was no longer asked to deliver the prayer. The following specimen, a translation from MW's reproduction of the 1933 fall Bread Dance prayer, was read in Shawnee to a few ~~informants~~ who immediately assumed that it had been transcribed at the Bread dance. It is, as a matter of fact, considerably shorter than the actual prayer.

Well now, all of you, my sisters and my brothers, you must come close around here to our seats, you must listen. That's the place we are coming to. For that reason, the one who is called *paapooθkwe* created our lives for us. That, to repeat, is why you (addressing Creator) created us, for us to pray to you at this season. For that again you must have pity. You created for us the Corn Person, and another thing (addressing Pumpkin), you, Pumpkin Person, you should lie still and [14] grow beautifully. For that also you (addressing Creator) have pity. Our Corn Person (addressing Creator) you created to produce more food. And another thing. Earth Person, you (addressing Earth Person), the Creator created you to be still and hold us on your lap for eternity. You must grow out well and settle down with a green head. For that also you (addressing Creator) have pity. Now all of you around here who are sitting down and facing us (addressing the winds), my grandfathers, carry us along slowly. For that reason the Creator created you when you go by at all times, you North Wind Person. Now also you. Summer Man, that's why she created you so that you could carry along heat for your grandchildren in that way as you slowly pass along Because of that again (addressing Creator) you have pity. And all you Tree Men, you who are standing up growing and producing for us. And also you. Water Person, what I am asking you is to be still as you lie down floating along. Because of that also (addressing Creator), you must have pity. All of you Thunderers, my grandfathers, you all quietly bring water and sprinkle for us at the places where we live, as you go slowly around. But because of that again (addressing Creator), you must have pity. Also you, you Cyclone Man, you take pity on us out here where all of us are created. Because of that also (addressing Creator), you must have pity. That is a pitiful way in which I am supplicating you, my grandfathers and my grandmothers. Because of that also (addressing Creator), you must have pity. Now also you (addressing fire in center of dance square), you who are Fire Person, and you (addressing tobacco), Old Man, you witnesses whom the Creator created for us, you are carrying us along, you are working for us in that you take up there our message, the prayers of your grandchildren. Now from here on, give our life some more (in addition to the things already possessed and mentioned) for eternity, as you create for us. Because of that also, you must have pity.

Because (addressing spectators) she created us and took pity on us that way, we pray to her when the time comes for us to give a dance and pray to her at that place up there. In that way we make her feel good, as we are being interesting to the one who created us. She said that she would feel good over there if she saw her grandchildren having a lively dance and prayer. Because of that also, (addressing Creator) you must have pity. That's why too (addressing spectators) that if she is forgotten by her grandchildren for eternity *paapooθkwe* says, "I will feel badly." If she finds only the tracks of insects on our dance-ground at such a time, she would not hear her grandchildren praying to her any more. What she would do next would be to come and discard us in some way that would be frightful for us.

And also all you young men and my sisters, you must respect this way in which we pray. It might be better even for the time being if you did not get drunk. And also, you must not speak the white man's language. After the dance nothing that you want to do will be harmful.

That's all that I am able to say to you this evening. All of you, my sisters and now also our brothers, tonight we must borrow the way our relatives dance.[206] But that's the way you must all stay with it, all of you, everybody who stays over here. That's how we must try to dance until morning. Then let's go home. That's the last part of what I tell you who are around here.

Comparable but shorter prayers are offered at other ceremonies. Some of these, like the ghost feasts and the retirement of the ball at the end of the football season, are annual; [15] others, as peyote meetings, naming ceremonies, and funerals do not fall in a calendrical series.

Brief prayers are made and tobacco is offered at the grave of an especially beloved child with the request that the deceased child be returned as one of the future children of the parents. This ceremony is a specifically religious expression of the mythological theory concerning life after death with Our Grandmother and rebirth in general. Marks on the ears of a baby which might suggest ear slits made in a former life or the child's general resemblance to a deceased individual are taken as evidence of rebirth.

In addition to prayers addressed to Our Grandmother at the retirement of the football, ball games themselves are certain to have Our Grandmother as an audience. She always looks through her sky-window while a game is in progress. She smiles in approval when in the speech preceding each game it is said that ball games are played because they were ordained by her rules.

The beneficiary of a ghost feast is primarily the spirit of the dead to whom food *is* offered; the obligations of the feast giver are quite intricate and include the offering of appropriate food and drink, as for example whiskey to the spirit of one who was a drunkard during life, as well as the inheritance of obligations of deceased feast givers. The relation between the feast giver and Our Grandmother is indirect, through the spirit recipient who dwells with the Creator. When an old woman was on her deathbed, she said to her children, "Whenever you raise anything you enjoy, prepare me a dry roasting ear with meat, simply cooked, and the Creator will help you, through me, to get along in this world."

Those occasions on which Our Grandmother comes to earth to be present at Shawnee ceremonies are rare. The former First Fruit ceremony is still preserved by some individuals who set out, cooked, the first corn, beans, squash, melons, etc., of the season for Our Grand' mother to taste. This she does during the night, and the next morning those who set the food out eat it. Opinion is divided as to whether the Creator comes down to every feast. The common way for her to receive food from feasts given in her worship is by means of the spirits, those who are dead, who eat in her behalf except at the ghost feast which is not given in worship of the Creator

---

[206] The speaker is here referring to the secular, all night stomp dances some of which were borrowed from the Creeks, presumably the relatives mentioned in the prayer.

but directly for the benefit of the dead. In order to nourish the Creator, the feast must be specifically in her honor, and certain types of food must be prepared, or at least some foods which are especially nourishing. Buffalo meat is such an especially nourishing food. Since buffalo are no longer available and other feasts are frequently neglected nowadays, the Creator is hungry, an unhappy condition which reflects on the Shawnee. Reasoning here is somewhat circular: because the Shawnee are poor, the Creator is hungry; because the Creator is improverished, the Shawnee are poor.

Before the Civil War, the Creator always came down to attend the Bread Dances. Two men were stationed in the neighboring forest, and as the women danced and sang with the Bread Dance singers, the two men would hear Our Grandmother singing above the dance, directly above the brush arbor; this was reported later to the people. She has ceased to at' tend the Bread Dances of the Absentee Shawnee, but still attends those of the Cherokee [16] Shawnee where her function is merely to voice her approval while prayers are made. FD heard her while he was praying in the 1934 Green Corn Dance, was much elated, and eagerly asked several of us who were present if we had not heard her.

At the Men's Dance of the Absentee Shawnee, mounted warriors ride around the dance ground four times just to amuse Our Grandmother who comes to earth for the day with her grandson, Rounded-side, and her little dog.

While apparently unrelated to ceremonies, the gift of prophecy by the Creator is really a subtle means of insuring the continuation of old time ceremonies.

Mechanical reading of signs has nothing to do with the more important prophetic in' sight peculiar to certain individuals. An individual may read signs, and knowledge gained in this way concerns none other than the individual reading the sign. Thus, a man may take the "appendix" out of the first deer he kills in the beginning of the season and throw the appendix in the fire. As many times as the "appendix" pops, so many deer will he kill for that season.

In contrast, those individuals having prophetic insight do not learn about their own personal future but the future of all Shawnee, or all people, or even the future of the world as a whole. This foreknowledge is rather exclusively dispensed by Our Grandmother, and since she no longer lives on the earth, it is necessary for people living on the earth to journey to her home to communicate with her. A distinction is sometimes made between those who flit, as it were, to the Creator's home in a prophetic trance, and those who make the long Journey going by the well established path which the visitors in the Orpheus tale took. The latter way is extraordinarily difficult and could not be made by an ordinary mortal without the aid of a powerful guardian spirit. Sweat house doctors or other individuals who have received on their vision quest an unequivocal guardian spirit are particularity well equipped for making the difficult journey. But it is always possible that such individuals may, in the name of prophecy, relate what the guardian spirit rather than what Our Grandmother said; in this sense the guardian spirit would presumably act as an intermediary between the Creator and the individual. The latter would be likely to make the complete journey if his guardian spirit were able to cope with all the difficulties on the way. Wind, sun, moon, and perhaps water are specified as guardian spirits who are especially successful in overcoming obstacles on the journey. There is no reason why a given individual may not make more than one journey to Our Grandmother. However, if instead of making the difficult journey, he approaches Our Grandmother in a prophetic trance, he could not repeat his visit because only one prophetic trance is granted in a lifetime. The resulting prophecy is thought of as coming directly from Our Grandmother; no lesser influences, as those from a guardian spirit, are involved. Many older Shawnee remember the following occurrence reported by E.B Townsend, Special Agent at Shawneetown, Indian Territory, in a letter dated April 6, 1883, addressed to Hon. W Price, Commissioner of Indian Affairs.[207] [17]

About a year ago an old Shawnee woman while in a cataleptic state received a revelation from the Great Spirit to the effect that the Shawnees were adopting unwisely and in too great measure the ways and habits of the white man; that unless they changed their course, abandoned the following and teaching of the whites, and returned to the ways of their fathers and the traditions of their forefathers, they would dwindle away and be lost; but if on the other hand they abandoned their evil course and returned to the old Indian way; adhered to their own traditions and the teachings of their fathers all would yet be well with them; they would yet be prosperous and happy; would be re-united (the Eastern Shawnees, the Black Bob Shawnees, the Absentee and Upper Shawnees) and become a mighty people, dominant upon the face of the earth and powerful among all the races thereof, not excepting the Latter Day Saints. Strange and weird as this story sounds it was received by the Shawnees as a work of inspiration, as much so as Christian whites accept the Inspired Word, and so strong was the influence it exerted that it threatened to bring about serious results. Children were taken out of school; many of the Indians (for a time) abandoned their civilized dress and pursuits and large numbers gave themselves up to feasting and dancing with a religious abandon which promised well for the woman's prophecies.

Prophetic insight was sometimes vouchsafed to individuals who had not visited Our Grandmother during their lifetime. Instances of this type are thought of as belonging definitely with the past and not even potentially with the present. Warrior men and women, defined as people who were bom with no special powers and who had had various misfortunes in war which were in a sense compensated for by a gift of prophecy from the Creator, attended councils and advised the chief and his councillors as to the future. A warrior woman would not be reluctant, as an ordinary woman would, to get up and speak in council. Less frequently, an individual was bom with a complete or partial knowledge of the future which he gained from the Creator during his residence with her as an unborn soul. *Teenškwaatawe*, the Shawnee Prophet and brother of Tecumseh, was such an individual. Before automobiles were invented, an old Cherokee Shawnee was able to tell that they were to appear in future because he was created with this foreknowledge.

The ceremonies reviewed are supported by prophecy and freely discussed.

There still remains to be considered the status of the Creator in respect to religious forces like magic, sacred bundles, and guardian spirits which are occasionally cultivated in ceremonies yet constitute essentially independent powers of an intimate but none the less potent nature.

Magic, which is employed chiefly to control weather and game, appears at first blush to be in a self-sufficient cause and effect system of its own, not at all integrated in the general system of Shawnee religion. Thus, an intricate string figure, symbolically "tieing up a star," is talked to and untied in order to secure cool weather; a buffalo tail is carried to a spring by a calm man, and shaken very gently in order to secure rain; other overt acts, accompanied by the proper

---

[207] This letter is from a copy of the original in the possession of Miss Martha Bunton, of Norman, Oklahoma.

words, cause a deer to stop so that he may be conveniently shot, make a deer more than normally visible, make the hunter shoot straight, and so on. Magical practises are clearly enough mechanical in a symbolic sense: as the buffalo tail is [18] shaken gently by a calm man, so the subsequent rain will be gentle and calm; but the words accompanying the overt acts are always addressed to a personified power or chief of weather or game who was created by Our Grandmother to benefit the Shawnee. Such an address is made while the buffalo tail is being shaken over the water of a spring.

> Our Grandmother put this water for people to use on this earth as long as they are on earth. This water was created a grandfather to take care of the people. Everybody will be glad to see it rain. And Our Grandmother created this water for all kinds of animals, big and little. But now it doesn't rain. People are dissatisfied and talk to you, Grandfather, to come and make it rain all over so that people may drink.

To describe the relationship between the Creator and the sacred bundles abstracted as one element of Shawnee religion falsely minimizes the extreme sacredness of the bundles. Their sphere of influence is all embracing rather than specific; they overshadow the Creator herself, and in many ways the attitude of the Shawnee towards the bundles contrasts sharply with their attitude to the Creator. The latter is known intimately to every child; the bundles are shrouded in mystery even to their custodians, their history and origin varies with each political division, and totemic name groups have various duties in respect to them. One senses that at the ceremonial dances the Shawnee talk about Our Grandmother but think about their bundles. If a study of the Creator is the prolegomenon to Shawnee religion, then the ultimate insight into this religion must rest on a study of the sacred bundles.

In addition to her creation of the bundles. Our Grandmother maintains a potential control over them. Whenever she wishes, she may inform the Shawnee how the bundles are to be changed or disposed of.

The bundles provide the most sacred approach to Our Grandmother. Before the war with the Tonkawa, the bundle of the *θwikila* division was opened and four ceremonial songs were sung. At the end of the fourth song, the small wooden figure of the little boy in the bundle became animate. He took up his bow and arrow, and then the Shawnee asked him to tell the Creator what they wanted. Then the child shot four arrows, showing that there were four big Tonkawa warriors. He shot one big warrior twice, annihilating him. Then he took up his blanket and became dormant again. The Shawnee concluded they would be victorious, went forth to war, and shot four of the big Tonkawa warriors.

Conversely, the bundles provide for extremely holy, possibly esoteric communications from the Creator to the Shawnee. Immediately preceding the end of the world. Our Grandmother will recall the bundles.

The bundles are a holy mystery and attract the inarticulate interest of the entire tribe. In comparison, guardian spirits are secret powers which an individual possesses and the individual is interested only in the particular guardian spirit which he himself possesses.

Shawnee children some time after their seventh year are sent out on vision quests to find a guardian spirit which is expected to benefit the individual rather than the tribe as a whole. At this time of life children are, or until recently were, subjected to various purification [19] and scarifications which are in a sense a preliminary to the vision quest. Boys of the *θwikila* division were given a purifying herb concoction in a sweat lodge. The Eastern and Cherokee Shawnee burned round scars on the forearms of boys and girls which would act as lamps on the way to the Creator. The protracted and often repeated seeking of a guardian spirit, and the hidden relationship which exists between the powers sought or received and the visionary is an experience which affects the individual deeply; but into this experience the Creator scarcely enters.

In contrast to this the Fox visionary has at least a secondary contact with the Great Manitou.[208] But even this secondary contact is lacking among the Shawnee, possibly because the vision quest and power derived from it has remained a purely individualistic matter; the blessing obtained by a visionary never becoming semi-public property, as it does among the Fox.

When, however, a Shawnee visionary is extraordinarily sensitive to the powers about him in his quest, and is accordingly favored by an especially powerful guardian spirit, he may then cultivate the power he has found for half a lifetime in order to become a sweat lodge doctor and in this profession cure the sick. Indirectly, then, his vision quest will be beneficial to others. And in his new usefulness he has divine precedent: as far back as the period before the flood, Our Grandmother was herself a sweat lodge doctor. It would seem that almost as a corollary to the extension of the visionary's powers beyond the sphere of the individual. Our Grandmother enters the scene and *is* called upon directly in prayer and indirectly in the employment of things which she has created, as herbs, fire, water, and tobacco. Sweat lodge doctors often engaged in curing with partners, women who knew herbal remedies, although this collaboration was not essential.

Information was not volunteered about guardian spirits, which the Shawnee do not even discuss among themselves, nor about sacred bundles. In these matters information was reluctantly given only after being solicited. And however carefully solicited, no individual was willing to recount his personal experiences beyond hinting that his own experiences were peculiar and probably completely different from those of any other Shawnee. To tell about these experiences would, as ~~informants~~ intuitively sensed, be tantamount to revealing the most intimate aspects of one's personality.

Information regarding other departments of religion was freely given together with descriptions of cultural peculiarities as contributions to an understanding of the Shawnee way of doing things. An attempt was made in gathering Shawnee texts to allow the ~~informant~~ to dictate whatever seemed of interest or importance to him. Spontaneous interest not censored by a compulsion of secrecy inspired ~~informants~~ to dwell on Our Grandmother more than any other single subject in texts whose subject matter covered a very wide range. Many of the texts about the Creator are in the form of personal anecdotes. It should be noted, however, that these attitudinal experiences concern a department of Shawnee religion which stimulates no great variety in individual responses. In recounting these [20] experiences, individuals are in a very real sense not revealing their own personalities; their behavior is such as might be expected from any proper Shawnee in like circumstances, and is therefore impersonal.

> FD tells that while his white neighbor was treated in a hospital, he received religion during a sleep (i.e, while under the influence of an anaesthetic) and also the mission to convert FD to Christianity. The latter was deeply impressed by the very Shawnee-like experience of his neighbor but explained that he had to believe in the one who created him, Our Grandmother, because he was

---

[208] Michelson, *Contributions to Fox Ethnology*: 135, 137; *Contributions to Fox Ethnology* II: 95, 87 et seq.

an Indian.

Various appeals are made to Our Grandmother in times of crises, as in the droughts of 1901 and 1934, and in the World War.

A little boy is scolded because he cut a tree. It is explained that Our Grandmother created Our Grandfathers, the trees, to be made use of by Indians, not to be wantonly harmed; the tree has feelings which may be hurt even as we have. Then the little boy promises never to hurt a tree again.

At another time a turtle was scolded because he was going up hill, away from the water. He was told that Our Grandmother did not create him to travel up hills. It was subsequently realized that the turtle wished to give warning of a minor flood which came shortly after the scolding.

Again, when a snake is killed, an explanation is made to him about Our Grandmother's intentions, which in this instance does not very well explain why the snake was killed.

When walking alone, FD sings because he knows Our Grandmother will listen attentively as she does when he sings at ceremonies.

Whenever tabus are mentioned, they are described as instructions of Our Grandmother.

While translating, ~~informants~~ sometimes supplemented the contents of their texts with remarks about Our Grandmother. Thus, in a concrete description of Shawnee costume it is said that in the manner described a Shawnee is properly dressed so that he may look like an Indian. The implication intended was that Our Grandmother would recognize a properly dressed individual as a Shawnee Indian and not mistake him for a white man.

In dictating texts of their own choice ~~informants~~ did not resort to relating inconsequential, trivial detail. One might, indeed, have wished for more detail and less of the characteristic, synoptic presentation of material. Significantly enough, an occasional irrelevant reference to Our Grandmother is one of the few luxuries ~~informants~~ allowed themselves in the rush of bare outline. Thus, a description of the movement of Shawnee from Kansas to Cherokee lands in what is now Oklahoma is interrupted with an elaborate explanation that such a movement was possible because the one who created us intended that we should think of one another, i.e, be mutually helpful. The account then explains, realistically enough, how the Cherokee played the rôle of extortionists with the Shawnee immigrants.

Basking in the Creator's good intentions, the Shawnee are no less miserable than their humble admissions specify, but the cause of an imperfect world, namely a serious disturbance of Our Grandmother's creations and instructions, is ascribed to others. It was the Creator who arranged that Indians might kill animals four times. After each killing, the Indian performed the proper ritual, and the animal spirit was refurnished with a new body [21] which could be used again in successive killings by Indians. But white men regard animals as targets, kill when they have no need for animals, and so defeat the purpose of Our Grandmother. Hence, game is scarce.

It is perhaps in respect to punishment that the attitude of the present day Shawnee towards the Creator and the things she stands for is most clearly expressed. Shawnee ceremonies were created by Our Grandmother; accordingly, contempt, negligence, or light hearted performance of any ceremony is subject to punishment. Instances in which punishments are directly ascribed to Our Grandmother are not frequent. Tom Bullfrog lost his legs (incidentally through freezing) because he made fun of his grandmother who was preparing a Ghost feast.

This violent expression of displeasure on the part of the Creator seems to conflict with her originally benevolent nature. One ~~informant~~ who felt this conflict said that the wrongdoer should not really hold the Creator responsible, meaning that the punishment is a reasonable penalty for violating a known code, avoidable by merely following the Creator's rules. In another instance the parents of a child followed the Name Giving ceremony in a halfhearted way, and as a result the Creator caused the child to be sickly.[209] The father (BW) recognised the fault as his own and renamed the child with the proper procedure, after which the child was no longer sickly. It is noteworthy that the ceremonies in both these instances were not for the benefit of the Creator but for the soul of a dead person and for a child; the Creator's punishments are more in the nature of a cruel sentence passed by an impersonal judge than of vengeance of one personally injured.

Mythologic punishments include a purgatory, with obvious Christian influences, which is administered by the devil as well as by the Creator. The dead who are not virtuous do not choose the proper path, which is a narrow one, in the bifurcation of the road to the land of the dead. Those who arrive safely find the Creator weaving a basket. During the night her little dog (with her grandson, in a Cherokee Shawnee variant) unravels the weaving of the previous day and thus prevents the Creator from completing her basket. Some day, not too distant now say the present day Shawnee, Our Grandmother will complete this basket. Then the virtuous living will be gathered into the basket, and those who are remaining will be destroyed with the world, but those in the basket will be used to repopulate a new world.

In view of the growing neglect of the Creator's rules, it is expected that the impending catastrophe will be actualized before long. This arouses anxiety among some and gleeful anticipation among others. Schematically considered, those individuals who are ceremoniously punctilious should expect to be rewarded by being gathered into the basket. However, punishment for negligence is meditated more than reward for obedience. Perhaps those who express pleasure in anticipation of the world's destruction contemplate the punishment of others and have the happy faculty of excepting themselves in such phantasy rather than dwelling on positive rewards for themselves. An intense Shawnee feeling of abject humility would, at any rate, prevent an individual from regarding himself as a successful candidate for Our Grandmother's basket of the virtuous.

---

[209] C.F and E.W Voegelin, *Shawnee Name Groups* (American Anthropologist, vol 37, no. 4: 617-35), 626.

Shawnee

Yale University Publications in Anthropology

Number #10

The Shawnee Female Deity

C.F Voegelin

Edward Sapir
Leslie Spier
Editors

Reprinted from the 1936 edition

Library of Congress Catalog Card Number: 79-118243
Published simultaneously in Canada by Burns & MacEachern, Ltd, Toronto

Printed in the United States of America

Reprinted by

Human Relations Area Files Press

New Haven

1970

The Shawnee Female Deity in Historical Perspective*
CF and EW Voegelin

Present-Day Shawnee groups now residing in Oklahoma hold their own religious ceremonies which are little influenced by while contacts. The observations of Black Hoof, a distinguished Shawnee chief, made more than a century ago, are as relevant today as they were in 1824. When white men first came to this continent, Black Hoof remarked, they gave the Indians assurances of perpetual friendship and

> proposed to establish a missionary among the Indians and endeavoured to convince them of the propriety of embracing the Christian religion, but the red men replied that the Great Spirit had already furnished them with a religion suited to their nature and capacity, that they were perfectly satisfied with it, that they might reciprocate the offer of their religion to the whites with propriety, but they thought it best to keep the ways which the Great Spirit had given them.[210]

Despite this conservative attitude, there has been a notable change in the Shawnee concept of their creator. Between 1824 and the present time emphasis on the relative importance of certain characters in the Shawnee pantheon has shifted; in this paper we shall examine this shift and suggest the time and condition of its occurrence.

Present-Day Concepts of the Creator

The characteristics, accomplishments and position of the Shawnee creator in the present-day religious ideology of the tribe have been described in a paper published in 1936.[211] We shall here summarize points necessary for our present discussion.

In the first place, the Shawnee creator as envisaged today is said to be a woman. She is known by various names, but is usually referred to simply as "Our Grandmother." A series of creation myths obtained from various Shawnee ~~informants~~ credit Our Grandmother with:

(1) the first creation of the world,

(2) residence on earth during this first creation,

(3) the peopling of the first world,

(4) escape to an upper region at the time of the flood,

(5) the creation of a second or new world after the flood,

(6) the creation of the first man and first woman on the new earth,

---

[210] * American Anthropologist 46: 370-75 1944.

Vernon Kinietz, and Erminie Wheeler Voegelin, eds, *Shawnese Traditions ~ CC Trowbridge's Account* (Occasional Contributions from the Museum of Anthropology of the University of Michigan # 9 1939): 63.

[211] CF Voeglin, *The Shawnee Female Deity* (Yale University Publications in Anthroplogy # 10 1936).

(7) misplaced genitalia on first humans,

(8) the gift of fire, food, tobacco, the sacred bundles and other cultural items to the first couple created,

(9) residence in a world above this earth after the work of creation was finished. [371]

Companion to Our Grandmother during the first and second creations and the time of the flood is a powerful little boy, the creator's grandson, whose personal name is *Haapočilaweeθa*. This grandson does various things, some good, some willful; he is responsible for releasing impounded water and thereby causing the first world to be flooded; he slays powerful giants and monsters; he even creates the progenitors of one or two of the Shawnee political divisions. Although powerful, he seems at all times subordinate to his Grandmother who, in all mythological accounts save one, is the dominant figure in the story of creation.

In the one exceptional account just referred to, the actual task of creation is accomplished by Our Grandmother, but the idea of the creation of the world emanates from another deity. This exceptional myth is brief:

> In the beginning there was the Great Spirit, formed of wind, invisible, but in the shape of a man. He lives above the sun. There was just space; no earth, no water. The Great Spirit said, "Let there be a woman" and as soon as he spoke there was a being formed like a woman. Then to this woman the Great Spirit gave the work of creating this earth, light (the sun), water, people, animals. She is the one the people saw and knew. Before the flood she and the devil and her grandson and the great giants were all on this earth which she made, and the people talked to them. In this first creation people lived a long time and died four times, but not so today. The Great Spirit must have made the sky, or again it might mean that the Great Spirit was the sky. The female creator is under the Great Spirit. Afterward the female creator did her creating and made the rules which are to be fulfilled.[212]

Aside from our own field data on the subject, sonic references to the Shawnee female deity and her role as creator are to be found in recent published and unpublished material on the Shawnee. Thomas Wildcat Alford, an educated member of the Absentee Shawnee group, writing in 1936, refers to Our Grandmother specifically as the creator.[213] Several field workers beside ourselves have unpublished material on Our Grandmother which corroborates the prominent part she plays in Shawnee religious ideology, despite the fact that comparative work shows the Shawnee to be unique among all the Eastern Woodlands Algonquian-speaking peoples in possessing a female supreme deity and creator.

Nineteenth Century Concepts of the Supreme Deity

Since the publication of our paper in 1936 on the Shawnee female deity two 1824 manuscripts on the Shawnee have been discovered and published. The material on Shawnee

---

[212] EW Voegelin, Shawnee *Myths,* Ms; narrated in English by James Clark, Absentee Shawnee, now deceased, of the Kišpoko political division. Clark learned the myth from his father.

[213] Thomas Wildcat Alford, Civilization, as told to Florence Drake by Thomas Wildcat Alford (Norman, Oklahoma 1936): 18-19.

creators contained in these manuscripts indicates that the present prominent role played by Our Grandmother is a recent development [372] in the history of Shawnee culture. The two 1824 accounts are based on data obtained by C.C Trowbridge in interviews with two reputable Shawnee ~~informants~~, Black Hoof, a chief, and Teenskwaatawa, the Shawnee Prophet and brother of Tecumseh.

The Prophet's account begins with the statement that

> When the Great Spirit made this Island he thought it necessary to make also human beings to inhabit it, and with this in view he formed an Indian.[214]

Then follows the misplaced genitalia motif which also occurs in our own recent field accounts. However, according to the Prophet's version of 1824, the first couple were made in a region above the earth and only later were they and their offspring set down on the earth island; this was after the male Great Spirit had finished creating everything on this island, and after he had provided the twelve original Indians with vegetable and meat foods. Having been put on earth the Indians pray to the male creator; later this creator himself visits the Indians. During his visit he gives them a tribal name and tells them where to live; he then informs them that he is

> going to leave them and would not be seen by them again, and that they must think for themselves & pray to their grandmother, the moon, who was present in the shape of an old woman.[215]

Nowhere in the origin myth as given by the Prophet is there any mention of a Creator's grandson. However, in a section dealing with religion the Prophet relates that the Shawnee

> believe in one Supreme being who has a moral superintendence over the affairs of the world. He is called Müyaataalemeelārkwau, or the Finisher, and is served by two Subordinate deities, one to take charge of the Indians and the other of the whites. The first of these is called, "Waupōāthee Skeelauwaathēēthar" or "The boy of Waupōāthee," an old woman, his grand mother, of that name. (Skeelauwaathēēthar is the proper name for boy.) This old woman seems also to have charge of the affairs of Indians and is allowed to be nearer the residence of the *Great* Spirit than her grandchild, whose location is immediately above the Indians and so near as to enable him to distinguish them & supply their wants.[216]

Black Hoof's 1824 account of the creation confirms and supplements that of the Prophet's. Black Hoof states that

> when the waters of the deluge had entirely overspread the earth, all its inhabitants were destroyed but an aged woman who ascended to the clouds, where she gave way to grief at the loss of her grandchildren. ... The great spirit witnessed her

---

[214] Kinietz and Voegelin, *Shawnese Traditions*: 1.

[215] *Ibid*: 5.

[216] *Ibid*: 40-41.

affliction and bid her cease to mourn.[217]

The Great Spirit then collected twelve kinds of roots for a medicine to purify [373] himself and resuscitate his powers of thought and invention. He washed his body with the medicine and became very pure and white; then he determined to renew and re-people the earth. The renewal was accomplished with a tiny bit of mud brought from beneath the water by Crawfish. Large animals were treated by the Great Spirit and put at the four cardinal points of the compass to keep the earth steady; "the Indians lie next formed".[218]

Certain amplifying remarks by Black Hoof and the Prophet are of particular interest for their implications which we will discuss in the following section. Black Hoof says in his account,

> When the Great Spirit had created the Indians, he endowed them with a knowledge of their formation, and the purposes for which they were brought into existence. *This intelligence was not communicated to them by any one commissioned for that purpose*, but by the Great Spirit himself, who held personal communication with the Indians of the early ages.[219] (Italics are ours.)

The Prophet's remarks are of a similar nature; he says that the male Great Spirit said to the Indians he had created, "Remember who made you and these [animals and plants] *and do not at any time attribute the formation to any but me*".[220] (Italics are ours.)

Change from Male to Female Supreme Deity

When we contrast the beliefs the Shawnee entertained in 1824 with those they now hold concerning their creator, we find that the male Great Spirit concept is at present obsolescent (indeed, obsolete for most of our Shawnee ~~informants~~), and that a once minor female deity has come to occupy the most important position in the Shawnee pantheon. This emphasis on a female supreme deity is startling, since it is the older Shawnee concept — that of a male being as supreme deity and creator — which is currently encountered in the mythologies of all other Eastern Woodlands Algonquian-speaking peoples.[221] A "Creator's grandmother," as Stith Thompson has pointed out, is widely but casually mentioned in Central and Northeastern Woodlands mythologies;[222] nowhere except among the present-day Shawnee is such a character accorded any great prominence in the religious ideologies of the eastern Algonquians.

The change, in the Shawnee instance, from male to female supreme deity has al least

---

[217] *Ibid*: 60.

[218] *Ibid*: 61.

[219] *Ibid*: 60.

[220] *Ibid*: 2.

[221] Both MR Harrington and Frank G Speck have noticed this anomaly for the Shawnee, but neither have commented further upon it; see Harrington's Religion and Ceremonies of the Lenape (Indian Notes and Monographs # 19: 1921): 20; and Speck's A Study of the Delaware Indian Big House Ceremony (Publications of the Pennsylvania Historical Society, # II, Harrisburg 1931): 2 note # 2.

[222] *Tales of the North American Indians* (Cambridge, Mass 1929): 275.

three possible explanations. The first of these, and to our minds the most convincing, is that it reflects contacts which the Shawnee had with [374] various Iroquoian-speaking groups during the historic period. There run through Iroquois mythology, especially Huron mythology, quite occasional references to a female divinity, *Ataentsic*, and her son, *Iouskaha*; the female divinity is accredited with the creation of heaven, earth, and mankind; and both she and her son superintend the world after creation.[223] The Seneca, another Iroquoian tribe, tell of the woman who fell from the sky and for whom the earth was created as a resting place; this woman had two sons who were always scuffling together.[224]

We may have here another example of what Kroeber has called "stimulus diffusion",[225] that is, the borrowing of cultural outline rather than cultural detail, and the recasting or adjustment or filling in of the outline to suit the detail of the borrowing people. In the case under discussion, the Shawnee female deity may have increased in power and importance during the course of a century by analogy to (or stimulus from) Iroquoian female divinities known to the Shawnee; but without at the same time taking over any Iroquoian detail, such as falling from the sky. There is abundant evidence of Shawnee-Iroquoian contacts during the last century.[226]

Two other historically possible sources of stimulation should be considered:

First, that Our Grandmother and her grandson are Shawnee embodiments of the Virgin Mary and the Christ child. Against this possibility is the fact that the Shawnee have had few contacts with Catholic missionaries; what nineteenth century missionizing was done among them was done chiefly by the Quakers, the Baptists, and the Methodists; and the Virgin Mary would scarcely appear to the Shawnee to be an especially powerful female divinity.

Secondly, the Shawnee may have been influenced by the Yuchi, a Southeastern tribe with whom some of the Shawnee divisions, at least, had close contact during the historic period. In a recent collection of Yuchi tales, the deeds of a "supernatural boy" who kills fierce animals are related in some detail.[227] This supernatural boy and his grandmother bear certain resemblances to the Shawnee Creator and her grandson. The boy is, furthermore, accompanied on his goings-about by a "dwarf dog" just as was the Shawnee boy. However, the tale in which he appears is one which concerns whites as well as Indians, and one in which the European story of the treaty of the oxhide [375] strip (often told by the Shawnee, the Delaware and other eastern tribes)[228] is included; also, it precedes another tale in which the Shawnee and other tribes are mentioned; also, it is chiefly the boy

---

[223] Louis Hennepin, *A New Discovery of a Vast Country m America* (2 vols, Chicago, 1903), vol. # 1; 450, note. See also Emma H Blair, *Tribes of the Upper Mississippi Valley and Region of the Great Lakes* (2 vols, Cleveland, 1912), vol. # 1: 40-41, note 15.

[224] Hennepin, *A New Discovery,* vol. # 1: 451ff, and note.

[225] A.L Kroeber, *Stimulus Diffusion* (*American Anthropologist*, n.s vol # 42: 1-20 1940).

[226] See article, *Mingo* by James Mooney (Bureau of American Ethnology, Bulletin # 30, part 1: 867-68.

[227] Günter Wagner, *Yuchi Tales* (Publication of the American Ethnological Society, vol # 13): 157-164.

[228] See Kinietz and Voegelin, *Shawnese Traditions*: 10.

whose exploits are dwelt upon. On the whole, therefore, it seems likely that it is the Yuchi who reflect Shawnee influence here, rather than the other way around.

Of the three possibilities discussed, that of Iroquoian influence is surely greater than Christian or Yuchi influence; but whatever may have led the Shawnee to ascribe additional functions and accomplishments to Our Grandmother, it is almost certain that no sudden change look place at one time. In the two 1824 manuscripts there is evidence that the groundwork for the shift to a female deity had been laid previous to 1824, for both the Prophet and Black Hoof state explicitly that the Great Spirit is to be credited with the creation of the world and of humans, *and no other being is to be so credited.* Such statements would seem uncalled for unless there were, even at that time, certain confused notions as to the identity of the creator, and perhaps a tendency on the part of some Shawnee at least to credit Our Grandmother with unusual powers. In the reversal of status, Our Grandmother as a female supreme deity is much more secure today than was the Great Spirit as a male supreme deity in 1824. The present-day Shawnee speak of Our Grandmother without feeling it necessary to protest that she is the only creator or supreme deity since the time when things were created; her importance is taken for granted. Of numerous Shawnee ~~informants~~, only one knew the tradition of an earlier male supreme deity.

INDIANA UNIVERSITY
BLOOMINGTON, INDIANA

Note Bene >> In the Shawnee Ohio homeland, the alignments of earthworks, thousands of years old, along the path and cycles of the Moon strongly suggest an ancient, ancestral female sky deity, whom the teachings of the Shawnee Prophet sought to demote even as his brother θθa was making classic statements about their all-embracing Mother Earth.

Shawnee Laws:
Perceptual Statements for the Language and for the Content

C.F Voegelin, John P Yegerlehner, and Florence M Robinett

WE ARE OFTEN told by our ~~informants~~ that a certain part of culture has a folkloristic origin, has existed in their own society' before contact with whites until today; and here we can confirm our ~~informants~~ to the extent of knowing that the part of culture being discussed is indeed aboriginal − aboriginal in the sense of being non-European. Such persisting parts of culture we designate as stable to distinguish them from acculturational changes, from culture which has appeared since White contact.

Shawnee Laws (*šaawanwa kwteletiiwena*) represent such a stable part of culture in a society in which some people are still trying to live like Indians rather than like whites. A point by point morphemic transformation of *kwteletiiwena = advise-animate-reciprocal-inanimate thing-plural = laws;* hence, *šaawanwa kwteletiiwena = Shawnee Laws.*

The "language of the law" among us is specialized and in part archaic. To compare the language of Shawnee law with that of English law, we need first to produce a legal glossary in Shawnee. Legal glossaries in English are plentiful. From *Black's Law Dictionary* (third edition, St. Paul, 1933), we abstracted a few terms and categorized them as either externally perceived or internally experienced. The procedure for selecting the terms was to read the entries under the first ten letters of the alphabet and to note on separate slips a few English entries whose specialized meaning was recognized by us; we excluded all Latin terms and also all English terms which appeared to lack legal specialization. After collecting some fifty slips in the way, we read the definition of each, to confirm our guess as to the use of the term. We then classified the terms as either externally perceived or internally experienced, with an unexpected result − a neutralized category had to be added, as shown below.

Of a total of fifty technical terms selected, about half (24) fell into our externally perceived category, while less than a third (14) fell [33] into our internally experienced category. For more than three fourths of the terms (38) there was coincidence in our independent judgments for these two categories. For the remaining one fourth of the terms (12) there was lack of agreement. Such terms, failing to gain confirmation for either of the two categories, have the effect of being neutralized in respect to the opposition set up by these categories.

Our externally perceived category includes: *abandonee, abator, back* (as in *indorse;* and again as in *back taxes), backwards and forwards* (as between ports at sea), *bail, cabotage, carrying away, case* (as in *case agreed upon;* and again as in *case for motion); damages, decision, earnest, ebb and flow, effluxion of time, ejectment, factor, grant, habitual, harbor, immovables, jetsam, John Doe,* and *joinder.*

Our internally experienced category includes: *bad* (as in *bad behavior), capable, capacity, civil death, easement, efficient cause, fabricate, faculties, false witness, fault, hang* (= remain undetermined), *illegal, immunity,* and *jeopardy.*

Our neutralized items are: *abandon, abet, bad* (as in *bad debt), debenture, debt, general exception, genuine* (as in *genuine bond), give notice, good* (as in *good cause), hearing, impeach,* and *judgment.* Our nonagreement suggests postulating a nonabsolute factor or, in other words, a relative factor, namely, the previous experiences of the perceivers. Whorf was on the side of regarding perception of Gestalt as absolute and hence universal. (All peoples see Ursa Major as one figure, he said; though we call this constellation of stars the "dipper," ways of speaking in other cultures may vary the figure to suit the culture. We question, however, whether all references in all cultures are to 4 + 3 stars. The Chukchee see 6 + 1 stars, with the last called a "double star"; moreover, they see two figures, the 6 = *men hunting* and the "double star" = *fox chewing on antlers.*)

Whether or not Gestalt gives us an absolute which can be used as a meter for universal measuring, some scholars have postulated one or another kind of absolute in semantic work, instead of resting content with translation meaning which merely switches codes from one language to another. Thus, in semantic studies of grading, totality, and end-point relation – more or less in collaboration with others who want ultimately to construct an international language – Edward Sapir tacitly assumed a kind of semantic absolute, which was in part configurational (Sapir 1930, 1944; Sapir and Swadesh 1932). The configurational absolute in Gestalt psychology can be discussed in terms of language structure, as well as in its traditional terms such as the equivalence of stroboscopic with mechanical movement. [34]

If, like H.G Barnett in *Innovation: The Basis of Cultural Change* (1953), we can convince ourselves that it is possible to have non-absolute Gestalten – configurations whose perception is determined by the prior experiences of the observer – then we can simply regard our neutralized terms as removed from the evidence which remains good in the agreed-upon categories. These suggest that the law in English is more inclined toward terms which are externally perceived; the terms in the Shawnee Laws, on the other hand, lean toward what we classify as internally experienced.

Whorf wrote a paper (1940) in which he exemplified his theory of the application of Gestalt techniques to the discovery of subtle features of the grammar of any language. Thus, in English, Gestalt considerations tell us why we use the simple present for certain verbs (*I hear you*) rather than the present progressive (*I am hearing you*) and why we use the present progressive for other verbs (I *am working}* rather than the simple present (*I work).* In Whorf's theory, Gestalt considerations and grammatical considerations from English structure are integrated into one statement. But for Shawnee it appears to be more difficult to state any integration between classes of distribution within the structure of the language – analogous to the simple and progressive present in English – and classes or subclasses of Gestalt distinctions. The results obtained by Whorf do not, in fact, integrate with Shawnee structure; they can, however, be stated in their own right, as, indeed, Whorf stated them.

We try again to obtain some integration or correlation between (1) grammatical categories and (2) perceptual categories; also between the latter and (3) the content of Shawnee Laws, which might be called the culture of the document, in contrast to the language of the document. If, now, we were to give our translation of the text called Shawnee Laws, we should obtain, *inter alia,* what is generally called "the content" of the document. But here we are not seeking ethnographic information as a whole, or specific legal-folkloristic points embedded in the document; instead we are seeking a procedure which will enable us to categorize morphological features of Shawnee in terms of perception, and a procedure which will allow us to categorize "the content" of our document in terms of perception too – "the content" of the document in contrast to the morphology of the language in which it is written.

The categorizing of legal terms into two opposing groups is of dubious value, even for English, because the categories set up are invulnerable (not subject to being proved wrong). At best, we can get [35] slight comfort from the fact that, though independent in our judgments, we generally agree. We do not attempt a vote to test agreement on Shawnee legal terms because, however we voted, we would fail to find a rationale for giving significance to the result; any such rationale would have to assume that the judges reacted in part from :, their intimate knowledge of the language being judged. In the case of Shawnee, the language whose terms were to be judged would be nonnative to the voters.

What we want for Shawnee is a procedure for arriving at categories relevant to some perceptual psychology like Gestalt, but we want our categories to be vulnerable. Perceptual categories are, in general, vague in definition, however clear they may look when projected visually. In order to have these more or less vaguely denned categories susceptible to being proved wrong, we correlate them with morphological features which are relatively precise and specific in definition. The latter then become the defining property of the former.

To this end, we set up two perceptual categories, defined by Shawnee morphemes which mark gender of nouns and actor of intransitive verbs, and which mark voice of transitive verbs; particles are selected for one of the categories irrespective of their referents, but their referents are always subsidiary to verbs and nouns.

1. All animate nouns are categorized as defining what is externally perceived, and as implying activity. In most instances Shawnee nouns are animate when their referents are animals, including humans, which are capable of mobility; in the common ancestor of Shawnee and the other Algonquian languages, according to Bloom-field, animate nouns included "all persons, animals, spirits, and large trees, and some other objects, such as tobacco, maize, apple, raspberry (but not strawberry), calf of leg (but not thigh), stomach, spittle, feather, bird's tail, horn, kettle, pipe for smoking, snowshoe" 1946: 94). In addition to animate nouns, intransitive verbs are categorized as defining the externally perceived when the actor is animate, irrespective of their meaning otherwise − whether of activity or of inert descriptiveness. So, also, all transitive verbs are categorized as defining the externally perceived, provided only that the transitive is nonpassive and noninverse, but irrespective of whether the verb marks animate or inanimate goal.

2. Every transitive verb that includes a preinflectional passive or inverse marking suffix is categorized as defining what is internally experienced; the same verb stem would accordingly fall into our [36] category 1, above, when lacking passive or inverse suffix, but into category 2, when so suffixed. So also all intransitive verbs with inanimate actor are categorized as defining the internally experienced. Besides these two types of verbs, both inanimate nouns and free particles are put into the category of the internally experienced or background phenomena rather than into the category of what is perceived as figure in the foreground.

When particles leading to one perceptual category are compounded with verbs leading to another, the word in question is neutralized so far as falling into one or another of our contrastive categories is concerned; so, also, when the translator introduces or injects an additional term into the record.

Morphological criteria for our perceptual categories are tentatively selected and subject to both revision and addition (in anticipation of obtaining more fruitful correlations). Though we throw all animate nouns into the externally perceived category, for example, we might, in another selection, distinguish between those animate nouns which are marked as more conspicuous from those which are marked as less conspicuous. The latter, known in Algonquian languages as "the obviative," might be placed in our internally experienced category in contrast to the other animate nouns, which would remain in the externally perceived category.

The first two paragraphs of Shawnee Laws are given below by way of illustration. Sentences are numbered consecutively, without breaks between paragraphs. The latter are marked by initial scope notes indicating the general range of content rather than a précis or itemization of content. The sentences themselves are printed in varieties of type; roman for Shawnee words whose defining morphology throws them in category 1 (externally perceived); *italics* for words whose Shawnee morphology indicates that they belong to category 2 (internally experienced); SMALL CAPS for what has been described above as neutral or neutralized terms. As will presently be noted, fewer words appear in roman than in italics and small caps; this is true not only for the seventeen-sentence sample given here, but also for the entire text, which is now being prepared for publication in the *International Journal of American Linguistics*. The reader of this paper will understand, of course, that the following translation (like all translations) suggests only in part morphological criteria which serve to classify the translated words into two opposing categories besides a neutral one.

Scope Note 1-6 (Creator gives laws for men who are assured guidance [37] from *manitos*): "(1) *Thus are* men *presented with a way provided by the Creator* that they may follow − so THAT HENCEFORTH THEY WILL LIVE IN A SATISFACTORY MANNER, if they adhere to *the law* which she devised. (2) *Certainly, the law was made up for all of those* who are traveling in the direction *intended for* man. (3) *Thus* does one earn the right to the earth when he follows *these laws in the way arranged for him.* (4) *That is the reason* the Creator gave out THE LAWS and the reason men know them. (5) *That is the reason* she gave them out − so that those *manitos turned loose* IN THE WORLD may take pity on men. (6) *That is the reason* she provided men with a way to live."

Scope Note 7-17 (Sexual initiation with wife helped by husband's mother): "(7) Henceforth men teach one another *everything, in order that* they may respect their sisters. (8) WHEN a man is TWENTY-FIVE YEARS OLD, *at the time he is customarily married off,* he *doesn't* know a *thing about the* way to have intercourse with his wife. (9) At the time they must marry, therefore, YOUNG MEN *are given personal instruction* in the way EACH ONE should try to act when having intercourse with his wife. (10) *It seems that once* a woman helped her son LEARN the way he should try to act. (11) 'You must pull over *your clothes like this,'* she said to her daughter-in-law, 'and you must lie *still,'* she told her. (12) She helped her son get an erection. (13) When he had an erection, he got on top. (14) 'Crawl off,' she told him. (15) *Properly* she directed HIS PENIS to the woman's vaginal orifice. (16) *'Now,* if you get it to go in, say *"all right"* to me, *and* I'll turn the two of you loose.' (17) *But* PEOPLE *become frenzied* when they do not follow exactly *the way as it was arranged for them, the way* they ought to follow, *the way it was intended for them."*

Until publication of the actual Shawnee forms from which the above translation is derived, it is impossible for the reader to confirm our count − namely, that what is morphologically defined as falling into italics (internally experienced) and into small caps (neutralized) well exceeds what falls into roman (externally perceived). A traditional translation of the type here given is still suggestive; yet to extend this from the first seventeen sentences of the text to the entire text (1,214 sentences) would transform the present paper into a monograph.

The above procedure concerns perceptual categories correlated with morphology; the procedure following concerns perceptual categories correlated with content.

Though space limitations preclude continuation of the sample above − the sentence-by-sentence translation − it is possible to give [38] all the scope notes for the entire Shawnee Laws text, and to classify them according to whether they are mostly Contemplative or most Eventful; or whether the two classifications are each conspicuous within one scope note, as in half-and-half proportion (C + E or E + C); or whether they are mixed (alternating between C and E). It is of course the translated sentences which are classified; then all sentences comprehended under one scope note (covering the content of one paragraph) are characterized as all Contemplative, or Eventful, or mostly the latter with one or two paragraph initial sentences which strike a Contemplative tone as an introduction to sentences which are Eventful. By reading all the scope notes for Shawnee Laws, we can gain an overview of "the content" of the document − the culture of the document − and then compare this with the perceptual categories into which the language of the document falls.

First Law

All Contemplative (1-6): as above, Creator gives laws for men who are assured guidance from *manitos*. [Our definition of Contemplative includes what is normative rather than a statement of actualized event; also what is clearly fantasy rather than what is actualizable; also, whatever draws attention to moralistic desiderata rather than to actually overt, or as though overt, cultural happenings.]

Mostly Eventful (7-17): as above, Sexual initiation with wife helped by husband's mother. [The first sentence within this paragraph (7) is Contemplative, as is the last sentence (17); the others (8-16), flanked by the initial and final sentences, are Eventful. With subscript numbers to give the total of sentences within the scope which are Contemplative (C) and which are Eventful (E), we write $C_1 + E_9 + C_1$. As a category opposing Contemplative, the Eventful comprehends what is said to be possible as a cultural happening, without regard to frequency or to typicality and without regard to overtness or to covertness − except for that part of the covert culture which is said to be entirely confined to what is talked about and hence is not included in the Eventful.]

Half and half (18-25): Wife separates from husband for eight days each month. [One of the rarest things in the Shawnee Laws is an even division within a scope, as here ($C_4 + E_4$); the first four sentence Contemplative (e.g, "That's the way people live"); the second sentences are Eventful (e.g, "Eight days is the length of time a man does not sleep with his wife"). This raises an interesting question as to whether we have paragraphed advantageously; it might be [39] cogently argued that this $C_4 + E_4$ scope proves nothing more than that the two paragraphs are called for; the first, all Contemplative; the second, all Eventful. *Per contra*, the sentiments of our C_4 are related to the action of our E_4; hence we have decided to combine the two into one paragraph.]

Mostly Eventful (26-28): Husband forbidden intercourse with pregnant wife; penalty for violation given. [This is the only scope begun and concluded by Eventful sentences, with intervening Contemplative ($E_1 + C_1 + E_1$)]

All Eventful (29-32); Test for boy arriving at manhood. [This is the only paragraph in which all sentences are Eventful.]

All Contemplative (33-36); Girl arriving at womanhood marries.

Mostly Contemplative (37-43): Infrequent intercourse conducive to health of husband, wife, and children. [This is an example of $E_1 + C_6$, the first sentence being Eventful, the rest Contemplative.]

All Contemplative (44-47): Men following the law will talk about the nature of things.

Half and half (48-60): Old men doctor overly virile young men. [This is an example of $E_6 + C_7$.]

All Contemplative (61-69); Socially beneficial laws oriented in direction of fire person.

Mixed (70-82): Injunction to talk about and to listen to laws of Creator; penalties mentioned. [This is an example of $C_{10} + E_2 + C_1$.]

The next two paragraphs are all Contemplative. First (83-94): Laws oriented in direction of earth person; then (95-109): Dualism, with hell for non-followers of law.

The next two paragraphs are mixed. First (110-123): Law prohibiting intercourse for six months after birth of child; then (124-138): Law against adultery for husband; penalties for violation specified.

The next two paragraphs are all Contemplative. First (139-143): Law is for the good of humans; then (144-153); Creator gives laws specifically for women.

Mixed (154-183): Law for women when menstruating; penalties specified [$C_1 + E_4 + C_{25}$]

The next three paragraphs are all Contemplative. First (184-202): The mystery of the law in relation to the mystery of motherhood; then (203-215): Law which recommends twelve children; then (216-219); Explication of four *manitos* or grandfathers.

Mixed (220-233): Grandfather in the winter. [This is an example of the most frequent mixed type, that with one or two Eventful [40] between two longer stretches of Contemplative sentences; thus, $C_6 + E_2 + C_6$.]

A solid block of twenty-two paragraphs now follows, which is all Contemplative. (234-241); Grandfather who sits in the west; (242-245): Grandfather who sits in the south; (246-252): Grandfather southerner of Spring; (253-257): Heaven is the end-point of law; (258-264): Creator and her *manitos* helpful when asked for help; (265-270); Heaven is objective, earth is a memory; (271-274): All kinds of languages spoken but Shawnee involved in repeating the laws; (275-280): Benefit from prayer in terms of paths or alternative directions; (281-286): Prayers which reach up to our grandmother in heaven are related to survival; (287-295); All are equal to the Creator who may not be all-powerful; (296-299): Devil tempts away; (300-324): Penalties (including insanity, half-witted visitors, sadism) for following what the Devil devises (e.g., liquor, different languages, different laws); (325-331): Plan of creation, including levels of heaven, not for benefit of men who are thoughtless of plan; (332-339): Benefit for those who follow laws, with provision for misunderstanding; (340-354): Instruction on how to receive knowledge of laws with notification (prophecy) year ahead of time to be interpreted as laws; (355-365): Fire person and water person, corn, bean, pumpkin created to help man; (366-373): Being humble, saying prayer, and "pity" gladden Creator and strengthen man; (374-390): Good results flowing from Creator's plan, as rain from water person, and as alternation of night and day; (391-409): Laws are good because Creator loves all, sees all (but is not herself seen until afterlife), and because they, as all created things, will never stop; (410-413); Do not doubt, because doubting makes duty and language appear disagreeable; (414-434): Hunting laws conveyed to animals as well as to humans; (435-447): Travel laws for humans and animals encountered in traveling to be learned before starting out on travels.

Mixed (448-459): Laws regulating women, with penalties (failure in health and hunting). [The actual mixture of sentences for this paragraph is $C_3 + E_1 + C_8$]

The next eight paragraphs (the rest of the First Law) are all Contemplative. Their scopes are (460-470): Laws are unforgettable, but weakness and insanity result from neglect, in contrast to fulfillment for obedience; (471-493): Interpretation of laws in council and by grandfathers, as Eagle; (494-512): Omniscience of grandfathers, especially of the Thunderers, and their protective role toward man; [41] (513-517): Frequent prayer beneficial for Creator and grandfathers who listen, as at dances; (518-536): Grandfather Sun and Grandfather {??} Moon carry man through day and urge preparation for following day, so all will be well; (537-562): Creator promises unidentifiable sound as signal to good persons among chiefs and councilors who are created with special insight, are faultless in speech, and able in translation of Creator's thought; (563-574): Leader to take his people for sojourn to father in heaven and after twelve days of rain to return to earth populated with animals, as at first creation; (575-594): Laws direct followers to little road on which all goes well until the earth burns, destroying all life, which will be re-created as at the first creation, with people descending from two men and two women.

Second Law

Mixed (595-638): Continuity from generation to generation; from infancy to maturity, with sympathy from Creator, with constant values − all toward the increase of life $[C_{13} + E_2 + C_{29}]$.

The next five paragraphs (the rest of the Second Law) are all Contemplative. The scopes are (639-649): Foods have savor because men possess laws for caring for everything and will transmit the laws to their children; (650-660): *Manitos* remember their grandchildren (humans) and are in sympathy with the laws, and humans remember *manitos* who talk to them; (661-677): Sun sees all, helps all in living now and into the future − as long as men follow rules handed down by the Creator who sits watching in heaven; (678-700): Law for snake and insect to serve as medicine to help those who have encountered the non-beneficial − as long as Creator allows the earth to exist; (701-704); Man to live and multiply, never disappear entirely, and arrive in heaven.

Third Law

Mixed (705-715): Law regulating deer to serve man by being eaten $[C_6 + E_1 + C_4]$.

The next five paragraphs (the rest of the Third Law) are all Contemplative. (716-733): Deer's freedom from disease (gained by eating medicines) good for humans whose kind talk is good for deer; (734-751): Deer created as children of Earth Person; rules given so that no me will ever come to destroy deer; (752-761): Longevity of laws not known to Creator, who is gladdened when laws are currently followed; 762-778): What is sacred and what is to be pitied − both deer and man, for both will eventually go to heaven, in the morning, crying; [42] (779-791): Speech made on arriving at place where our grandchild lives gives prophecy of end of world, followed by the dead rising, and even the trees being renewed.

Fourth Law

Mostly Contemplative (792-801): Law regulating bear to serve man by being killed by him $[C_9 + E_1]$.

Mixed (802-816); Disposal of bear entrails and their use by humans; fate of bear after being killed four times, and his speech to bear overseer $[E_2 + C_6 + E_4 + C_3]$.

The remaining three paragraphs in the Fourth Law are all Contemplative. First (817-832): Bear to relay information from Creator to man, who passes information along to others with Creator notified by bear of man's action; then (833-837): Bear to live in wilderness; then (838-848): Bear to aid in bringing mankind to heaven at date unknown even to Creator.

Shawnee

Fifth Law

All Contemplative (849-854): Dog to help men when they him The next two paragraphs are mixed. First (855-866): Man is not to abuse dog but dog to be fed occasionally by man, who in turn to profit by dog's premonitions $[C_7 + E_1 + C_4]$; then (867-873) Man enjoined never to kill dog; penalties mentioned $[C_1 + E_1 + C_5]$.

The next five paragraphs (the rest of the Fifth Law) are all Contemplative. (874-877): Dog to be man's friend; (878-891); How the behavior of a certain dog will indicate the approach of the world end; (892-902); Dog to be dressed and shod exactly like his grandchild; (903-914); Reason given why man hunts animals and how do is to help man when man hunts; (915-927): Not all of the laws apply equally to all beings who populate the earth, but all beings are brought to heaven.

Sixth Law

The first two paragraphs are all Contemplative. First (928-939] Birds to warn men of things not beneficial to them; then (940-948) Birds are to pity men, especially when they pray.

Mixed (949-961): Birds and man to aid one another; birds to pray for man $[C_1 + E_1 + C_{11}]$.

The remaining two paragraphs of this law are all Contemplative. First (962-968): Birds eventually to go to heaven, but while on earth they are not to wonder about things; then (969-976): Birds and men to dress in similar fashion; Creator gladdened and birds brought to heaven by following this rule. [43]

Seventh Law

The paragraphs of the Seventh Law total two; both are all Contemplative. (977-988): Wolf to live in wilderness and to act as intermediary between the guides and man; (989-1004): Man is notified of how the law applies to wolf so that both man and wolf know how they are to aid one another on mutual road to heaven.

Eighth Law

The single paragraph of the Eighth Law is mixed. (1005-1041): Buffalo to be grandfather to man, who will not say anything bad about him, will feed him, and will kill, cook and eat him on earth, and share with him in heaven $[C_7 + E_1 + C_{13} + E_2 + C_{14}]$.

Ninth Law

The paragraphs of the Ninth Law total three, which are all Contemplative. (1042-1050): Creator interrogates raccoon as to what he will look like and how he will live; (1051-1071): Raccoon will never counsel his grandchild, but will help him find water; (1072-1078): Raccoon notified of where he is to live and when he will roam about.

Tenth Law

All Contemplative (1079-1082): Turtle to live in water.

The two remaining paragraphs in the Tenth Law are mixed. First (1083-1091); Man kills turtle to make medicine and is strengthened by turtle's strength [$C_2 + E_3 + C_4$; then (1092-1101): Turtle to be a rain maker for man [$C_3 + E_1 + C_6$].

Eleventh Law

All Contemplative (1102-1107): Turkey to live in wilderness and sleep on tree.

Mixed (1108-1118): Turkey to be in same clan as man, to be leader of man's prayers, and to be eaten by him [$C_2 + E_1 + C_8$].

Mostly Contemplative (1119-1127): Man forbidden to use grease of turkey or to fry squirrel; penalty for violation given [$C_8 + E_1$].

Contemplative (1128-1134): Injunction to pity man.

Twelfth Law

Mixed (1135-1146): Crow to receive information in dreams which he will tell to man, who will eat him [$C_9 + E_1 + C_2$].

The remaining paragraphs in Shawnee Laws are all Contemplative. (1147-1155): Crow will dispose of the carcasses of dead animals at the beginning of winter and feed snakes and birds; (1156-1162); Crow will aid man in hunting and be fed by him; (1163-1165); Crow [44] to have dreams after man defeats enemy in battle; (1166-1172): Crow to pity man and become a *manito*; man to respect crow and n(come near him; (1173-1182): Creator will tell crow to warn man of things he will not be benefited by; crow will give man this warning and advice on children; (1183-1197); Laws given and *manitos* created so that Creator will keep man in mind and won't wonder about him, and so that man won't wonder about things; (1198-1214): *Manitos* promise to help man by listening to him through smoke from their place under the sun, and to give him Creator's instructions. [Though our phrasing of the scope notes for the first two paragraphs above − (1147-1155) and (1156-1162) − read as though the content were full of action, the Shawnee phrasing of the sentences in the paragraphs gives an opposite impression − mystical, allusive, other-worldly.]

In the perceptual categorization proposed above, two sets of single categories are opposed − in consideration of the linguistic structure alone (externally perceived versus internally experienced), and consideration of the ethnographic content alone (Eventful versus Contemplative). "We now suggest the possibility of an integration between the two sets which might lead to a contrast of greater depth than when single categories are opposed. Something less than equation, perhaps a relationship of implication, might be expected between the members of the opposition set up for the language and the content, respectively. If a contrast of greater depth were obtainable, it would come out of combining, as pair (1), the externally perceived (1.1) with the Eventful category (1.2); and opposing this to pair (2), a combination of the internally experienced (2.1) with Contemplative category (2.2).

In general, everything attributed to (1), both under (1.1) and (1.2) is concerned with the outline of Gestalten, with what is figural, either directly visual or inferred in space as figures projected from another sense. Everyday experiences − like the Doppler effect in hearing higher pitch when a train is coming than when it is going away, or childhood experiences as discovering the shape of some object in playing blind man's touch − lead to an association of touch shape, of sight and space, of sound and space, and of time and space. These associations must surely enter into our comprehension of motion, since motion goes on in space, and space is a characteristic component in such associations. [45]

In general, everything attributed to (2), both under (2.1) and (2.2), is concerned with the field of Gestalten. with the filling-in of outline, the less conspicuous, the background. The associations for (2) can be stated as the converse of those for (1). The non-figural, the field or background, is associated with the non-active, with the passive, with what remains unmoving – this for the negative side; on the positive side, categories of type (2) are concerned with what is internal to the perceiver, and Whorf and others have extended this to include ego considerations – the egoic.

It is still not certain whether the proposal for combining categories in pairs would lead to useful correlations, or whether the categories are independent variables in respect to each other. We have not given the evidence on the distribution of (1.1) and (2.1), the morphologically defined categories; but we can anticipate that they might well be more evenly distributed throughout the document than (1.2) and (2.2), the content-defined categories.

As the record shows, nothing is more striking in the style of Shawnee Laws than the way the second kind of categories are scattered, beginning with some apparent alternation, and then proceeding to clusters or blocks of one category, with the Contemplative characterizing the larger blocks of paragraphs and also occurring more frequently than others. The first paragraph in the document is all Contemplative; this is followed by paragraphs which are mostly Eventful, then half and half, then mostly Eventful again, then all Eventful. Thereafter, and for the remainder of the document, blocks of Contemplative paragraphs are, in effect, merely flanked by paragraphs which are otherwise characterized as Eventful (E), mixed generally (M), or mixed half and half (HH). The inventory for the remainder of the document is given in tabular form to show the stylistic dominance of the contemplative over the other categories.

3 Contemplative paragraphs + HH + C + M paragraphs

2 Contemplative + 2M paragraphs

2 Contemplative + M paragraphs

3 Contemplative + M paragraphs

22 Contemplative + M paragraphs

8 Contemplative + M paragraphs

5 Contemplative + M paragraphs

6 Contemplative + M paragraphs

4 Contemplative + 2M paragraphs

7 Contemplative + M paragraphs

4 Contemplative + 2M + C + M paragraphs

2 Contemplative + M paragraphs

7 Contemplative paragraphs [46]

References Cited

BARNETT, HOMER G
    1953   *Innovation: The Basis of Cultural Change.* New York, McGraw-Hill.
BLOOMFIELD, LEONARD
    1946   "Algonquian." *Linguistic Structures a/Native America*: 85-129, Viking Fund Publications in Anthropology, No. 6.
SAPIR, EDWARD
    1930   *Totality.* Linguistic Society of America, Monograph No. 6. 1944 "Grading, A Study in Semantics," *Philosophy of Science,* 11:93-116,
SAPIR, EDWARD and MORRIS SWADESH
    1932   The Expression of the Ending-Point Relation in English, French, and *German.* Linguistic Society of America, Monograph No. 10.
WHORF, BENJAMIN L.
    1940   "Gestalt Techniques of Stem Composition in Shawnee," Prehistory Research Series, Indiana Historical Society, 1, # 9: 393-406.

The American Anthropologist

Language in Culture

Proceedings of a Conference on the Interrelations of Language and
Other Aspects of Culture

Edited by Harry Hoijer

With Papers By

Franklin Fearing   Norman A. McQuown   Joseph H. Greenberg
Stanley Newman   Charles F. Hockett   C.F Vocglin
Harry Hoijer   J.F Yegerlehner   Florence M Robinett

The American Anthropological Association
Vol. 56   No. 6   Part 2   Memoir No. 79

December 1954

Our Grandmother, The Creator[229]

Much more important in Shawnee worship today, and more clearly conceptualized, is the Shawnee female deity, commonly called Our Grandmother (*Kokomthena*) or the Creator. Intact would appear that between 1824 and the 1930s the emphasis on the Supreme Being or Great Spirit, a male deity, shifted to Our Grandmother, a female, which is a most interesting phenomenon. The earliest mention of the Shawnee female deity is found in Trowbridge (*Shawnee Traditions:* 41). He calls her *Waupoathe* and says, "This old woman seems also to have charge of the affairs of Indians, and is allowed to be nearer the residence of the Great Spirit than her grand child, whose location is immediately above the Indians and so near as to enable him to distinguish them & supply their wants." Morgan (*Indian Journals*: 47) has little to say about the Creator: "The Supreme Being of the Shawnee is a woman. Her name is *Go-gome-tha-na* meaning Grandmother." Later in the same work (Morgan *Indian* Journals: 49) he records that Tooly, a Shawnee, told him that the "Great Spirit" of the Shawnees was a woman.

Joab Spencer (*The Shawnee Indians*: 383) provides a Shawnee origin legend collected from Charles Bluejacket in the period between 1858 and 1860. It shows obvious European influence, but provides our first account of Our Grandmother's role in the Creation.

> Our traditions of the creation and the antediluvian period agree in all essential points with the Mosaic record. The first real divergence is in connection with the flood. The tradition gives an account of the white man's great canoe and of the saving of a white family, just as the Bible has it, but in addition it states that an old Indian woman was also saved. After the flood she lived in a valley, with a hill intervening between her and her white brother and his family, over which she could see the smoke rise from the white man's wigwam. When the sense of her loneliness and destitution came over her she began to weep very bitterly. There then appeared a heavenly messenger and asked her why she was so sorrowful. She told him that the Great Spirit had left her white brother his family but she was just a poor old woman alone, and that there was to be an end of her people. Then said the visitor, 'Remember how the first man was made', and then left her. From this she knew that a new Creation was meant, so she made small images of children from the earth as directed, as the Great Spirit had made the first man. But when she saw that they had no life she again wept. Again her messenger appeared and inquired the cause of her [165] grief. She said she had made children from clay, but that they were only dirt. Then said the visitor, 'Remember how the Great Spirit did when the first man was made. At once she understood, and breathed into their nostrils and they became alive. This was the beginning of the red men. The Shawnees to this day venerate the memory of the one they call their Grand Mother as the origin of their race' (Cf also J Spencer, Shawnee Folklore: 319).

Alford (Civilization: 19) distinguished between "*Mo-ne-to*", the Supreme Being, and the Great Spirit, or ruler of destinies, and speaks of the latter saying that she; "was believed to be a Grandmother who was constantly weaving an immense net which was called *Ske-mo-tah*, and it

---

[229] James Howard, Shawnee! The Ceremonialism of a Native American Tribe and Its Cultural Background, Athens: Ohio University Press 1981: 164-171.

was the Shawnee belief that when the great net was finished it would be lowered to the earth, and all would be gathered into its folds who had proven themselves by their actions to be worthy of the better world, the happy hunting ground. The world would then come to an end, and some horrible fate awaited those who were left."

The best account of the Shawnee female deity is that of C.F Voegelin, *The Shawnee Female Deity*, based upon fieldwork done by himself and E.W Voegelin and also on the field notes of Truman Michelson. He notes that in the Shawnee pantheon Our Grandmother (*Kokomthena*) reigns supreme, and that the three bands of Shawnees are remarkably consistent in their attitude towards her (*The Shawnee Female Deity*: 3), an observation that has been confirmed by my own field work: "To a greater or less extent, she establishes, observes, or participates in every aspect of Shawnee religion upon which information was secured ... She enjoys only nominal association in parts of Shawnee religion which concern the individual qua individual; quest for guardian spirit and witchcraft, for example; she is firmly integrated in those parts of religion which are communal in expression or interest, as for example with the future of the group, prophecy, and with ceremonial dances."

Our Grandmother is described as an anthropomorphic female being with gray hair (sometimes one of the hairs from her head is found on newly born babies). At times she is conceived of as a giant who can pick up adult men and hide them in cracks in the lodgepole of her house. Other descriptions, however, depict her as being small. That she wears short skirts may be seen when her shadow is reflected in the full moon. In one folktale she is painted with the traditional Shawnee woman's face paint, a round red spot on either cheek, and she has her hair parted down the middle. Her personal name is most frequently given as *Papoothkwe*, [166] "Cloud-woman," but also *Shikalapikshi* and *Lithikapo'shi*, which are both untranslateable except for their feminine endings (ibid: 4).

The Creator is thought to speak her own special non-Shawnee language in addition to Shawnee and other Indian tongues. This special language is thought to be intelligible to children under four years of age but is unlearned as soon as they begin to speak Shawnee. Formerly certain Shawnee priest-shamans, those who attended the ills of children, could speak this infant-language, but when these doctors died, opportunities to secure specimens of the dialect were lost (ibid: 4).

Our Grandmother lives in a spacious lodge in heaven, described as a typical Shawnee bark house in one tale (ibid: 5), and as a log cabin by my ~~informant~~ Mary Spoon. Now and then prophets and visionaries, and persons close to death, have visited Our Grandmother's celestial abode and returned to tell of it. As described in the Orpheus tale cited by C.F Voegelin (ibid: 5) the lodge has the typical sleeping and lounging platform at one side. The four mortal visitors find the Creator sitting upon this platform weaving a special basket *(shkimota)*, undoubtedly the same item as the "net" in Alford's description. Other features of her house are the typical furnishings of an aboriginal Shawnee dwelling: a central fire, pottery vessels, bark platters and plates, and carved wooden spoons; but she prepares her food in a little "inexhaustible food supply" pot. Her visitors are surprised when they find that they cannot consume all of the food contained in the little pot, which is emptied only after she has eaten (ibid: 5).

The locale of Our Grandmother's house is variously described. In one tale several men travel west until they come to "a lot of water at the end of the earth" ("the edge of the ocean" or "the end of the earth") which they must cross to reach the abode of the Creator (E.W Voegelin, C. Rafinesque, C.F Voegelin, and E Lilly, *Walum Olum*: 9). In an Eastern Shawnee variant of the Orpheus tale an ocean is crossed and much land is also traversed because several pairs of moccasins were worn out on the journey (Voegelin *The Shawnee Female Deity*: 5). In an Absentee Shawnee variant the visitors go to a western region beyond the end of the earth, crossing four oceans, with the passage over the last one being possible only as the rhythmically rising and falling sky rises and leaves a gap. The journey seems to have been over flat terrain, but upon arriving the visitors find themselves high [167] above the earth and Our Grandmother shows them a "sky window" through which she observes her earthly children to determine whether they are obedient. On their return journey the visitors take a shortcut, being lowered from the "sky window" in a basket and passing through a region between heaven and earth where birds and others live (ibid: 5). This suggests various "levels of heaven," and in this sense Our Grandmother does not live in the highest level, but on the next lower one, as the Supreme Being is presumably higher than she (Trowbridge *Shawnese Traditions*: 40); likewise the sun, the same sun that passes over the earth, passes over the land to which the Shawnee dead go, the place where the Creator stays and lives (Voegelin *The Shawnee Female Deity*: 5). Edward J McClain, an Eastern Shawnee, makes this explicit in a 1937 interview (Indian Archives, Oklahoma Historical Society 6: 483) stating that there are "three heavens, one on the bottom of the sea, one on the surface of the earth, and one in the air. My own ~~informant~~ Esther Dixon mentioned that the Milky Way is the road traveled by the dead on their way to heaven, adding that people who on this earth are always kicking and abusing dogs will be set upon by a pack of vicious dogs as they traverse this route, and the dogs will prevent them from entering heaven.

Trowbridge describes this heavenly abode, shared by Our Grandmother and her household and the spirits of the dead '*Shawnese Traditions*': 41): "They entertain a confused idea of a future state of punishment & rewards, which seems to originate in a mixture of their own opinions and creed with those taught by the whites. Agreeably to their notion of such things the Great Spirit inhabits a rich, fertile country, abounding in game, fish, pleasant hunting grounds and fine corn fields. Four days after death the soul of the deceased takes her departure for this place, where they remain, pursuing the same course of life which characterized them here. They plant, they hunt, play at their usual games & in all things are unchanged. The soul inhabits a similar tenement of day. This is the fate of the *good*."

My ~~informants~~ described the other world, the home of Our Grandmother, as resembling this earth *in every way* except that it is lacking the influences of white civilization. Mary Spoon said that the Shawnee heaven was "open country" or a "bare place" in the sense that there were no highways or towns. Each family lives in its own dwelling, a log cabin according to Mary. There are no [168] doors or locks there. The people live by hunting deer and other game "like the way Indians lived years ago." This heaven, located in the west, in the heavens. For this reason the Shawnee are still buried today in an east-west orientation, with the head the west. E.W Voegelin (Voegelin, Rafinesque, Voegelin, and Lilly *Walum Olum*: 86) secured a similar interpretation for the orientation of Shawnee graves from her ~~informants~~.

Those who arrive safely in the afterworld find the Creator weaving her *shkimota* ("basket" or "net"). During the night her little dog (with the aid of her grandson, in a Loyal Shawnee account) unravels the weaving of the previous day and thus prevents Our Grandmother from completing it. Some day, however, she will finish it and this will signal the end of the world. The virtuous living will be gathered into the *shkimota* but those who are evil will be destroyed. Those in the basket or net will be used to populate the new world (Voegelin *The Shawnee Female Deity*: 21).

Conservative Shawnees believe that the growing neglect of the Creator's rules means that the impending catastrophe will occur before long. This belief leads to the punctilious performance of the yearly cycle of ceremonies on the part of traditionalist Shawnees, lest they be omitted from Our Grandmother's *shkimota* when) doomsday dawns. The dead, and the living when they participate in ceremonies, should always be painted and dressed in Shawnee costume so that Our Grandmother will not mistake them for whites. Formerly the Eastern and Loyal bands of Shawnees burned round scars on the forearms of boys and girls to further mark them off. These scars were said to act as lamps on the way to the Creator (ibid: 19).

C.F Voegelin (ibid: 10) notes that even though Our Grandmother does not take sweat baths herself, she maintains a sweat lodge for doctoring her visitors. The souls of the virtuous dead are segregated by tribes and further subdivided into kin groups. An especially attractive portion of Our Grandmother's domain is reserved for the souls of warrior men and women, who spend their time in constant dancing and feasting. From this heaven, a soul travels to earth and jumps through the mother's vagina and into the body of the child through the fontanelle just before birth. A variant concept from the Eastern Shawnees has it that babies live rather on the little stars of the Milky Way before birth. Heavenly bodies are thought of as "suburbs" of Our [169] Grandmother's residence. The moon, apparently, is considered close enough to her home to be her reflector or shade, through which her image is seen, and so ceremonies are held at full moon when she can be observed bending over a pot cooking. Permanent associates of the Creator are her Grandson, her little dog, her "Silly Boys," and sometimes a bantam rooster. The Devil and Cyclone Person are also sometimes present (*ibid*: 6).

After the Creator retired to her present abode, following her recreation of the Indian race, she continued to dispense benefits to the Shawnees, supplementing her creations in the postdiluvian period. The origins of most specific items of nature and culture are generally attributed to Our Grandmother. She habitually gives visitors to her lodge useful knowledge to take back with them when they return to earth. These bits of knowledge range from herbal remedies through sacred ways of making fire to important additions to tribal ceremonies. All accounts stress her omniscience; she can read the thoughts of her visitors before they speak.

The Shawnee laws, a very important part of the knowledge and instruction received from Our Grandmother, number twelve (C.F Voegelin, J.F Yergerlehner, and F.M Robinett, "*Shawnee Laws*"). The first law sets forth their origin and purpose, describing their benefits and the consequences of failing to observe them. It also outlines modes of sexual conduct involving intercourse and such states as menstruation and pregnancy. The second is also general in scope. Each of the remaining ten laws centers on a particular animal such as deer, dog, bear, bird, wolf, buffalo, raccoon, turtle, turkey, and crow, spelling out the service it performs for humans and the manner in which it should be treated.

All of the major Shawnee ceremonies except for the Buffalo Dance of the Loyal Shawnees and the Peyote ritual were supposedly originated by Our Grandmother, and sometimes she descends to earth to observe their performance. Even if a ceremony is not primarily devoted to her she will punish its neglect. To this day when the women sing with the men during the *Kokeki* or Women's Cluster Dance, a part of the Bread Dance, an extra female voice, the voice of Our Grandmother, is sometimes heard above the brush arbor.

A number of writers have noted and some have suggested possible reasons for the shift in emphasis from the male Supreme [170] Being to Our Grandmother, the female deity. This shift occurred sometimes between 1824 and the time of the Voegelins' work in 1933-35. The Shawnees appear to be unique among all Eastern Woodlands Algonkian-speakers in possessing a female supreme deity and creator, hence the subject is of considerable theoretical interest (Cf. Voegelin and Voegelin "*The Shawnee Female Deity in Historical Perspective*"). This shift from a male to a female supreme deity is difficult to trace to any great change in Shawnee economic or social structure. Inter-tribal acculturation is a possibility, and the Voegelins suggest Iroquoian influences as the most likely one. They point out that there runs through Iroquoian mythology references to a female deity, Ataentsic, and her son Iouskaha. This Iroquoian female deity is credited with the creation of heaven, earth, and mankind, and both she and her son superintend the world after the creation (*ibid*: 374). They also suggest possible Yuchi or Christian (i.e, the Virgin Mary) influences as less likely possibilities (*ibid*: 374-75). In a recent article Jay Miller has suggested that the Shawnees may have changed from a male to a female deity because they wished to differentiate themselves from the Delawares, who believe in an all-powerful male creator (Miller "The Delaware as Women: A Symbolic Solution": 513). I find this last suggestion to be totally absurd.

If the shift in emphasis from a male Supreme Being to Our Grandmother is due to outside influence, I would agree with the Voegelins that an Iroquoian model is the most likely source. In this case the close association of the Eastern and Loyal Shawnees (and their ancestors) with the Oklahoma Seneca-Cayugas (and their ancestors, the Mingo Iroquois) would have provided ample opportunity for such borrowing. More likely no outside influence need be sought. Perhaps the shift merely represents an evolution in Shawnee belief, a movement away from a male Supreme Being who is too remote from human affairs to be of any great religious concern and toward a more immediate and approachable female deity by the harassed nineteenth century Shawnees.

Our Grandmother's Grandson

Though distinctly subordinate to Our Grandmother, Creator, in the minds of present-day Shawnees "Waupoāthee Skeelauwaathēēthar [*Wapothi Skilawethitha*] or "The boy of Waupoathee", the grandson of Our Grandmother, was apparently [171] considered one of the two principal subordinate deities by the Shawnees in Trowbridge's day, the one who was in charge of the welfare of Indians (Trowbridge *Shawnese Traditions*: 40). The other subordinate deity, whose business it was to take charge of the Whites "has so little connection with the Indians that they do not pretend even to know his name" (*ibid*.).

When he was demoted from his high position and replaced by his grandmother we do not know, but present-day Shawnees assign only a minor role to Our Grandmother's Grandson. His personal name is Rounded-Side (*Haapochkilaweetha*), according to the Absentee Shawnees and Cloudy-boy (*Peputhichkilaweetha*) to the Loyal band (Voegelin *The Shawnee Female Deity*: 6). In some Shawnee folktales Our Grandmother's Grandson originates evil creatures and happenings but at the present time he is no longer the source of catastrophes. Instead, he innocently plays with cumulus cloud formations, fashioning them into ephemeral animals for the amusement of people on earth (*ibid*: 6, 9). In some variants there are two grandsons, Rounded-Side and his evil brother, who represent a dualism that is common to the stories of other Algonkian-speaking groups. Whether good or evil, Our Grandmother's Grandson is the protagonist in some important tales, such as the one in which he precipitates a great flood by piercing either a giant with a huge belly or a transparent fish monster that has stored up all the waters of the earth in its body (*ibid*: 9). With the Shawnees this tale is a preliminary to the flood and Earth-diver myth.

Our Grandmother's Silly Boys

Sharing Our Grandmother's celestial abode are two "Silly Boys," who are giants whose feet make tracks that are five feet in length (ibid: 6). In the Orpheus tale these Silly Boys have somewhat the same character as the giant in the European tale of Jack and the Beanstalk. Thus, when Our Grandmother has hidden four mortal visitors to her home; "Her Silly Boys enter and criticize her housekeeping, remarking that they detect a very evil smell, an allusion to their pretense at being cannibals. They are of course aware of the visitors whom they attempt to frighten. When Our Grandmother tires of her Silly Boys, she picks up a poker and hits them on their legs" (ibid: 3). Thus Our Grandmother tolerates the nonsense of her Silly Boys, but manages to control them when they threaten the peace of her home.

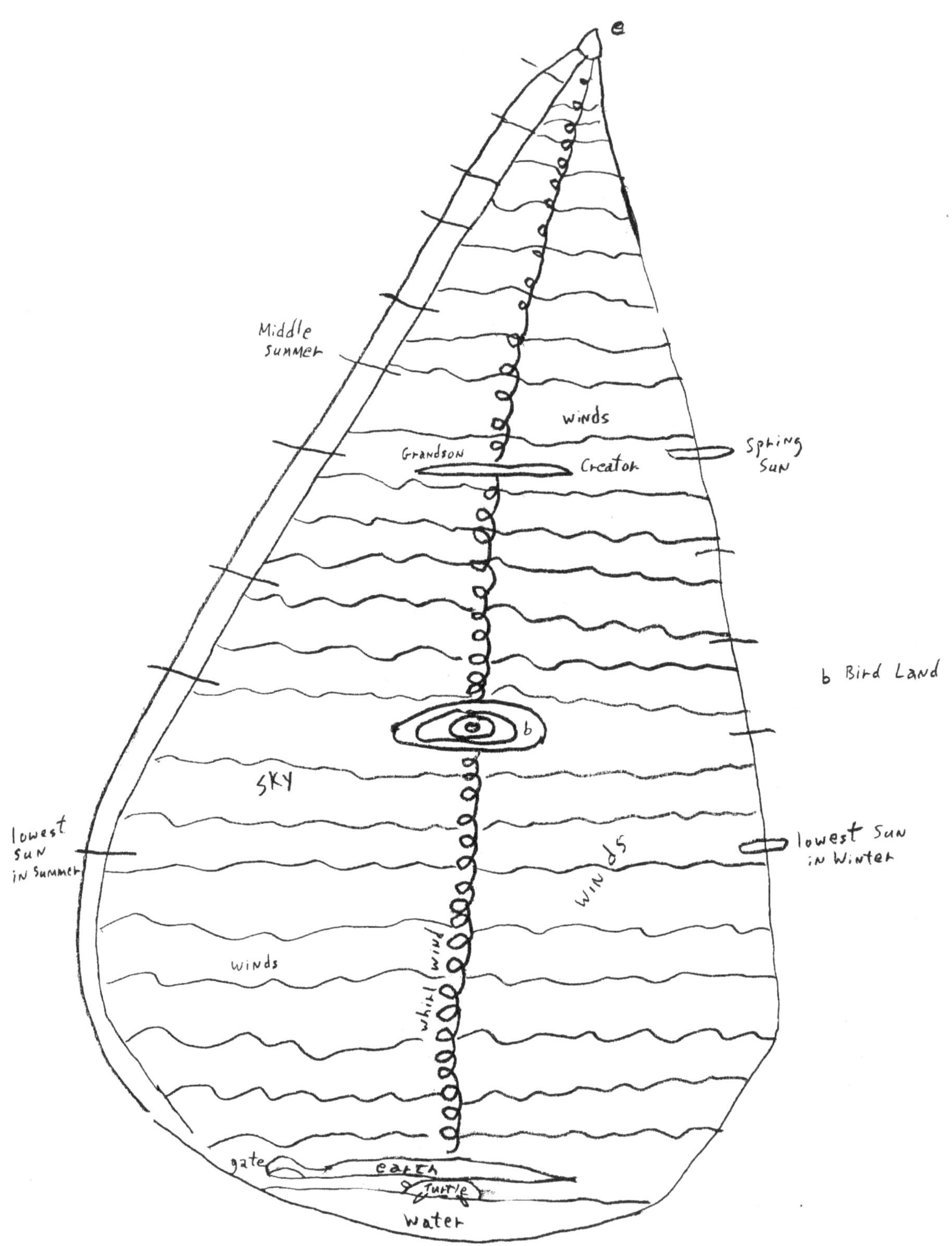

Shawnee Cosmos

Shawnees

The term Shawnee, in their own Central Algonkian language, refers to 'warmth, south, southern climes' because that was their location in terms of their other Central Algonkian speaking neighbors (see Lakes chart). After the devastation of their Ohio River homeland in the 1600s, however, some of them did move into the US Southeast and spent decades among the Muskoke Creeks. To survive, they made huge changes in their society, to make it more flexible and adaptable during horrific changes. They scattered from their Ohio homeland, but began to reclaim it in the 1700s. Originally, they traced kinship and residence directly though the father (patrilineal, patrilocal). Later, clan membership became based on personal names. A yearly series of rituals based in the growth cycle of maize and other crops, also gave spiritual strength. They seem to have numbered about 2500 during recent centuries, but their cultural and political impact was much larger and more wide ranging than their population might indicate, due largely to the efforts of men like Nika, Blue Jacket, and then the brothers Tekumtha and Tenškwatawa before and after AD 1800 (below).

The famous French explorer and trader, Robert Chavelier (1643-87), Sieur de la Salle, relied on a Shawnee slave, purchased at Lake Ontario in 1669, known only as Nika(na), Shawnee for "friend (my)". He guided the French through the Great Lakes, and probably helped to congregate the Shawnees and others in 1683 at Fort St Louis (Starved Rock) on the Illinois River. Late that same year, Nika went to France with La Salle's delegation, including another Shawnee who died there. After their colony shipwrecked in Texas, he was murdered beside La Salle in March 1687.[230]

Creations

Shawnees recognized several (re)creations of the world. Today, the most significant one occurs after the Flood, under the care of female creator usually called "Our Grandmother" (*Kokumthena*), though her personal name is Cloud (*Paapoothkwe*). Indeed, the Shawnee are distinctive in world cultures for revering this woman deity, whose twelve laws (commandments) consist of two concerned with 1) marriage and family, and 2) all-pervading care and sympathy, as well as ten with the rules laid down by species for 3) deer, 4) bear, 5) dog, 6) birds, 7) wolf, 8) buffalo, 9) raccoon, 10) turtle, 11) turkey, and 12) crow and dreams.

During their yearly series of rituals, Our Grandmother is thanked for continued bounty. This epic explains the origins and founders of each of the six tribes (Shawano, Chalaakaa(tha),[231] Thawikila, Mekoche, Pekowi, Kishpoko) of the Shawnee Nation, as well as the six clan clusters (phratries), both inherited through the father's line. Each of these tribes had a bundle (*maasawi*) that contained its medicines, such as twelve roots and other healthful ingredients, as well as other sacred items enabling it to fulfill its obligations toward the wellbeing of the cosmos.

---

[230] Interest in La Salle again peaked in 1996-97 when his supply ship *Belle*, intended for a colony at the mouth of the Mississippi, was excavated in Matagorda Bay (Texas). It produced a million artifacts, but the extensive La Salle web site from the Texas Historical Commission (Austin) /thc@thc.state.tx.us/ does not mention Nika. Robert studied to be a Jesuit, but entered the world instead equipped with both analytical and recording skills.

[231] Because this is the source for the famous name of Chillicothe the term for a member of the Chalaakaa(tha) has come to replace that of the Chalaakaa tribe itself.

Crawfish[232] brought up dirt from the bottom of the sea, and from this the earth was made by the Creator, who placed the island on the back of a turtle. Then she formed beings to populate it, and provided food – twelve kinds of meat animals, along with twelve primary plants.

The very first version of humans had all the usual parts but some were in unlikely places, so they could not have children. They were to live for 200 years, with any remaining years left over from a premature death added to that of a youngster. To make sure that some part of humans was always good, the Creator took some of her own heart and added it to the heart of each human. Everything had a heart except the earth itself, but then she gave it some of the heart from the oldest man, humanizing the landscape.

Twelve hearty men were formed in the sky, along with two old men who were given grey hairs. The oldest man, addressed as "grandfather", acted as leader, with the second older man as his deputy. These 14 men were lowered from the sky in a basket, set down on a shore across from the earth island, and sent off to find the earth's heart at a place in the north.

The oldest leader's backpack held the foods and gifts from the Creator. From it, he took out a gourd and shook it as a rattle. The men sang and fasted for twelve days to make the water recede so they could cross over the sand to the earth. Before they left, however, the oldest man passed on the pack to a strong, new leader named Chalaakaa (Chillicothe). Then he sat down and turned to stone. Once they were across, the other old man sat down and he too turned to stone. The two elders still look across the sea passage at each other. Later, the Thawikila also came across the sea.

Marching on, increasing in numbers, the men got to the heartland, where the Creator said they would be named the Shawnee, after that river and place. Thereafter, they must think for themselves and pray to their Grandmother, the Moon, who was something like a shield and shadow for the Creator herself.

In the most frequent version, Pekowi sprang up from the ashes of a fire to found the priesthood who conduct the annual rituals, because they come from "nature" and understand its cycles.[233]

A council was held to decide who would care for the great medicine bundle sent down by the Creator inside the oldest man's pack, until then kept by the Chalaakaa. They debated for days until a man appeared, naked except for a covering of white paint, who became the Mekoche founder. Undecided, the council, as a precaution, provided him with only half the contents. As a test of this medicine, Shawnees killed some Creeks, but then revived them, calling them "brothers".

Later, during warfare, Shawnee rival killed a Mekoche, and scalped him supposedly to see if such men were really pure white and bloodless. He was. Remorseful, the murderer gave the scalp and a Catawba woman prisoner to that Mekoche's own father, but lied that both were

---

[232]   Crawfish (crawdad) is an appropriate 'earth diver' because it raises a tiny mound of dirt every time it flicks its tail to move around on the bottom of a creek.

[233]   The Shawnee Prophet gave CC Trowbridge another version. Young men were sent out to hunt, with strict instructions to bring back all they killed. One elk was so large, however, that they left the backbone behind, after packing up all the meat, hide, and head. When the elders found out, greatly alarmed, they sent the hunters back. There, instead of the backbone, they found a man who was all red and became the Pekowi founder. He led the warriors because he came from an animal, not the Creator, and so could kill and die. Tenškwatawa, a failed prophet, very much had his own agenda and this colors his ethnography. He wanted to replace Our Grandmother with a Biblical God the Father, and disliked the Mekoche, and probably the Pekowi too.

enemy trophies. Years later, after she had learned to speak Shawnee, the Catawba woman told the old man about the murder of his son, setting off a war among and against the Shawnees. To restore unity, elders took the other half of the medicine bundle back from the Mekoche, returning it all to the care of the Chalaakaa.

Almost overcome during an attack by Six Nations, Shawnees turned the tide to victory by dressing their women in the garb of slain warriors. Since then, like other Ohio tribes (such as the Miami, Myaami, or Meearmear), Shawnee have had both peace and war matrons as well as female doctors mirroring those male ones.

Over time, the Shawnee Nation came to include six patri-tribes, but only five continued into today. The Chalaakaa (Chillicothe) provide the national leader, backed up by the Thawikila as deputy. Both tribes were founded by men from across the sea. The other four tribes were founded on the earth island it(her)self. These were the Shawano subtribe proper (now vanished); the Mekoche − who once had half the great medicine bundle and continue a concern with general health and ritual; the Pekowi (Piqua) − who are tied to the hunt, ritual, and oratory (bellowing) because of their origins from an elk backbone; and the Kishpoko − who are charged with warfare.

Though they are never regarded as full moieties (the dark/light halves common to other Central Algonkians), these tribes were contrasted (technically called "opposition", using / as the divider) in various ways to create shifting dualities. These include leading Chalaakaa *čalaakaa* and Thawikila *θawikila* / specialized Mekoche *mekoči*, Pekowi, and Kishpoko *kišpoko*, or hostile Chalaakaa and Mekoche / friendly Thawikila, Pekowi, and Kishpoko.[234]

There also seems to be a concentric patterning, which can be traced for thousands of years in Ohio archaeology. Each tribe and its founder stands at one of the four directions, with the Chilaakaa north of the Ohio River, and the Thawikila to the south, as attested in their histories. The Mekoche are in the east (upriver), and Pekowi to the west (downriver). The Kishpoko defend the outside edge, and the Shawano once stood at the center.

Today, Our Grandmother lives in the sky, with her grandson and his dog. Though unspecified, for good reason, it is likely that the grandson has a twin, whose intentions are bad or disruptive. Our Grandmother is constantly weaving a "net" (*skemotah*), probably something like the basket that brought the first men to earth. When it is finished, the world will end but all those faithful to the Shawnee community of past and present will be saved in the net by Our Grandmother.

Diet

Varying by seasons, Shawnees lived by a mixed economy of farming, fishing, hunting, and wild harvesting. Men did the hunting and women did the gardening. Kentucky was Shawnee hunting ground, and the Cumberland was known as the Shawnee River.[235] During the summer, families lived in a long oval house with gabled roof, spacious to hold stored foods and

---

[234] Charles Callendar (1978, 622), who has devoted his life to understanding Great Lakes ethnography, noted that these tribes functioned much like Creek town-tribes (*talwa*) and saw an even more ancient inspiration for both of these expressions in the prehistoric organization of Mississippian societies, including the huge council house. While the Shawnees and Mvskoki have long had close ties, the Thawikila actually joined the Creeks for some time.

[235] The most famous version of this name, however, is the river draining Georgia and Florida known by a variant of the tribal name – Suwanee River, as in "Way down upon …". The name derives from the Shawnees who lived among the Creeks.

possessions. The winter house was small, round, and domed, making it easier to heat. Small huts were used by women when they gave birth or menstruated, secluding them until ritual restrictions were lifted. For ceremonies, families camped around sacred precincts, positioning themselves as a microcosm of their world. In other words, families living northeast of the ground camped in the northeast sector, those from the south in the south, and so forth − to make sure the ceremonial grounds mirrored their whole territory.

Clans

Like other natives of the Great Lakes, the Shawnees had to cope with huge population loss and disruptions. Like the Ojibwa, they probably once had patrilineal clans, each predominating at certain villages and regions. Clans had the characteristics of their namesake animals as well as duties within the larger cosmos.

Biology – in the face of infertility, infant mortality, and human catastrophe – could not assure the continuity of clans. Instead, the solution for balanced ratios of membership is based in the rituals of naming. Parents select an elder to name a new son or daughter, and the infant then belongs to the same name group (quasi-clan) as the namer. The name is suggestive of the namesake animal or being. Boys are named ten days after birth, and girls on the twelfth day.

Though as many as 36 patriclans can be identified, six naming groups (*m'shoma*, phratries, clan clusters) are basic. These are, with their cosmic equations 1) Turkey = all birds 2) Turtle = all aquatics 3) Round Foot = all mammal carnivores 4) Horse = hoofeds (formerly named Elk) 5) Raccoon = paweds 6) Rabbit = peaceful, quiet, calm, timid folk, making ideal Peace chiefs. Again, interclan joking and special duties that formed certain pairings or dualities suggest former moieties.

During warfare, subgroups of the Round Foot had varied responsibilities. The Panther clan led war parties out, while the Wolf head warrior led them home.

Laws

As noted, Grandmother gave twelve laws to Shawnees which consist of two for the conduct of 1) marriage and family, and 2) all-pervading care and sympathy, as well as ten rules with regard for certain species; such as 3) deer, 4) bear, 5) dog, 6) birds, 7) wolf, 8) buffalo, 9) raccoon, 10) turtle, 11) turkey, 12) crow and dreams. More generally, snakes and insects are to serve as medicine to help those who have encountered them – as long as Creator allows the earth to exist.

Death

A man was buried by male nonkin attendants, while a woman had both male and female nonkinspeople arranging her funeral. After an all-night wake, the body was placed in a grave lined with wooden or stone slabs, then covered with mounded earth. Later, a grave house was built over its length and width.[236]

Good souls went immediately to the abode of Our Grandmother, but bad ones went off on a side path, where they were punished accordingly. They still had a full sense of feelings, assuring their pain and suffering. A soul's torments depended on its wickedness and selfishness during life. Most were maimed or hurt for a time, cured, and sent on. The worst were actually consumed in flames, then revived and improved until they could finally enter the sky among the good.

Like other Great Lakes tribes, the Shawnee once had a version of the Midewiwin

---

[236] Today funerals involve morticians, coffins, and hearse, but the grave house is still built over the surface of the entire grave.

(doctoring lodge), whose new members were initiated during a rite that enacted their being killed, dismembered, eaten by dogs, and revived.

War

The most famous Shawnees, the brothers Tekumtha and Tenskwatawa the Prophet, belonged to the Kishpoko tribe and the Panther clan. Their father was killed during the battle of Point Pleasant, when the Shawnees took on Virginians in Lord Dunsmore's War to hold off the European settlement. Eventually the aggressive occupation of Ohio permanently split apart these five tribes. The Chalaakaa (Chillicothe) and Mekoche remained hostile, staying in Ohio during 1774-94. The other tribes, both more friendly and concerned to get out of harm's way, moved to Missouri, which was then Spanish territory. Tekumtha and his allies lived in Indiana from 1798 to 1805. They moved to Greenville (Ohio) until 1808, then settled Prophet's Town at Tippecanoe (Indiana) on a branch of the Wabash. There, in 1811, William Henry Harrison led an attack that he called a victory but that was really more of a draw. The brothers then moved to Ft Malden in Canada until Tekumtha was died in battle as a British general in 1813.[237]

Whenever a Shawnee war party arrived outside a village with prisoners, those to be tortured to death were painted black, but those to be adopted were painted red. Others were left to fate as the shouts of these arriving warriors set off a race between the women peace chiefs and four old women, painting their lips bright red as they rushed from their homes, who led the cannibal cult. Whichever woman first touched each prisoner would determine his or her fate. A Peace Woman assured adoption into a Shawnee family and perhaps release, but a hag doomed a ritual meal of human flesh, after protracted torture as a test of bravery, stamina, and courage.

Each town had a council house, a huge rectangular building with six standing timbers, set in three pairs down the middle, holding up the roof. After prisoners were painted and ran the gauntlet (racing between two rows of Shawnees holding weapons), they were brought into this hall and tied to the inner posts. A War Woman stripped them naked, and they were subjected to other humiliations. Each post probably represented one of the six clan clusters. The post that a prisoner was tied to probably indicated who would be his or her likely adopters or torturers, according to their luck at that town.

For days after their return from the warpath, Shawnee men secluded themselves in the Council House, off limits to their families and especially their wives, whose life-giving abilities were endangered by this supercharged (macho) warrior condition. After fasting, prayer, and purification, they returned to ordinary life, and were expected to use their bravado only on the enemy.

Rites

The Shawnee year is marked by a series of important rituals, appropriate to the harvesting cycles and seasons. Twelve months were named by seasonal bounty ('strawberry, raspberry, blackberry, plum, pawpaw') and by weather conditions ('long, cold, erratic, hard').

The Shawnees are still intensely devoted to their traditional religion, and absolutely certain that the entire world will end if they ever forego their rituals. All of their efforts are done

---

[237] Elected President in 1840 as a US hero, Harrison died almost immediately. As other US presidents elected at the end of decades (years ending in zero 0) also died in office, newspapers hyped "Tecumsah's curse". In 1889, however, Harrison's grandson Benjamin was elected president and served a full term, so the "curse" was on the office not the family, as it should be.

before spiritual witnesses (*tipwiwe*), who receive prayers and return goodwill. Tobacco and fire usually witness for men; as water does for women.

Though Shawnees gave up the council house, they have maintained its outline at their ceremonials. The dimensions of this rectangular floor plan are outlined by railroad ties stacked to sitting height, with gaps like doorways left in the short sides at the east and west. Men enter this sacred space through one gap, and women through the other. Family camps had the same alignment by direction as their homesteads, as noted, so the whole camp was a mirror of their entire territory.

Two Bread Dances are held each year. The Spring one honors women and their farmed crops, while the other in the Fall respects men and their hunting. At the Spring Bread Dance, men and women divide into teams to play a version of Football (as a ritual not a sport), whose goal is to transfer energy from the players to the growing crops. The loser provides the firewood for the dance.

Twelve women serve as cooks, twelve men as hunters providing game meat for the dances. A man and a woman pair are selected from each of the six naming groups. In the spring, the leaders must be Turtle or Turkey because both lay eggs and promote fertility. In the fall, the leaders are Horse or Roundfoot because both are allies in the hunt. The Loyal Shawnee community also hold a Green Corn dance just before this crop is harvested. The Absentee Shawnees, about the same time, hold a dramatic Ride-in War Dance to honor the opening of the Kishpoko tribal bundle.

After the harvest, Shawnee families will host a memorial (death feast) for all their deceased kin. Food will be cooked, served, and left on a table, often in the dark, for several hours until the dead have had their fill and the living can partake.

A short time later, the Buffalo Dance is held outside the dance ground to the south because it was not given by the Creator. Instead, it is often traced to Tekumtha, who had bison as a spirit helper. Men have a buffalo head painted on the chest, and act as bulls, while women take the role of bison cows. Two huge kettles of corn mush, one sweet and one not, are cooked over open fires, and the men and women jostle each other to grab handfuls of the hot gruel. Afterward, the cooks formally served this mush in bowls to seated dancers.

Before the Fall Bread Dance, instead of Football, a dice game using marked peach stones (six, for the naming groups) inside a wooden bowl is played by the twelve hunters against the twelve cooks. The loser provides the wood for the fires at the Fall dance.

Today

Today, the five tribes are included within three federally-recognized Shawnee communities, each of whom once had land and a reservation until these were "abolished" by the state of Oklahoma and US. The Eastern Shawnees in Northeast Oklahoma derive from those at Lewistown (OH), who left with the Mingo Iroquois in 1832. Nearby are the Loyal Shawnee with their ceremonial ground at Whiteoak. In central Oklahoma, the Absentee Shawnee have two ceremonial grounds, with the older one at Little Axe to the south and the newer Little River one to the north. Until recently, the community at White Turkey was largely composed of the Thawikila and held rites in honor of that bundle, which has since joined the Absentee.[238]

---

[238] Federal Indian law is a legal specialization, based on claims to sovereignty by many tribes and nations which place them above the laws of states and below those of DC. All three branches of government impact tribes and reservations. Dealings with Congress include treaties, which have international standing, and agreements (after 1871); those with courts and judges work their way from hostile local situations to the Supreme Court,

Shawnee language, kinship, religion, and traditions remain strongly embraced in these communities, devoted to keeping the goodwill of Our Grandmother in a world abounding in witnesses for all of their actions. Intensely proud of their traditions, Shawnees have struggled long and hard to keep them alive with meaning and purpose.

Alford, Thomas Wildcat
    1979 *Civilization, and the Story of the Absentee Shawnees*. Norman: University of Oklahoma Press. [1936]
Callander, Lee A and Ruth Slivka
    1984 *Shawnee Home Life*: *The Paintings of Ernest Spybuck*. New York: Museum of the American Indian.
Callender, Charles
    1962 *Social Organization of the Central Algonkian Indians*. Milwaukee Public Museum Publications in Anthropology 7.
    1978 Shawnee Handbook of North American Indians, *Northeast*, 15: 622-635. Bruce Trigger, ed. DC: Smithsonian Institution Press.
Clifton, James
    1984 *Star Woman and other Shawnee Stories*. Latham: University Pres of America.
Trowbridge, Charles Christopher
    1939 *Shawnese Traditions*. Vernon Kinietz and Erminie W Voegelin, ed. University of Michigan, Museum of Anthropology, Occasional Contributions 9.
Voegelin, Carl F, John F Yegerlehner, and Florence Robinett
    1954 Shawnee Laws; Perceptual Statements for the Language and for the Content. *Language in Culture*. Harry Hoijer, ed. American Anthropologist 56 (6), part 2, 32-46. Memoir 79.
Warren, Stephen
    2005 *The Shawnees and Their Neighbors, 1795-1870*. Urbana: University of Illinois Press.
Warren, Stephen, and Randolph Noe
    2009 "The Greatest Travelers in America" ~ Shawnee Survival in the Shatter Zone: Chapter 7, 163-187. Robbie Ethridge and Sheri Shuck-Hall, eds. *Mapping the Mississippian Shatter Zone, The Colonial Indian Slave Trade and Regional Instability in the American South*. Lincoln: University Nebraska Press.

---

which is not always just; and those with the White House include executive orders and opinions. In Federal law, tribes retail all those rights and privileges not explicitly given up in official documents. Reservations are lands therefore kept back in "reserve" by native officials, not something provided for them by the US government.

English translations of French in Cooper
page numbers refer to original text

Archbishop Taché {49-51} wrote his account in 1851, after four or five years spent among the Chipewyan, at the time of the first opening-up of missionary work among them. He had, therefore, ample opportunity to observe them in their pagan state, and his exact and minute account of general Chipewyan culture shows him an exceptionally good observer.

"Aussi nos Montagnais [that is, Chipewyan, not eastern Montagnais], sans autres lumières que celles de leur raison, son parvenus á la connaissance de Dieu, sans y joindre ce mélange grossier d'absurdités qui captivait les peuples les plus éclaires de l'antiquité.

"Therefore, our Montagnais [{mountaineers}, that is, Chipewyan, not eastern Montagnais], without other enlightenment than that of their {own} reason, have come to the knowledge of God, without adding to it this gross mixture of such absurdities which captivated the most enlightened peoples of antiquity.

Ils croyaient en un seul Dieu, créateur et conservateur de tout, rémunérateur de la vertu et vengeur du crime, en un Dieu éternel dont les soins providentiels s'étendaient á tout ce qui existe.

They believed in one God, creator and conservative of everything, remunerator of virtue and avenger of crime, in an eternal God whose providential care extended to all that exists.

Seulement, peu faits aux idées purement spirituelles, ils supposaient ce Dieu revêtu d'une forme humaine, dont les proportions gigantesques répondaient á son pouvoir, et dont la délicatesse des organes lui permettait de voir et d'entendre du haut du ciel tout ce qui se faisait et se disait sur la terre."

Only, a little inclined to purely spiritual ideas, they supposed this God to be clothed in a human form, whose gigantic proportions corresponded to his power, and whose delicacy {refineness} of the organs allowed him to see and hear from heaven all that was done and said on earth. "

He was called by "les noms de Créateur (*Niottsi*) et de puissant (*yeddariyé*)".

He was called by "the names of Creator (Niottsi) and of mighty (yeddariyé)".

"II est surprenant qu'avec ces idées sur la divinité, les Tchipeweyans n'eussent aucun culte, ni aucune cérémonie religieuse quelconque.

"It is surprising that with these ideas on divinity, the Tchipeweyans had no worship {rites}, nor any religious ceremony whatsoever.

Seulement aux reunions, surtout aux festins, quelqu'un des vieillards exhortait l'asseniblée à reconnaître la libéralité de Dieu, à éviter le mal qui seul peut suspendre le cours des bienfaits du Tout-Puissant.

Only at gatherings, especially at feasts, one of the old men exhorted the assembly to recognize the liberality of God, to avoid the evil which alone can suspend the course {flow} of the blessings of the Almighty.

Suivait une fervente prière pour demander la santé, le succès a la chasse et autres choses nécessaires à la vie présente.

Thereafter followed a fervent prayer asking for health, success in the hunt and other things necessary for this life.

On jetait ensuite au feu et on enterrait sous le foyer quelques bouchées des aliments qui devaient être offerts aux conviés.

Then we threw in the fire and we buried under the hearth a few mouthfuls of {the} foods that were to be offered {served} to the guests.

Quelques sacrifices plus considérables avaient aussi lieu, mais si rarenient qu'ils n'étaient, pour ainsi dire, point d'usage.

Some more considerable sacrifices also took place, but so rare that they were, so to speak, useless {pointless}.

Tel est absolument tout le culte public que cette nation rendait à la divinité.

Such is absolutely all the public worship that this nation rendered to the divinity.

On trouve pourtant quelques traces de jonglerie ; mais, outre qu'il est permis de les croire de fabrique étrangère [Cree ?], ce [50] n'étaient guère que des prières, accompagnées de plus de bruit que les autres.

There are, however, some marks of juggling {conjuring}; but, apart from being allowed to believe them of foreign fabric [Cree?], they [50] were hardly more than prayers, accompanied by more noise than the others.

Les jongleurs avaient, sans doute, la prétention de passer pour des hommes extraordinaires; mais ils ne s'adressaient jamais qu'a Dieu, et ces superstitions n'avaient jamais les résultats fâcheux qu'elles ne présentent que trop souvent chez les peuples voisins.

The jugglers undoubtedly pretended to be extraordinary men; but they only addressed to God, and these superstitions never had {any of} the unfortunate results they all too often had among neighboring peoples.

Le culte particulier était assez universel. Quelques personnes adressaient tous le jours à Dieu de ferventes prières, d'autres ne le faisaient que dans les circonstances critiques.

The particular cult was fairly universal. Some people prayed earnestly to God every day, others only did so in critical circumstances.

"J'ai entendu raconter plusieurs exemples, qui prouvent combien les prières de ces âmes simples étaient puissantes auprès de Celui qui a dit: 'Demandez, et vous recevrez'.

"I have heard many examples recounted, which prove how powerful the prayers of these simple souls were {to} with Him who said, 'Ask, and you will receive'.

Voici un fait entre plusieurs.

Here is one fact {case} among many.

J'examinais un jour le main d'un vieillard privé de son pouce; s'étant aperçu de mon attention, il me dit d'un ton de conviction qui me toucha:

I was one day examining the hand of an old man deprived of his thumb; perceiving my attention, he said to me in a tone of conviction that touched me:

'Vois cette main. J'étais un jour à la chasse, en hiver, loin de ma loge.

'See that hand. I was hunting one day in winter, far from my lodge.

Il faisait froid.

It was cold.

Je marchais; tout-à-coup j'aperçois des caribous; je les approche, je les tire, mon fusil crève, et m'emporte le pouce.

I was walking; all of a sudden I see caribou; I approach them, I shoot them, my rifle bursts, and takes {off} my thumb.

Déjà beaucoup de mon sang n'était plus.

Already a lot of my blood was gone.

En vain, je m'efforçai d'en tarir le source : impossible.

In vain, I tried to dry up the source: impossible {hopeless}.

Peu à peu je prenais froid.

Little by little I caught cold.

J'essayai d'allumer du feu: impossible.

I tried to light a fire: impossible. {hopeless}

Alors j'eus peur de mourir; mais, me souvenant de Celui que tu nommes Dieu, et que je ne connaissais pas bien, je lui dis:

So I was afraid of dying; but, remembering Him whom you call God, and whom I did not know well, I said to him:

'Mon graud-père, (Se tssiyè,) on dit que tu peux tout ; regarde-mois, et *quisque* {puisque} tu es le Puissant, soulage-moi'.

'My grandfather, (Se tssiyè,) they say you can do anything; look at me, and as you are the Mighty one, {give} me relief'.

Tout-à-coup, plus de sang, ce que me permit de mettre ma mitaine.

Suddenly there was no more blood, which allowed me to put on my mitten.

Je regagnai ma loge, ou j'écrasai de faiblesse en entrant.

I returned to my lodge, where I was crushed {overcome} with weakness upon entering.

Je compris alors, ajouta-t-il, profondément ému, je compris quelle est la force du Puissant.

I understood then, he added, deeply moved, I understood what is the strength of the Mighty.

Depuis ce moment, j'ai toujours désiré le connaître.

{Ever} Since that moment, I have always wanted to know him.

C'est pourquoi, ayant appris que tu étais ici, je suis venu de bien loin, pour que tu m'eiiseignes à servir Celui qui m'a sauvé cette fois et qui seul nous fait vivre tous".

This is why, having learned that you were here, I came from afar, so that you could teach me to serve the One who saved me this time and who alone makes us all alive".

The Chipewyans, according to Tache, also believed in a multitude of malicious spirits,

"ennemis de Dieu et des hommes; toujours en guerre avec le premier, sur lequel ils avaient quelquefois l'avantage, ce dont ils ne se servaient que pour nuire à l'homme.

"enemies of God and of men; always at war with the former, over whom they sometimes had the advantage, which they used only to harm man.

Aussi attribuaient-ils à ces esprits mauvais tous leurs revers, leurs maladies et surtout [51] la mort, quand elle arrivait avant la décrépitude de l'âge.

So they attributed to these evil spirits all their setbacks, their illnesses and especially [51] death, when it happened before the {full} decrepitude of age.

Ils croyaient que ces esprits n'avaient pris naissance, qu'-après le déluge; qui, de plus, ils avaient une union très-ètroite avec les animaux, ennemis de l'homme ou qui lui inspirent de l'horreur, entre autres les serpents.

They believed that these spirits did not take birth until after the flood; who, moreover, they {these} had a very close union {bond} with {bad} animals, enemies of man or which inspire him with horror, among others snakes.

De là une extrême attention à ne rien dire contre ces animaux, dans la crainte d'exciter leur courroux.

Hence {their} extreme care not to say anything against these animals, for fear of arousing their wrath.

Quoique le mot de blasphème se trouve dans leur langue, ce crime si commun parmi les chrétiens était inconnu parmi eux.

Although the word 'blasphemy' is found in their language, this crime so common among Christians was unknown among them.

Ils croyaient que de paroles injurieuses contre la divinité ne pouvaient qu'augmenter leurs peines". <#11>

They believed that abusive words against the deity could only increase their punishments. <#11>

The foregoing is Tache's description in full of Chipewyan religion. There is no mention by him of a supreme evil being. A large number of the points in his general description of Chipewyan culture I have been able to verify independently, during a stay among the Chipewyans in 1931, but I did not get anything on their early theistic cult, being at the time on the trail of other information, namely, that bearing upon the general relationship of northern Algonquian culture to northern Athapaskan.

<11> *Alex. Taché, "Lettre de, à sa mère", dated* Isle à la Crosse, *Jan. 4, 1851, in* Rapport sur Le missions du diocèse de Québec, *Mars, 1853, no. 10, Quebec, 1853, 7-10; also in* Annnales de la propagation de la foi, *Lyons, 1852, xxiv, 333-36.* The Rapport sur les missions, *just cited, will hereafter in the present paper be cited as RMQ. The Rapport ended with no. 21, March, 1874, being continued as* Annales de la propagation de la foi pour la province de Quebec, *Montreal, beginning n.s. I, Feb, 1877 (hereafter cited as APFQ).*

53 Marest >> "'Ja'i su qu'ils ont des espèces de Sacrifices; ils sont grands jongleurs; ils ont, comme les autres, l'usage de la pipe, qu'ils appellent *calumet;* ils font turner le Soleil, ils font fumer aussi les personnes absentes".[15]

Marest >> "'I know they have a kind of Sacrifices; they are great jugglers; they, like the others, use the pipe, which they call *calumet*; they make the Sun turn, they also make absent people smoke".

53 La Potherie >> "Ils reconnoissent comme ces anciens heretiques [the Manicheans] un bon et un mauvais esprit. Ils apellent le premier le *Quichemanitou.* C'est le Dieu de prosperité. C'est celui dont ils s'imaginent recevoir tous les secours de la vie, qui préside dans tons les effets heureux de la nature. Le *Matchimanitou* au contraire est le Dieu fatal. Ils l'adorent plus par crainte que par amour . . . Ces deux Esprits selon la croyance de la plûpart, sont le Soleil et la Lune. II y a de l'aparence qu'ils reconnoissent le premier pour le Souverain maître de [54] 1'Univers: aussi quand ils se trouvent dans quelques afflictions publiques, ils lui font des sacrifices".

La Potherie >> "Like these ancient heretics [the Manicheans] they recognize a good and an evil spirit. They call the former the {*Kichi manitu*} *Quichemanitou*. He is the God of prosperity. He is the one from whom they imagine they receive all help of life, which presides over all the happy effects of nature. The *Matchimanitou*, on the contrary, is the deadly fatal God. They adore him more out of fear than out of love... These two Spirits, according to the belief of most, are the Sun and the Moon. There is an impression that they recognize the former for the Sovereign master of [54] the Universe: also when they find themselves in some public afflictions, they make sacrifices to him".

54 "Ceux, qui les ont phis fréquentés, assurent qu'ils ont, comme ceux du Canada, l'idée d'un bon. & d'un mauivais Genie, que le Soleil est leur grande Divinité".

"Those who have spent the most time with them assure that they have, like those in Canada, the idea of a good and bad Genie, that the Sun is their great Divinity".

54 Father Laverlochere, writing about the same time as did McLean, states: "Les tribus indiennes du nord de l'Amerique, celles du moins que j'ai pu visiter, n'ont point de fétichisme. Ils croient qu'il y a un esprit supérieur et bon qui ne peut point faire de mal, et pour cette raison, ils ne s'en mettent nullement en peine; mais ils croient aussi qu'il y a le génie du mal, presque aussi puissant que le premier; qu'il a une multitude de satellites qui se trouvent partout pour faire du mal, et qu'il faut les apaiser et se les rendre favorables en leur sacrifiant quelques restes de tabac, ou un chien que l'on pend par les pieds de derriere, ou quelques [60] entrailles d'un castor".

Father Laverlochere, writing about the same time as did McLean, states: "The Indian tribes of North America, at least those that I have been able to visit, have no fetishism. They believe that there is a superior and good spirit which cannot do harm, and for this reason, they do not bother at all; but they also believe that there is the Genie of evil, almost as powerful as the first; that there is a multitude of satellites which are everywhere to do evil , and that it is necessary to appease them and make them favorable by sacrificing to them some remains of tobacco, or a dog which one hangs by the feet from behind, or some [60] entrails of a beaver ".

60 he reported that one Albany Indian, a young man nineteen or twenty years old, whom he had just instructed and baptized, said to him: "Il est vrai que nous sommes bien malheureux dans nos forêts, ensevelis dans la nuit profonde de la magie, nous venons au monde, nous grandissons et puis nous cessons de vivre comme les bêtes des nos forêts. Nous ne savons pas que là-haut dans sa grande lumière le Grand-Esprit veille sur nous".

he reported that one Albany Indian, a young man nineteen or twenty years old, whom he had just instructed and baptized, said to him: "It is true that we are very unhappy in our forests, buried in the deep night of magic, we come into the world, we grow up and then we stop living like the beasts of our forests. We don't know that above us the Great Spirit in his great light is watching over us."

60 Father Charles l'Allemant, writing in 1627 of the Indians around Quebec, states: "Aux festins qu'ils font pour la mort de quelqu'vn ils font la part du defunt aussi bien qu'aux autres, laquelle ils iettent dans le feu". "Il leur semble que comme eux nous addressons nos Prieres au Soleil.... Ils n'ont aucun cult diuin, ny aucunes sortes de Prieres. Ils croyent neantmoins qu'il y en a Vn qui a tout fait; mais pourtant ils ne luy rendent aucun honneur. Entr'eux ils ont quelques personnes qui font estat de parler au Diable; [61] ceux là font aussi les Medecins, & guarissent de toute maladie".

Father Charles l'Allemant, writing in 1627 of the Indians around Quebec, states: "At the feasts they make for the death of someone they form the aspect of the deceased as well as the others, which they put into the fire". "It seems to them that like them we address our Prayers to the Sun.... They have no divine cult, no kind of Prayers. They nevertheless believe that there is One who has done everything; but yet they do not not give honor. Among them they have some people who presume to speak to the Devil; [61] those also confirm the Doctors, & are immune from any disease".

61 Father Paul Ie Jeune writes in his 1633 Relation, of the "Montagnais": "Il disent qu'il y a vn certain qu'ils nomment *Atahocan*, qui a tout fait: parlant vn jour de Dieu dans vne cabane, ils me demanderent que c'étoit que Dieu, ie leur dis que c'estoit celuy qui pouuoit tout, & qui auoit fait le Ciel & la terre: ils commencerent à se dire les vns aux autres *Atahocan, Atahocan,* c'est *Atahocan.* Ils disent qu'vn nominé Messou repara le monde perdu dans les eaux", referring here to the flood story in which Messou plays the rôle that Wisekwedjak plays among the eastern Cree.

Father Paul le Jeune writes in his 1633 Relation, of the "Montagnais": "They say that there is one certain person that they name Atahocan, who did everything: speaking one day of God in a hut, they asked me what was God, I tell them that it was the one who could do everything, & who made Heaven & Earth: they began to say to each other Atahocan, Atahocan, it's Atahocan. They say that one nominated Messou will repair the world lost in the waters," referring here to the flood story in which Messou plays the rôle that Wisekwedjak plays among the eastern Cree.

61 On a later occasion, however, when le Jeune questioned two of the Indians, they answered "qu'ils ne sçauoieiit pas qui estoit le premier Autheur du monde, que c'estoit peut-estre Atahocham, mais que cela n'estoit pas certain". "Dans leurs festins, ils iettent par fois quelques cuillerées de gresse dans le feu, prononcant ces parolles *Papeouekou, Papeouekou,* faites nous trouuer à manger, faites nous trouuer à manger; ie crois que cette priere s'addresse à ces Genies, ausquels ils presentent cette gresse comme la chose la meilleure qu'ils ayent au monde". The "Genii" referred to by le Jeune are the *Khichikouai;* at the present time the word *Kijiko* is used by the Tête-de-Boule Cree and the Abitibi Algonkin for guardian spirit or for the being(s) who used to come into the shaking tent during this conjuring rite. *Papewe* is still used in many places in the northern Algonquian area, in the meaning of "good luck!", as when a bit of meat or grease is thrown on the fire.

On a later occasion, however, when le Jeune questioned two of the Indians, they answered "That they did not know who was the first Author of the world, that it was perhaps Atahocham, but that that was not certain". "In their feasts, they sometimes put a few spoonful of fat in the fire, uttering these words Papeouekou, Papeouekou, make us find food, make us find food; I believe that this prayer is addressed to these Genies, to whom they present this fat like the best thing that they have in the world". The "Genii" referred to by le Jeune are the *Khichikouai;* at the present time the word *Kijiko* is used by the Tête-de-Boule Cree and the Abitibi Algonkin for guardian spirit or for the being(s) who used {sic} to come into the shaking tent during this conjuring rite. *Papewe* is still used in many places in the northern Algonquian area, in the meaning of "good luck!", as when a bit of meat or grease is thrown on the fire.

62 Father Henri Nouvel, in the Relation of 1663-64, referring to the Ouchestiguetch, a band living north of the Papinachois country, whom he met and preached to for three days during his pioneer journey into the Labrador hinterland, wrote: "Ayant esté aduerty que parmy ces Cathecumenes il y en auoit trois, qui auoient ionglé autrefois; ie les appellay en particulier en la Chapelle; & les ayant examinez sur ce qu'ils auoient fait en ionglant, & qu'elles estoi[en]t leurs pensées, ils me dirent qu'ils auoient eu cette pensée, qu'il y auoit vn bon & vn mauuais manitou, qu'ils hayssoient le mauuais, & aymoient le bon; que tout ce qu'ils auoient fait, ce n'auoit esté que pour honorer le bon manitou". <27>"

Father Henri Nouvel, in the Relation of 1663-64, referring to the Ouchestiguetch, a band living north of the Papinachois country, whom he met and preached to for three days during his pioneer journey into the Labrador hinterland, wrote: "Having been warned that among these Cathecumenes there were three, who had formerly juggled; I called them in particular in the Chapel; & having examined them on what they had done while juggling, & what were their thoughts, they told me that they had had this thought, that there was a good and a bad manitou, that they hated the bad, and loved the good; that all they had done, it was only to honor the good manitou ". <27> "

Two-thirds of a century later, Father Pierre Laure, writing in 1730 of the Mistasini Indians, mentions a sacrifice they offered to the dead, but gives nothing clear in his Relation on any Supreme Being or offering to Him: "Rarement entre eux ils boivent ou mangent sans donner avant aux morts une petite portion de leurs mets qu'ils jettent au feu".

Two-thirds of a century later, Father Pierre Laure, writing in 1730 of the Mistasini Indians, mentions a sacrifice they offered to the dead, but gives nothing clear in his Relation on any Supreme Being or offering to Him "Rarely do they drink or eat among themselves without first giving the dead a small portion of their food which they throw into the fire".

64 At the time of Father Charles Arnaud's first visit to them in 1853, they were nearly all still pagan. He wrote as follows of them: "En général, les sauvages infidèles de ces contrées [upper interior Labrador Peninsula] croient à l'existence de deux divinités qu'ils appellent *Manitous* (esprits); mais cette croyance est si confuse dans leur esprit qu'ils ne peuvent guères en rendre compte. Suivant eux, il y a le bon et le mauvais *Manitou.* Le bon est bon essentiellement. C'est lui qui accorde le succès dans toutes les entreprises; ils n'ont done rien à en craindre. Mais ils redoutent le mauvais *Manitou,* car c'est a lui qu'ils attribuent tous leurs malheurs. Ils n'ont, cependant, aucune manière propre pour rendre a ce mauvais Manitou ce qu'on dirait un culte, si ce n'est quelques petites pratiques superstitieuses, auxquelles ils attachent beaucoup d'importance, et qui forment tout leur bagage en fait de religion extèrieure".

At the time of Father Charles Arnaud's first visit to them in 1853, they were nearly all still pagan. He wrote as follows of them: "In general, the unfaithful savages of these lands [upper interior Labrador Peninsula] believe in the existence of two deities which they call Manitous (spirits); but this belief is so confused in their minds that they can scarcely convey it. According to them, there is the good and the bad Manitou. The good is essentially good. It is he who grants success in all enterprises; they therefore have nothing to fear. But they dread the bad Manitou, because it is to him that they attribute all their misfortunes. They have, however, no proper way to render to this bad Manitou in what one would say a cult, if it is not a few small superstitious practices, to which they attach a lot of importance, and which form all their baggage in terms of external religion".

65 "Nous avons entendu dire par nos ancêtres que de pareils signes présageaient le colère du Grand Esprit". <32>

"We have heard from our ancestors that such signs portended the wrath of the Great Spirit." <32>

: "Le Naskapis sait qu'il existe un grand Esprit et que celui-ci a un antagoniste, l'esprit du mal qu'il redoute plus que le Grand Esprit. . . . Le Grand Esprit avait un fils qui était né de sa tête".

: "The Naskapis know that there is a great Spirit and that this one has an antagonist, the spirit of evil which he fears more than the Great Spirit.... The Great Spirit had a son who was born of his head".

"Le Grand Esprit crea le Naskapis quand il crea les autres hommes".

"The Great Spirit created the Naskapis when he created the other men."

"Tu tueras mon corps, mais mon âme repassera dans le corps d'un autre caribou façonné par *l'ombre* qui plane au-dessus des forêts et qui veille sur la destinée de la nation des caribous".

"You will kill my body, but my soul will pass back into the body of another caribou shaped by the *shadow* that hangs over the forests and watches over the destiny of the caribou nation."

66 "Nos pères mangeaient tout ce que leur envoyait Ie Grand Esprit, et nos pères étaient *fins,* nous faisons comme nos pères.... Je tues dix caribous; c'est le Grand-Esprit qui me les envoie parcequ'il voit que j'ai faim; il a un gros coeur pour moi, le Grand Esprit, et il veut que je mange ... je mange tout. Le Grand Esprit rit, et m'engraisse encore mille caribous là-bas, dans les terres des Naskapis. Tu voudrais ... que je cache le *pemican* que le Grand-Esprit m'envoie? Mais cela insulte le Grand Esprit. Si je meurs cette nuit, après l'avoir fait, je paraîtrai devant la face du Grand-Esprit, son oeil sera fâche, et il me dira tu es un mauvais fils, tu n'as pas eu d'esprit. Tu me traites comme un *matshimanitou....* Tu fait pitié à ton Père d'en haut.... Il n'enverra plus ses caribous dans ton chemin de chasse".

"Our fathers ate whatever the Great Spirit sent them, and our fathers were astute, we do as our forefathers.... I kill ten caribou; it is the Great Spirit who sends them to me because he sees that I'm hungry; he has a big heart towards me, the Great Spirit, and he wants me to eat ... I eat everything up. The Great Spirit laughs, and fattens me a thousand more caribou out there in the Naskapi lands "Would you like ... that I hide the *pemican* that the Great Spirit sends me? But this insults the Great Spirit. If I die tonight, after I have done it, I will appear before the face of the Great Spirit, his eye will be angry, and he will tell me you are a bad son, you had no spirit. You treat me like a matshimanitou... You should pity your Father from above.... He will no longer send his caribou to your hunting path".

Merci Thanks to Marie Futoso and Max Olmos

Please Help Wipe Out Typo Gnomes!